CODE BLUE

The Fragrance of Caring

A Collection of Nursing Essays

Jane Ha

Code Blue

First Edition, First Printing
Published June 23, 2011
Translation Korean to English April 18, 2025

Author: Jeonga Jane Ha
Editor: Robert Lennon
Translator: Robert Lennon

Korean Language: Published by HyunMoon Publishing
English Language: Published by Jane Ha

Email: JaneHaBooks@Gmail.com

Returns:
In cooperation with the author.

ISBN 979-8-9985637-0-6

Find Jane Ha online

CODE BLUE

Prologue

Becoming a nurse has brought me happiness. I nearly missed one of life's most precious experiences, settling instead for a half-lived existence. For a long time, I believed the mind was superior to the body, that caring for thoughts and emotions alone would be enough. I see now how mistaken I was. What a quiet and grave error that could have been.

This realization revealed to me the deep interconnectedness of body and spirit, and how caring for one without the other leaves something essential untouched. Nursing became more than a profession. It became a calling that reminds me daily of the beauty and dignity present in every human life.

In the ward, I have learned to love people as they are. Regardless of race or cultural background, I have come to believe that every human being is worthy of love. I remain in awe of the human body—its intricate structure, its physiological rhythms, its delicate senses. People are simultaneously fragile and resilient. I find that truly remarkable. Each day, I am reminded of the greatness and quiet wonder that defines what it means to be human.

Every time I step into the ward, I also return to myself. I practice the quiet discipline of examining my own body and mind. The hospital is more than a place of work; it is a stage where life's complexities unfold. It broadens my

view of the world and sharpens my awareness. Here, I learn not only about others, but also about myself. It is a place that cultivates humility and deepens thoughtfulness.

I am especially grateful to literary critic Yang-geun Park for his kind and generous review. Instead of harsh criticism, he offered a gentle and forgiving appraisal. He understood that someone as delicate as I am might not grow under sharpness, and so he graciously turned a blind eye to my flaws. I will always remember the grace and wisdom in his response.

My heartfelt thanks also goes to Dr. Won-taek Lee, a psychiatrist and literary colleague, who helped translate the English terms scattered throughout my writing into Korean. His silent yet pointed critique reminded me of the importance of cherishing and honoring my native language. I had not realized how often I relied on foreign words. This truth filled me with a deep sense of apology toward Korean, my mother tongue. Having never practiced nursing in Korea, the language of Korean hospital wards often feels unfamiliar to me, like a set of clothes that do not quite fit.

During my childhood, I lived for three years on Heuksan Island, where I first encountered the Pungran, a wild orchid that grows among rocks. Its gentle presence and the soft, sweet fragrance of its flowers left a lasting impression on me. My father once told me that the scent of the Pungran travels about two and a half miles, reaching distant people with its perfume like an invisible hand.

My father added, "The scent of a flower can travel five or ten miles, but the fragrance of a person travels ten thousand." As a child, I wondered whether a person's fragrance could truly be deeper and richer than that of a flower. Now I understand, it is. A person's fragrance is more beautiful and travels farther.

I hope my writing, like the fragrance of the wild orchid, can travel beyond mountains and seas, reaching others who, like me, may feel like simple and ordinary creatures. If, by some small chance, these words warm even a corner of your lonely heart, it would bring me immeasurable joy.

From Upland, a small town beneath Mt. Baldy.

Table of Contents

Chapter I

Covering

We use a lot of beautiful words in the hospital ward I work in. The phrase "my patient" carries with it a profound sense of responsibility. I also like the term "doctor aware." Within it lies a comforting sense of relying on a presence greater than myself. In clinical settings, this phrase is commonly used in nursing documentation to indicate that a physician has been informed about a patient's condition or a specific issue. For example, a nurse might document, "doctor aware of patient's elevated temperature," signifying that the physician has been notified. This practice ensures clear communication and delineates responsibility within the healthcare team.

Then there's "cosign." In nursing practice, the term "cosign" refers to the requirement for a second qualified healthcare professional to verify and acknowledge specific actions or documentation, particularly in high-risk procedures such as administering insulin injections, conducting blood transfusions, or disposing of narcotic pain medications. This practice serves as a safeguard, ensuring accuracy and adherence to protocols in critical situations.

The act of cosigning embodies trust and commitment within the healthcare team. It signifies a willingness to vouch for and bear witness to significant and potentially hazardous procedures. Moreover, cosigning reflects a collective responsibility, fostering a culture of teamwork and mutual accountability. By participating in this process, healthcare

professionals demonstrate their dedication to patient safety and the integrity of medical practices.

My favorite word is "covering." It refers to taking responsibility for a colleague's duties, or having them take over yours, when personal circumstances require being gone for a certain duration. Hearing someone say, "I'll cover you," always warms my heart. It's a gracious assurance: "Don't worry. I'll take responsibility for your patients and care well for them while you're out." No matter how busy you are, it's hard to refuse when a colleague asks, "Could you cover me?" When I am asked, it's difficult to say "no" when you've made the same request of a busy colleague. Both scenarios demand more than the usual amount of courage.

When I entrust my patients to a fellow nurse, I stake my reputation on it. I do everything in my power to handle complex tasks in advance so as not to burden the one covering for me. I make an effort to anticipate and meet my patients' needs ahead of time, saving my colleague valuable time. This is because I understand the generosity behind their willingness to step in for me during my absence, even when they themselves are overwhelmed and pressed for time. It's also a matter of survival. If you earn a reputation as selfish or lazy, it becomes increasingly difficult to find someone willing to cover for you. In the world of nursing, there's no room for underhanded shortcuts or superficial tricks. On the ward, nothing is swept under the rug. Everything is laid bare.

A nurse on the ward initials and signs documents more than a hundred times a day easily. But what does a signature truly mean? It's a declaration of responsibility, something no one can handle without an unwavering sense of duty. Nursing is a profession that demands exactly that. The life of a patient often depends on a nurse's quick and precise hands, their adaptable and integrative thinking, and their ability to act decisively in emergencies. These skills are not just technical; they are a lifeline, shaping outcomes in moments that matter most.

Amid all this, there is something called covering. It means stepping in for a colleague caring for a difficult patient—checking a blood sugar level, taking a blood pressure reading, or tending to others so they can focus on someone nearing the end of life. It's the quiet support offered without fanfare or recognition. It's listening with compassion to a wounded colleague's story, offering no lectures, no judgments—just presence.

Covering. It evokes the sweet thrill of escaping as the eagle's prey and finding refuge in the warm embrace of a mother hen. It's like the deep, calming breath you take when stepping into the shade of a towering pine tree, away from the scorching sun. It is a word that touches the heart of a mother's love, or even the heart of God. Covering is a solemn promise shared among those who understand that the ward's tranquility ensures their own peace. Quietly covering a colleague's mistake, bearing a little extra burden, or making a small sacrifice; these acts of love, born of humility and selflessness, are ultimately for your own sake as much as theirs. It is a secret code of compassion, spoken by those who know that giving grace to others enriches us all.

When I'm flustered by a mistake, the colleague who pats my shoulder and says, "It's okay. None of us are perfect," feels like an angel. The one who covers for me with a cheerful wink when I can't finish my tasks on time has the same glow of kindness. And when someone, even in the midst of their own busyness, responds with a heartfelt, "No problem!" instead of irritation, I feel so grateful I could cry. Every time I step onto the ward, I grasp the true meaning of the phrase "we must live together." I am who I am not because of what I possess, but because of the people around me. My well-being depends on the well-being of my neighbors. Their survival is intertwined with mine. And in those moments, I realize a profound truth: I am my neighbor.

Today, I dream of growth once again, hoping to expand my ability to cover those around me a little more broadly and deeply. I wish for the concept of covering, this beautiful act of selfless sacrifice, to spread throughout the community in which I belong. And I imagine beautiful words resonating like music, filling every corner: "It's okay. I'll wrap my arms around your deep wounds. I'll wipe away your painful tears."

Preference Card

Early in the morning, the surgical team is bustling with activity. The tension on their faces is unmistakable. The surgery is fast approaching, and it's the first time they're working as a team with a newly arrived surgeon. The problem is they don't have enough information about his preferences, or what it's commonly referred to as a preference card.

Usually, when a new doctor is hired, the surgical team is provided with a preference list outlining the cases he or she will handle. Yet, there always seems to be a blind spot when it comes to the very first case.

The surgical team keeps a preference card for each surgeon they work with. Even for the same type of surgery, each surgeon has their own specific preferences for instruments and brands. The card is a detailed list of these preferences, meticulously documented. When working with a new doctor, it's essential to find out in advance if they have any specific instrument preferences or requirements. If that information is not available, the team prepares multiple sets of diverse instruments to ensure they're ready for anything.

When the surgical team is well-acquainted with the surgeon's habits and preferences and has a reliable preference card, they can work with ease. This confidence stems from the wisdom gained through experience, confirming case by case that knowing both oneself and the other ensures success every time.

Surgeons prefer to work with technicians who can read their cues and hand them the right instruments at the right moment with precision. They also want a skilled anesthesiologist with excellent decision-making abilities who can take full responsibility for the patient's overall condition, allowing the surgeon to focus solely on the procedure. In addition, they value agile nurses who proactively fill any gaps to ensure the surgery flows smoothly and seamlessly. If the preferred team members are unavailable, surgeons may occasionally cancel surgeries citing other reasons. This is understandable, as the value of synergy achieved with a well-coordinated team and familiar tools cannot be overstated.

There are doctors whom the surgical team deeply respects. These are the ones who, even when the situation falls short of their ideal, whether due to a lack of preferred instruments or incomplete preparations, show patience and give their best effort. They understand that undue pressure on the staff can have the opposite effect, causing more harm than good. They are wise and gracious individuals who recognize the capabilities and limitations of the surgical team working alongside them.

In human relationships, there is also a kind of preference card. Those who possess an extensive list of preferences for others are truly wealthy at heart. They are thoughtful individuals who prioritize consideration for others over asserting their own preferences. Such people have the wisdom to understand that lifting the pride of others and making them feel at ease ultimately benefits everyone, including themselves. Being around individuals like this brings a sense of comfort and peace, creating a space where hearts can rest, and relationships can flourish.

I think about the preference card I've mentally written up for my neighbors. It's an old list, written long ago, perhaps only once. As time has passed, I wonder, have I unintentionally hurt their feelings by seeing and treating them through the lens of fixed ideas and assumptions. Was I insistent that this card I created is the best and only true representation of these people, rather than seeing them fully for themselves? Looking back, I think, if I had approached others without any preconceived notions, simply following where my heart led, I could have been more genuine and purer.

I also think about the preference card my neighbors may have written about me. After all, am I not a complex and sometimes incomprehensible person, even to myself? I can almost picture a long, messy list. It makes me wonder, do my loved ones sometimes feel perplexed or burdened, unsure of how to approach or deal with me? As time passes, I hope that the list of likes and dislikes about me grows shorter, clearer, and simpler.

Just as a surgical team contributes to the success of an operation by keeping an updated preference card, you and I can nurture more genuine and beautiful relationships by revisiting and rewriting the preference cards we hold for each other each day.

Chapter 1

The Heart of One Lying on the Operating Table

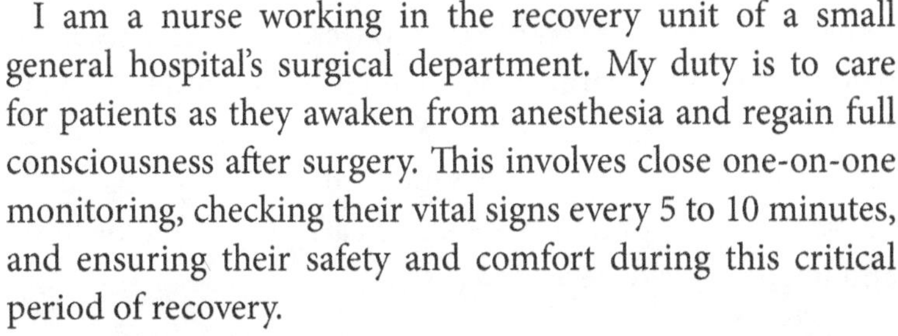

I am a nurse working in the recovery unit of a small general hospital's surgical department. My duty is to care for patients as they awaken from anesthesia and regain full consciousness after surgery. This involves close one-on-one monitoring, checking their vital signs every 5 to 10 minutes, and ensuring their safety and comfort during this critical period of recovery.

On one side of the recovery room is a waiting area where preoperative patients stay. This is where doctors and nurses interview the patients and perform final checks on the requirements for surgery. If a patient's condition is deemed unable to withstand the surgical process, the procedure is canceled on the spot. My heart is moved when I hear of a surgery canceled for the sake of a patient's safety and well-being; especially when it results in significant losses for the hospital due to the sterile surgical instruments that have already been opened for the operating room. Witnessing the professionalism and decisiveness of these life-saving experts is truly inspiring.

Introducing oneself and establishing a rapport with a patient in the waiting area is essential for quality care. For nurses, this interaction is a crucial opportunity to assess and compare the patient's mental state before and after surgery, ensuring that any changes in demeanor or mood are noted and addressed. For patients, encountering a familiar, caring face in their vulnerable moments offers reassurance and comfort during the recovery process.

In those brief conversations, I often glimpse their intellect, education, and character. In the rawness of a surgical setting, wealth, power, fame, and even knowledge or wisdom offer little help. What ultimately preserves human dignity is character—a truth reaffirmed every day.

The reactions of patients awakening from anesthesia can be remarkably varied. Even those who were polite and reserved before surgery sometimes become violent or rude, spewing crude and ignorant profanities. Such colorful outbursts often cause me to stifle my own laughter. Interestingly, regardless of the language, profanity seems to carry the same meaning and impact everywhere.

Without missing a beat, I gently held the patient's hand and smiled, saying, "I'm sorry, but I have no idea what language you're speaking. Latin? Oh dear, I'm afraid I don't understand that language." Depending on the situation, patients either escalate their behavior or calm down. Some may swing fists or even pinch, but with quick reflexes, like dodging a boxer's punch, I deftly evade their jabs and kicks while continuing to provide the care they need.

Every surgery, whether minor or major, carries inherent risks. Even young and seemingly healthy patients, who appear to be low-risk, can sometimes present unexpected challenges. There are cases where blood pressure suddenly plummets, creating an emergency, or where bleeding from the surgical site won't stop, requiring the patient to be rushed back into the operating room mid-transfusion. In some instances, even a simple surgical procedure can lead to complications, like an accidental injury to the lungs or a puncture to the bladder. Such possibilities remind us that

surgery is never entirely predictable and that vigilance is always crucial.

When a patient under the influence of anesthesia struggles to breathe steadily, I tilt their head back to open the airway. In more severe cases, airways are inserted into the mouth or nostrils to secure breathing passages, followed by oxygen delivery. Sometimes, a ventilator is necessary. Often, simply calling their name and rubbing their chest will awaken post-anesthesia patients. Wrapping them in a warm blanket, I place a hand on their chest to encourage steady breathing. When they manage to lift their heavy eyelids, signaling that they're awake, it's a moment of relief and joy that never fails to touch me.

Before surgery, patients must remove all accessories attached to their bodies—glasses, watches, rings, necklaces, earrings, toe rings, dentures, and even piercings on ears, eyelids, lips, tongues, or navels. Each time I encounter these many adornments; I'm reminded of how inherently lonely humans are. It strikes me that people use these items to soothe their emptiness, going to great lengths to comfort themselves. This thought fills me with a quiet sense of compassion. Yet, when all these items are set aside and the patient is left wearing nothing but an old surgical gown, lying on a simple makeshift bed in the waiting area, they often appear more at peace. They look humble and clear, sincere and grounded, as if the shedding of worldly trappings allows their true essence to shine through.

When I feel the urge to assert myself or when I sense my rights are being infringed upon, I picture myself lying on an operating table. In that vulnerable state, I begin to remove the cumbersome adornments that dress up my heart. I let go of the vanity that whispers, "It has to be me." I set aside the stubbornness and excuses that always start with "But" or

"Still." I strip away every embellishment life has added—the roles, titles, or positions that have made me ashamed of my true self and forced me to wear a mask. Left with nothing but my raw, unadorned essence, I find the experience both humbling and freeing.

Today, as I guide patients into the operating room and help them onto the surgical table, I reflect on the flawed traits within myself that need to be laid down as well. I hope that, with time, the list of these shortcomings will grow shorter, piece by piece, refining who I am and how I live.

Chapter 1

A Doctor's Kindness

Dr. Noh,

I watch you now, writing prescriptions just after finishing four consecutive surgeries. Every day, you face the blood, pus, and the acrid smell of burning flesh, enduring the grueling demands of your work. You look tired, yet your expression remains lively and gentle, a calm presence even in the chaos. When you quietly said, "I'm really tired today," my heart ached deeply for you.

When I first explained my mother's situation after her arrival from Korea, I didn't have high hopes. All I wanted was to know the diagnosis of her illness. Three years ago, she had received a traditional moxibustion treatment on her chest and suffered burns as a result. The injury left behind three small, pea-sized lumps, and despite the passage of time, the wounds never healed completely. Instead, they would occasionally swell red, burst open, and cause her persistent pain and discomfort. These symptoms tormented her, leaving us both searching for answers.

Why wouldn't she have sought help from doctors? She did. But they refused treatment, citing her diabetes, high blood pressure, and age as reasons. Some even responded dismissively, asking if she expected to live long enough for the wound to turn into cancer. My mother told me she was scared and didn't want to live any longer as they said the likelihood of it becoming cancerous would only increase over time.

Thinking about the worry and pain my mother had endured over the years, my heart ached with pity for her. I wanted to hear your opinion because of the deep trust I had in you after observing your work up close. You readily agreed, for which I was so grateful. She was more worried about the cost of treatment than the excitement of seeing an American doctor. It was because she was visiting and didn't have medical insurance.

I'm sorry, but I called your office and cautiously asked about the consultation fee. The response left me feeling disheartened. The staff member said, "But let's wait and see. He's always incredibly generous with the team members he works with."

Your diagnosis was simple and straightforward: keloid caused by the burn. Although the conversation was conducted through my interpreting, my mother was deeply moved by your demeanor and kindness. Then, you said something that left a lasting impression: "Schedule a date for the surgery. All consultations and the procedure will be free of charge. We'll do everything here in my office because, if we take it to the hospital, the costs will be beyond my control." Tears welled up in my eyes.

On the day of the surgery, you finally removed the source of my mother's long-standing pain and anxiety. I understood all too well how much courage and sacrifice your decision required; your time, your staff's effort, the sterile instruments, the medications, and so much more. As I stood there, overwhelmed by the enormity of your kindness, unable to find words, you gently spoke to me: "My father was a dentist. All his extended family received his care for free. I only regret that, due to the nature of my field, I cannot offer the same generosity as freely as he did."

On the way home, my mother and I talked about hope, gratitude, and love. Together, we made a promise: to pray for your blessed future. We vowed to ask that your extraordinary skill and compassion might continue to sow seeds of hope wherever you go.

In the evening, you gave us a call. Once again, your kindness moved us deeply. With such warmth, you asked if there was any bleeding or severe pain. Furthermore, you reassured us not to worry, saying that while it would take some time, the healing process would go well.

Doctor Noh, how could you ever fathom the tears my mother has shed, the pain she has endured, and the years of silent perseverance she has lived through? You will forever remain one of the utmost generous, giving, and memorable people whom we will forever be grateful for in our lives. You will be remembered and spoken of endlessly among my family, relatives, and neighbors, both in Korea and America.

Doctor Noh, today you healed not just a wound but a part of our ailing world. Thank you. I admire and respect you deeply.

Jane Ha

Jennifer's Tears

The February rain in California feels like a gift. It sweeps away the arid, desert-like air in an instant, replacing it with a refreshing vitality. The once-parched landscape, parched with thirst, now gleams with vivid colors, alive and revitalized. Everything is moist and alive. A calm despair, a bittersweet melancholy, gently washes over me, warm and comforting. Emotions long buried deep within stir, shaking off the dust as they gently rise to the surface.

I watch raindrops endlessly stream down the car window. As they hit the glass, the droplets seem to spread sideways before splitting into multiple trickling streams that slide down. It's quiet. Serene. The rain flows endlessly, yet there is no sound. It's a strangely familiar sight. Where have I seen this before? What could it have been? There is certainly a memory that resembles this.

Ah, that's it. It was Jennifer, a patient I met long ago at the hospital. It was her. She cried just like this rain, silently, calmly, endlessly. My heart suddenly feels desolate. Where might she be now? What could she be doing? Or perhaps… is she even still in this world?

Early that morning, her name was on the patient list I received in the ward, but I couldn't see her face. She had already been taken to the operating room. Was it because she was only forty? Or perhaps because of her troubling medical history? As I listened to the report from the nurse

who had cared for her earlier, I found myself inexplicably drawn to her case. At 11 a.m., she came to me from the recovery room. Her left foot had been amputated below the ankle, and the empty space where her ankle had been tightly wrapped in layers of compression bandages.

The doctor's order was for her to start walking that afternoon. Since she had lost her right foot in a similar manner two years earlier, she now faced the challenge of walking without either foot. I was at a loss as to how to approach her. I decided to delay as long as I could. For now, I resolved to give her the space to rest quietly, without any disturbance, allowing her to find a moment of peace in the midst of her struggle.

I expected her to be in severe pain so soon after surgery. The doctor had already prescribed several potent injectable pain medications. Yet, even after four hours, she hadn't asked for any pain relief. Each time I checked on her, she lay quietly, staring at the ceiling. Whenever I asked if she was in pain, she would give a brief response, saying she had a higher tolerance for pain than most people.

Late in the afternoon, I stopped by to administer her antibiotics and found her sitting up in bed. She told me she needed to use the restroom. When I offered to assist her, she declined. She said she didn't want to train herself to become dependent on others. "The first time is crucial," she explained. It was her first time going to the bathroom without both legs, and she believed that accepting help would cost her freedom in the long run. Calm and practiced, she first put on her right prosthetic leg, then the new one on her left. She tucked a crutch under each arm and carefully worked to walk upright as she made her way to and from the bathroom. She didn't let out a single groan or sigh.

I resisted the urge to help her lie back down in bed. She was cheerful, spirited, and composed. I couldn't help but wonder where her strength came from, given her significant medical history. Six years ago, she had a hysterectomy due to cancer; three years ago, she had her right breast removed; and two years ago, she lost her right foot to complications from diabetes.

Unable to contain my curiosity, I finally said, "I've never met anyone with such remarkable willpower. There's an indescribable strength about you. I can't help but wonder, where does it come from?" She burst out laughing and said she was relieved not to appear pitiful. Then, almost casually, she explained that she had been in regular therapy for several years. During countless painful moments, she had been fortunate to meet a good doctor who helped her hold onto her strength and keep living. Her candidness and resilience left me both inspired and humbled.

A little while later, I returned to her room and found her lying quietly on the bed. When I asked if she was in pain, she replied, "It's bearable." I told her that enduring pain isn't always the best course of action, gently explaining that there was no need to treat herself so harshly. I assured her that tolerating pain had nothing to do with strong willpower or self-esteem. I explained that severe pain causes the body's cells to tense, disrupting electrolyte balance and oxygen delivery, which can delay the healing of the surgical site. Her eyes seemed to brighten, and then she said, "In that case, please give me painkillers right away."

After two days off, I returned to the ward to find that she had already been discharged. I thought of her from time to time, but amidst the constant struggle of caring for patients suffering from various illnesses, she gradually faded from my memory.

A year later, I met Jennifer again in the ward. A new patient had just been admitted after undergoing a left mastectomy, and her name caught my attention. When I looked more closely, I realized it was her. Her face, worn and exhausted, had changed so drastically over the past year that I barely recognized her. Her once-soft, flowing hair now hung limply over her shoulders, brittle and uncared for, as if weighed down by the pain she must have endured. Despite everything, she recognized me and smiled.

As soon as she lay down, she asked for pain medication immediately. Blood pressure is not measured on the arm of the side where a mastectomy has been performed, nor is it measured on the leg of the surgical site. She had lost both breasts and both feet. Given her condition, even taking her blood pressure was not an easy task.

It was a busy afternoon, but I carved out a moment to sit by her bedside. Gently, I brushed her brittle hair away from her face with one hand. She clasped my hand tightly, turned her head toward the window, and gazed at the sky. In a self-deprecating tone, she said, "How long can I keep this up? Is it even worth living like this? My husband and children left me long ago. My mother spends her days in tears because of me. Maybe the kindest thing I can do for her is to let go of the will to live. If I weren't here at all, I'd eventually be forgotten, and her tears would dry." I listened quietly, unable to offer her any words in response.

I gazed silently at her pale profile, as still as plaster. A crystal-clear droplet seemed to form at the corner of her eye, then trickled down her cheek. At first, the tear lingered momentarily in a rounded shape near her eye, but as it flowed down her face, it spread, blending with other streams before soaking into the pillowcase. She didn't seem to realize she was crying, as her calm tone remained unchanged.

I thought about her life. Before her illness, she must have been one of the happiest women. The refinement and intellect etched into her well-defined facial features attested to this. She possesses remarkable endurance and exceptional self-control.

She is humble and polite, never succumbing to bitterness over her circumstances. Unlike many patients who might direct their anger at medical staff or the world at large.

Who could have foreseen her misfortune all those years ago? Everyone desires good health, yet no one is guaranteed it. Then, one day, without warning, the thunderclap of an unexpected diagnosis strikes. Who can truly grasp the weight of that suffocating weight of such a realization?

As I left her room, I found myself reflecting on my own life. How long would I remain healthy? The answer was clear: I had no way of knowing. It wasn't something within my control. I searched for what I could do, and the answer came quickly. Enjoy the life I've been granted, one day at a time. Be grateful for every moment and live each one joyfully.

It is about gratefully embracing the time we have now, living passionately in the moment, cherishing yesterday and being thankful to be alive today. Feeling moved by the fact that we have passed through autumn and are now welcoming winter. Rejoicing in the hope of awaiting spring.

The rain fell steadily all afternoon, and I couldn't pull myself away from the window. Jennifer's tears were there. The quiet, unending streams of rain rolling down the glass resembled her tears.

Chapter 1

Sunshine that Reflects on My Soul

It's the first day back at work in the new year, and I feel an overwhelming sense of joy as I step into the ward. The realization that I've returned to my workplace fills my heart with happiness. This is the place where I spend the most dynamic, purposeful, and productive hours of my day. I'm grateful to have a space where I am needed and surrounded by colleagues who feel like family. Their warmth and camaraderie make me truly happy to be here.

Maryann, a nurse from the gastroenterology department, greets me with a heartfelt New Year's wish. Overflowing with love and gratitude, I give her a big hug. I pat her shoulder, saying, "Let's live by the '3L' again this year." We encourage each other to fully embrace and enjoy the "blessings bestowed upon nurses."

3Ls — Live well, Laugh often, Love more. It's my guiding principle for the new year. I resolve to stay healthy, both physically and emotionally. I promise not to mistreat my body, mind, or soul. I remind myself to stop being my own harshest critic, to let go of unnecessary self-troubles. Above all, I vow to laugh more. Freely, fully, and often.

By taking a step back, perhaps I can let go of the relentless desperation to cling to things. But how can I love more? Haven't I accumulated an even greater debt of love over the past year? I'm clumsy when it comes to handling everyday matters; a simple call to check in, writing a single card, even these feel beyond me at times. How can I love and then convey that love to others? This year, I need to learn the wisdom of giving love beautifully and receiving it wholeheartedly. It's a lesson I must embrace, to offer love generously and to welcome it with gratitude and grace.

As a nurse, I resolve to renew my mindset this year. I want to rekindle the excitement and passion I felt when I first stepped onto the ward. I will confidently embrace the belief that nurses deserve to be blessed, with love to share with others, with a warm heart and compassion to care for people, and with the kindness to accept others generously. With love, compassion, and kindness, I can face the new year abundantly. And if humor and art accompany me along the way, all the better—it will be perfection.

I remind myself not to worry and to revisit the principles that can shield me from unnecessary anxiety:

See the world with a broad perspective.

Draw inspiration from the smallest creations in nature.

Do not worry.

Set priorities correctly.

Yes, I will not fret over an uncertain tomorrow. Instead, I will live fully and contentedly today. I will not anticipate misfortune in advance or exaggerate the challenges I face.

During lunch, I stepped out into the hospital garden. Roses the size of a baby's face were in full bloom. As I inhaled their fragrance, clear and radiant sunlight poured down on my head and shoulders like a blessing. It felt like sunlight shining on my soul. I lifted my face, closed my eyes, and stood in the middle of the lawn. I felt grateful, for being alive, for being able to breathe, for having limbs that move at will, and for

sensory organs that let me see, hear, touch, feel, and taste. I felt thankful for being able to easily recall the faces of those I love. I was grateful, too, for the ease with which I could call to mind those I love. It was a simple but profound moment of connection to life and all its blessings.

It is this New Year I received as a gift. It's a bonus time granted to me. I want to live a good life. I want to be kind to myself, extending grace to who I am. By doing so, I can approach others with ease and warmth.

I want to live with self-awareness, recognizing and accepting my emotions with honesty. "Ah, so I have feelings like this within me!" I want to live honestly, taking a sincere look into my heart. To be happy, one must forgive one's self of the wrongs they have committed throughout their life. It means forgiving even the part of oneself that refuses to forgive. Furthermore, forgiveness is about gently accepting all the circumstances and processes of life that have been given to us.

I hope that, throughout this year, my body and mind will align with my good intentions. I wish for a year as fragrant as the scent of roses, as warm as the sunlight now resting gently on my shoulders. Let it be a year filled with grace, peace, and quiet joy.

Jane Ha

A Nurse's Excuse

A recovering patient, after being urged by a nurse to walk to hasten recovery and avoid complications, wrote about his feelings following his effort to walk the hospital corridor: "I endured the pulling pain in my abdomen and walked 27 laps around the 80-meter ward. How wonderful it would've been to just launch out into space, leaving everything behind! Instead of clinging foolishly to life, I'd throw away all attachments to this earth and soar freely through the heavens." Patients who hear this would probably feel a deep sense of catharsis.

I'm well aware of the biases some people hold against nurses. They think we are emotionless, cold-blooded beings. They imagine that we remain unfazed at the sight of gushing blood or even a patient's death—our faces unchanging, our emotions hidden. And, in a way, they're right. But that's what makes a nurse a true professional. A nurse who openly displays every emotion in front of a patient, whether fear, sadness, or frustration, is not providing the best care.

I am a nurse with five years of experience. I began my career in general wards and cardiology units, later receiving training in Nursery, Maternity, Intensive Care Unit (ICU), and Long-Term Care Unit. Currently, I work in the Post-Anesthesia Care Unit (PACU) at a small general hospital in a suburban city. I held the hands of dying patients and closed their eyes for the last time. I have washed bodies and dressed them in burial garments according to the customs of their respective cultures.

I am constantly exposed to a wide range of diseases. When caring for patients with pulmonary tuberculosis, I collect and send samples of sputum, urine, and stool to the lab for testing. I provide equal and compassionate care to patients with AIDS, hepatitis, tuberculosis, and those carrying antibiotic-resistant bacteria, without discrimination. A number of years ago, I was pricked by needles in quick succession while working with an AIDS patient and a hepatitis C patient. For a while, my life revolved around countless tests and checkups. It was during that time I discovered, quite unexpectedly, that I had developed immunity to three types of hepatitis. The phrase "nurses are missionaries" is an accurate description. However, the term "angels in white" isn't as flattering as it may seem. It feels like a pitying expression, a bittersweet consolation for those in a life-risking profession.

A nurse is an advocate for the patient. Doctors rely on the information provided by nurses to determine the proper prescriptions and treatment needed. A good nurse works to correct any errors and ensures that the patient receives the most appropriate care.

A nurse's wise judgment can shorten a patient's recovery time or, conversely, lead to wasted time and resources if misjudged. However, if a nurse misinterprets or improperly carries out a doctor's order, it can result in devastating consequences for the patient.

As a nurse, I am well aware of my limitations. While I often feel conflicted when trying to judge what I must do and what I cannot, I always prioritize the patient's safety and well-being. This frequently leads to conflicts with doctors.

Even so, I am always confident because my actions are never motivated by personal convenience or gain.

Being a nurse in a cultural environment, vastly different from the one I was born and raised in, often leads to significant conflicts and internal discord. When caring for a 17-year-old girl who just had her second child via C-section, I find myself clenching my lips to keep from scolding her to get her life together. When I see teenage girls treating abortions as a casual form of birth control, coming to the hospital three or four times a year, my frustration boils over, even toward the doctors. I find myself frustrated, questioning how patient education is being handled. Sarcasm slips out unintentionally: "Well, she's your number-one customer keeping your life comfortable, so you should treat her well." The OB-GYN snaps back, telling me to try teaching them myself, shaking their head in disbelief.

Yesterday, I gave discharge education regarding post-operative care to a 15-year-old girl who had just undergone an abortion. When I said, "Pelvic rest for at least 2 weeks," she clung to her boyfriend's arm and pouted, "You're telling me to wait that long? I can't live like that." Suppressing my discomfort, I gently explained the risks of infection in a calm, quiet tone.

A pregnant woman with severe diabetes had refused to take her medication because she found it bothersome, tragically leading to the death of her 8-month-old fetus. After delivering the stillborn baby via C-section, she complained about being hungry, and I found myself at a loss for words. I could only assume she was in the denial stage of grief, too shocked to fully comprehend her situation. All I could do was embrace her with kindness and understanding.

Patients often see nurses as extraordinary beings, expecting that no matter how unreasonable their demands are, a nurse must comply unconditionally. Patients may harbor a general sense of resistance toward nurses, stemming from the feeling that it is unfair for them to suffer while the nurse remains healthy. A true nurse understands this unspoken dynamic and empathizes with the patient's inner turmoil with unwavering compassion.

Ten years ago, my fellow nurse, Molly, was diagnosed with ovarian cancer and had her right ovary removed. Just two weeks ago, she received the devastating news that the cancer had metastasized to her left ovary. For the past two years, she has endured excruciating pain that no pain medication could alleviate. A CT scan revealed abnormalities in her colon, and further tests are being conducted to check for metastasis to other organs. To prepare for further tests, she had to fast for two full days. Watching her continue to work without taking a single day off simply broke my heart. While caring for a patient who complained about minor pain following a routine endoscopy, Molly clutched her abdomen to manage her own unbearable pain. She spoke with calm resignation, saying she wasn't sure whether she should undergo surgery or start chemotherapy, though she needed to keep working because of financial pressures.

Nursing is a philosophy. Each time I put on my uniform and step onto the ward, I hold close the maxim: "To touch the human body is to touch the divine." No matter the age or gender of the patient, I insert catheters, treat wounds in intimate areas, and dress them with care. Through these acts, I learn the profound intricacies of the human body. Nurses do not work solely out of professional obligation. The privilege of touching a patient's body, from head to toe, is not something we take lightly. In caring for patients, we are given the opportunity to reflect on life and learn its deeper meanings.

Through the people and events, I encounter in the hospital, I have come to see the world anew, a world I could never have known before becoming a nurse. It is a place where tears, inspiration, anger, and patience coexist. Things that would be incomprehensible or unacceptable in ordinary society happen here every day, every moment. And yet, within the hospital's walls, these occurrences are accepted with a quiet understanding as the norm.

Though I am bound to protect the privacy of my patients, as well as the pride of my fellow nurses and doctors, there are stories that must be told. Stories revealed through them, about what it means to stand at the crossroads of life and death. These are stories of their thoughts, choices, and humanity. Stories that deserve to be shared.

Caring for patients has taught me, without hesitation, to release many of my lingering attachments to desires. In witnessing their suffering, their resilience, and their moments of quiet surrender, I have come to understand the impermanence of so many things I once thought essential. The relentless pursuit of material success, the need for validation, the longing for control—these burdens, which once weighed so heavily on my heart, have gradually loosened their grip. Instead, I have found a deeper sense of fulfillment in small acts of kindness, in the fleeting yet profound connections formed in the space between pain and healing. I have learned that true contentment does not come from holding on but from knowing when to let go. In the end, it is not what I cling to that defines me, but what I am willing to release in order to embrace something greater.

The Awe of All Living Things

At 7 a.m., I received a report from the night nurse about Peter's condition, and a sigh escaped me. Today is not going to be easy. A 37-year-old man is dying. The thought of watching him wage war with death fills this day with sadness before it even begins. He had refused CPR, leaving no interventions available. After being in a prolonged coma due to uncontrolled hypoglycemia, his family requested the removal of his ventilator two days ago. Yet, against all odds, he is still breathing, clinging to life. Is it the unfinished chapters of a life not fully lived that hold him here? Are there words left unsaid, or a longing for someone he can't let go of?

I stepped into Peter's room, where a subtle and chilling aura seemed to envelop him. His emaciated body was pale, and his hands and feet felt damp to the touch. Despite receiving oxygen at 10 liters per minute, he struggled for each breath. His half-open eyes remained unresponsive to both my voice and touch.

After checking on other patients and returning to the nurse's station, an alarm sounded on one of the monitors at the desk. The room number displayed for a patient with a pulse of 41 was Peter's. The time has come. The pulse numbers on the screen flickered and wavered—38, 30, 45—as if unsure of their next step. The graph on the monitor moved in a soft, slow, graceful rhythm. I ran to Peter's room.

He was no longer breathing. A minute passed, perhaps less, and then he took one long, deep breath. I held his hand tightly. He might long for the touch of another as he took his final breath. I gently touched his face, ensuring he didn't feel alone in his final moments.

A straight line. The monitor displayed a steady, unbroken line. An unwavering line, allowing no deviation. Silence, stillness, peace. Now I understand the reason we feel a sense of rest while gazing at the horizon at sunset by the beach; the reason an indescribable sadness washes over me in such moments.

Now it's clear, humans are part of nature, one form within its vast diversity, a lifeform that mirrors nature itself. At last, the mystery is resolved. The reason why gazing at the beauty of nature always brings thoughts of home, it's the memory of a lost legend. Aren't we all sorrowful strangers, cast away from the bright heavens and left to wander this dark earth?

The heart must have longed for rest. For an entire lifetime, 70 to 80 years, it beats tirelessly, 60 to 80 times a minute, without pause. When the body's chemical balance is disrupted, it races to 180 or even 200 beats per minute, pushing itself to its limits. It is the heart that drives the other organs, giving them life and motion. And it is the heart that continues to fight until the very end.

Only when the heart surrenders does a life truly come to an end. Even if legs are lost, kidneys fail, or cancer ravages the body, life persists. Even when the brain is damaged and consciousness is gone, as long as the heart keeps beating, we call it life. We might label such a state as vegetative, but we do not declare it death. The heart is the ultimate arbiter of life.

It is painful, but it is living. There is solace in knowing that being alive, even in suffering, still holds meaning. When the heart stops, it signifies the end of life. No matter how healthy or youthful the other organs may be, they cannot continue without the heart. When the flow of blood ceases, so does life.

The emergency room doctor had come and gone, leaving behind paperwork with the word "Expired" written in red pen. The term felt heavy with sorrow, a life past its term. When a life ends, we say they have "passed away." This implies there is a place they once departed from, a homeland, an origin. Where is the homeland of us all? What is our mother tongue? Perhaps our sorrow comes from having lost our heavenly home, our heavenly language.

Peter had passed away, yet the flow of fluids, medications, and nutritional liquids continued to be administered into his body at regular intervals. It was time to free him from the tangled web of medical interventions that no longer served a purpose. I carefully removed the IV needles from his hands and feet, untangling the tubes that covered his frail body. I took off the oxygen mask from his face, the feeding tube from his nose, the suction tube, and the catheter that had been collecting his urine. Lastly, I detached the electrical leads from his chest that had been monitoring his heart.

With the help of the nursing assistant, Lupe, I began to wash Peter's body. His face was as pale as a sheet of paper. Parts of his chest were still warm to the touch, while his fingers and toes had already grown cold. I regretted not touching his skin more before he took his final breath. Each time I care for a deceased patient, I am filled with guilt and remorse for not having given them enough care and attention.

As I watched Lupe's diligent hands gently clean Peter's eyes, nose, and ears, a wave of dizziness washed over me. Images of one of my elderly relatives in my hometown, carefully washing my late grandmother's body, came flooding back. In that moment, I was struck by the profound similarity between East and West. The act of cleansing and caring for every open orifice of a departed body felt deeply sacred.

As I washed my hands and stepped out of Peter's room, I felt composed. Perhaps it was because I had witnessed, touched, and felt the deaths of others so many times during my work at the hospital. Or maybe it was because I had ingrained in myself the belief that through death, we come to understand life. I thought I had become resilient, hardened even. But I was wrong.

Our head nurse, Chloe, patted me gently on the shoulder. I must have broken the unspoken nurse's rule about not letting one's inner emotions show. "It's probably for the best," she said. "Peter will be at peace now, in a place without pain. It's much better than here, no suffering. Cheer up. There was nothing more you could have done." She was probably right. But as she spoke to me, I could sense she was also reassuring herself, seeking her own confirmation that we had done all we could.

It is ironic that humans, with finite lives and no way of knowing when their own end will come, mourn the death of another. Perhaps the absurd sorrow or confusion I'm feeling right now isn't because I pity Peter, but because of my own compassion for my life. How many more years will I be able to sustain this existence? Can I even call it a truly living life? Is this time called life, which slowly progresses toward the final destination of death, truly something that belongs to me? If so, the sorrow and despair I feel now aren't absurd at all. Mourning and remembering the dead is, after all, an act of grace and duty for those of us who remain.

Peter's older brother came into the room. He quietly patted my shoulder, offering comfort. I placed my hand gently over his in return. Neither of us said a word. Words felt like unnecessary tools. Both he and I will someday fade away, just like Peter.

Standing before a lifeless body, it becomes easier to define death. And in doing so, the truth of life becomes clearer, loving and giving love are the essence of living. When I look at all that is alive, tears well up. Everything feels so precious, so fleetingly beautiful.

After Peter was taken to the morgue, I stood blankly in the empty room. How futile it all feels in the end. Love and hate alike will become nothing more than a wisp of vapor. I took a deep breath. Even so, I must do my best for as long as I am alive. What other choice is there? If life can deepen and grow, what couldn't I do? What couldn't I become?

My phone rang, and on the other end was Lupe's urgent voice. "Are you still in that room? Snap out of it! Get to Room 37 immediately. The patient pulled out both IV needles from his arms, and there's blood everywhere!"

That's right. My day isn't over yet. Her words jolted me back to reality. There are still living patients who need my care. Yet, even as I carry on with my work today, I won't let myself forget Peter's death. His life, his passing are a part of this day, every day, a part of the meaning I carry as I move forward.

Jane Ha

Code Blue

Early in the morning, I take a deep breath as I step into the ward. I hope for a peaceful day. I wish for the patients I care for to recover well and be discharged. It's selfish, though, not entirely for them, but also for myself. Every time I pick up the schedule at the nursing station, listing the room numbers of the patients I'll care for that day, a shiver runs through my fingers. It's a reaction born of a mix of light anticipation, excitement, and nervous tension.

I spot my name on today's Code Blue team roster. Code Blue, the alarm signaling a patient in critical condition. I silently pray that there won't be a Code Blue today. When the call goes out, the designated team members must drop everything and rush to the specified ward. The room quickly fills with the emergency doctor, respiratory specialists, the manager, the supervisor, and nurses from various units. People crowd closely around the patient's bed as if forming a protective barrier, as if determined not to let the angel of death take them away.

Being present at the scene where life and death hang in the balance leaves a profound impact. Each time I work on the Code Blue team, I am deeply moved. Watching everyone pour their heart and soul into saving a fading life with a shared determination strikes me as nothing short of beautiful. The sight of hands moving swiftly in response to urgent instructions from the doctors is truly inspiring.

When CPR is completed, the airway is secured, and the patient stabilizes, the room turns into a celebration, with high-fives exchanged all around. It's easy to believe that the patient's revival is the result of the collective, fervent efforts of everyone in the room. Even when the patient's family, who love them dearly, are present, they cannot participate in the Code Blue team's work. Instead, a separate team is assigned to comfort and care for them in an isolated space. This task belongs entirely to the specialized medical team. Every time I work with the Code Blue team, I feel a tangible sense of what it means to be part of the human family.

After finishing my rounds, I was checking an IV piggyback when the announcement came over the speakers: a Code Blue in the Emergency Room. I had a bad feeling. It was too early in the day for a Code Blue. Washing my hands, I rushed to the scene, where people were already gathering from all directions, busy with preparations. The patient was expected to arrive within seconds. Like everyone else, I put on gloves and a mask, focusing my gaze on the entrance. The piercing siren of an ambulance blared, and the stretcher carrying the patient was hurriedly wheeled into the room. He appeared to be a sturdy man, not yet fifty.

The room was a flurry of activity: someone performing artificial respiration, another administering chest compressions, someone else handing over medication, others repeating each order loudly, documenting procedures, and exchanging reports. The room was a whirlwind of activity, charged with energy and determination to save a life. I moved busily, my hands working while my mind observed. I watched the people in the room and felt awe. How serious and noble it is to save a life.

As I handed the medication tube to the director, I was jostled by the crowd and found myself next to the crash cart, stocked with every kind of emergency medication and equipment. Nervously, I scrambled to locate and hand over the medications the doctor requested. Beads of sweat formed on my forehead; I was just a rookie, only a few months into working on the ward. But being new didn't mean I could step back or claim ignorance about the medications. All I could do was do my best. Somewhere in the chaos, a voice quietly announced, "5 minutes, 40 seconds." Another voice confirmed that there was still no pulse. Yet, there was no sign of hesitation in anyone's movements. I've lost count of how many rounds of CPR have been performed. Is it because the patient is young? Perhaps the team is still holding on to the hope that his heart will start beating again at any moment.

The person supplying oxygen with the CPR Ambu Bag gave me a look, a signal to switch places. Taking the large rubber balloon in my hands, I delivered one breath every 6-8 seconds. His chest rose and fell in sync with my hands, creating a strange sense of unity. His wide-open eyes stared directly at me. In my heart, I begged him to live. "They say you collapsed on the street. No one knows how long you were there. Even when you were found, there was no pulse. What happened? Please, take a breath. Just one breath, please."

He gazes at me blankly, his expression unreadable. Shifting my eyes to the monitor connected to the crash cart, I see the heart rhythm tracing erratically across the screen. Still, I continue to supply oxygen at steady intervals, keeping my focus on his eyes. The others in the room remain unshaken, silently carrying out their assigned tasks with calm precision. Only the doctor's orders and the repetitions of those commands break the stillness in the air.

In a low but resolute voice, the doctor said, "Stop." For over 30 minutes, countless rounds of CPR and every possible medication had been administered, yet no pulse could be detected. The doctor, too, could not afford to spend more time on futile efforts. At his command, people began to step back from the man one by one. I held onto the oxygen bag, pretending not to hear. Letting go of it would mean giving up on his life. Then came a sharp, stern voice: "What are you doing? I said stop."

I hesitated, then stopped what I was doing and looked at the man. The ER nurse gently patted my shoulder. "Jane, go back to your ward. Your part is done. He's gone." I faltered, unsure. "Leave this room, now. Look at your pale face. At this rate, you'll be the next one to collapse, and there's no bed for you here. He didn't even have a pulse when he was found, and we don't know how long he'd been down. We did everything we could. Even if he had come back, his brain was too damaged, he would have been in a vegetative state. It's better this way."

What I longed to hear wasn't such a clinical, logical analysis. I longed for something more human, more emotional. Perhaps a warm thought or a gesture of condolence for the departed. As I removed my gloves and mask, I glanced around the room. I noticed how empty it had become. Where had all the people gone? Just moments ago, the room had been bustling, yet now it felt desolate, leaving behind a lonely corpse. How cold death feels. When there was a chance to save his life, there had been such passion and urgency, but the moment that life ended, everything turned so indifferent and detached.

I stepped backward out of the room. Those clear eyes, which seemed far too vivid to belong to the dead, were still fixed on me. On my way back to the ward, regret washed over me. I should have closed his eyes. How could I have left him so abruptly, without a proper farewell?

At 11 a.m., I admitted a new patient, "M." Transferred from the ER, his condition was clearly critical. Once all the paperwork was completed, the attending physician and a cardiologist burst in together. After a brief discussion, they decided the patient needed to be moved to the Intensive Care Unit immediately. Today feels heavy. I gathered the patient's medications and his chart, secured a portable oxygen tank to the patient's bed, and connected a mobile cardiac monitor before transferring them to the ICU. After handing over the report to the assigned nurse, I was about to leave when I suddenly thought of patient, "L" and asked how he was doing. I shouldn't have asked.

"L" was a patient I had cared for a week earlier who had undergone surgery. Considering the time needed to wake up from anesthesia, I thought he should have been back on the ward by then. I called the operating room, only to be told he was still in the recovery room. I assumed their recovery was simply taking a little longer than usual. An hour later, I received a call from the recovery room. "L" had been transferred to the ICU. They asked me to bring all the patient's medications and his chart, as it was unclear how long he would stay there. When I arrived, "L" was on a ventilator, relying on it to breathe. His complexion was pale, a stark contrast to how he looked in the morning. Despite calling his name, there was no response, he still hadn't regained consciousness.

During the few days I had off, "L" occasionally crossed my mind. Today, I happened to remember him because the nurse I was speaking with had cared for him. She subtly drew her right index finger across her neck and whispered, "Last night." "What happened?" I asked, my face growing tense. She shrugged and said, "Forget it. He'd been suffering from heart disease for a long time. Honestly, he lasted longer than anyone expected." As if there was nothing more to say, she hurried off to another patient's bed, without another word.

As I left the ICU, I felt the strength drain from my legs. "I hate this. I really do. This job as a nurse, why must I witness death so often? I hate how it makes my heart grow calloused." Truly, I despise it.

I loathe how indifferent and detached I've become while caring for patients hospitalized with terminal cancer and a slew of other diagnoses. I despise my hardened resolve as I fit prosthetics on patients who have returned from surgery after losing both legs to diabetes, lecturing them that walking more will help their wounds heal faster.

Early in the afternoon, I discharged patient "T". Dressed in a vibrant, floral Hawaiian shirt instead of his hospital gown, he looked like a completely different person as he paced around the room. In front of his wife and children, who had come to pick him up, he proudly declared, "I'm all better now!" Wasn't this the same man who, just an hour before the doctor gave the discharge order, had complained of pain and refused to walk to the bathroom on his own?

Discharging a patient brings me joy. As long as it's not one of those cases where discharge is the only option left because there's nothing more medicine can offer, it feels good. Although discharging a patient adds extra tasks like, writing discharge notes, completing the chart, and organizing the system, it is satisfying to see someone leave. Even though a discharged patient's empty bed quickly fills with a new admission, bringing with it endless paperwork, a history review, and new orders from multiple doctors, the process still feels rewarding. I enjoy explaining post-discharge care to patients and their families, what to do in this or that situation.

Watching them listen intently, not wanting to miss a single word, makes me happy. It's also a joy to witness the tight-knit bonds of family. Through this, I am reminded that human life is fundamentally the same for everyone and that humanity cannot exist without love. It's a lesson I learn over and over again.

As I stood at the entrance with the patient in a wheelchair, the sunlight felt harsh. While his caregiver brought the car around from the parking lot, I reminded him once again, no more drugs, no more alcohol, and quit smoking. He smiled awkwardly and replied, "I'll try."

Looking up at the sky, I noticed the palm leaves swaying vibrantly in the breeze, full of life and health. "Look at those trees," I said. "Even they look so healthy. You need to be just as healthy. Your body isn't just yours, you have a responsibility to care for it for the sake of your loved ones. Promise me you'll stay healthy!"

Instead of answering, he simply smiled.

He, his wife, and their two children each gave me a hug and a kiss on the cheek. I waved goodbye as I sent them off. "Don't come back here. I don't want to see you again." He responded with a bright smile and said, "Thank you."

Hospitals are such strange places. Words like "I don't want to see you again" are met with warm gratitude. The farewell stretched on, and I could already imagine Debbie, our head nurse, giving me one of her looks and saying, "Jane, how many times do I have to tell you not to spend so much time seeing patients off? If you manage your time like this, it throws off the rest of the schedule. Why haven't you learned this by now?"

As I turned the empty wheelchair and stepped back through the entrance, I saw it—the sky filled with the vitality

of life. And suddenly, I understood. I understood why life is often depicted as blue, why the effort to save a life is called Code Blue.

But why is life blue? Is it because life is sacred, and blue symbolizes nobility? I don't know, I really don't. Life is just... blue.

As soon as I stepped back into the ward, the announcement echoed again: "Code Blue, ICU. Code Blue, ICU!" Oh no, what's going on today? I turned to Kerri, our head nurse, for help. "Can you go this time? I've got a backlog of medications to administer to my patients." It wasn't true.

Kerri, I'm sorry. I'm just so exhausted. Today has already been more than enough. Please, give me a moment to breathe, before I collapse and end up being wheeled into the ER myself. And we both know there's no bed there for me.

Jane Ha

A Day in the Life of an On-Call Nurse

I was shocked awake by the screeching ring of my phone. The hospital's name flashed clearly on the screen. It's 1 a.m. I pulled the blanket over my head and turned away. I'm not on call tonight. It's my colleague Patrick's turn. If I answer, I won't be able to say no. Moments later, the phone rings again. I cover my ears, refusing to listen, and let the sound fade into the distance. Berating myself, I resolutely whisper in my head, "I should've put my phone on silent before going to bed,"

Meanwhile, my mind buzzes with restless thoughts. "Who's in pain and needs emergency surgery? Which surgeon is operating? Who's the anesthesiologist? And who's the on-call OR nurse tonight? For heaven's sake, Patrick, where is that guy? He's on call, so why doesn't he ever answer his phone, leaving me to deal with this?" By now, sleep is a distant memory.

Now the house phone rings. My heart sinks. As expected, it's Jerry, the house supervisor. An emergency room patient with a ruptured appendix has developed peritonitis, and immediate surgery is critical. His voice is urgent. Apologetically, he asks, "We can't get hold of Patrick. Do you know anyone else who might be able to come in?" I feel helpless. No matter how hard I think, no one comes to mind. Both Jerry and I already know the reality, I'm the only full-time nurse for the recovery room. No one else would want to be disturbed at this hour. The per diem nurses almost certainly have shifts at their main jobs.

I reassure him not to worry, that I'll head to the hospital shortly. As Jerry alternates between saying "Thank you" and "God bless you" in his warm voice, I forgive myself for the foolishness of answering the phone. I couldn't bear to disappoint him. On nights like this, when I'm pulled from bed to work, Jerry goes out of his way to make it up to me. He'll order my favorite sandwich from the kitchen and personally bring it to me. He even leaves notes for the morning shift supervisor, Lou, saying, "Jane worked late into the night or early morning, please take special care of her." Lou, in turn, always copies the note and hands it to me with a smile.

Grabbing my water bottle, I pause at the door for a moment. What if the surgeon is late? Or if I have downtime while waiting for the post-op patient to arrive in the recovery room? Since it's an abdominal surgery, it'll take quite some time. Reading poetry would be nice. I reach for the debut poetry collection of "S," my poet friend of 20 years who recently moved to "P" city and take it off the bookshelf.

As I back my car out of the driveway, an unexpected wave of loneliness washes over me. When will I ever reach a point where I can live as I please, unaffected by circumstances or obligations? Suddenly, I feel a surge of resentment toward Patrick. This is the third time. I felt okay when he apologized profusely, practically begging for forgiveness. His excuses weren't convincing, but I had no choice. If he doesn't step up, all the on-call shifts fall to me. Raymond, who works part-time three days a week, has been on vacation for three weeks, proposing to his girlfriend in the Philippines. There's simply no one to share the load with me.

Still, this time I find myself questioning his character. If he can't handle the responsibility, why did he sign up for on-call duty in the first place? Wouldn't it have been more decent to let me know his situation in advance? If he had, I could have covered for a fellow nurse with a sense of camaraderie rather than this heavy heart. I could have mentally prepared myself and gotten some rest earlier. Instead, here I am, stepping out of the house barely 20 minutes after falling asleep. It doesn't feel great.

I merge onto the freeway and turn on some music. "Love is lovely…." That's right, love is indeed lovely. The soulful, heartfelt voice of the male singer suddenly brightens my mood. "I love you like never before…." Of course. Naturally. Love always comes in new colors and scents. That's the magic of love. That's why even those who have been deceived by love countless times, or worn down by it to exhaustion, still find themselves falling into new love as long as they're alive. And that's what makes life worth living.

Driving along the empty freeway, I feel an unexpected rush of exhilaration for life. I take pride in the fact that I am still here, alive, at this hour. Even now, there are those taking their final breaths in this world. Earlier today, in the ICU, I spoke with a fellow nurse as we cared for a 92-year-old patient recovering from surgery under general anesthesia, entirely reliant on a ventilator. We questioned whether undergoing surgery in such a state was truly worth it. Where does human dignity lie? What about the quality of life? The answer was clear, there isn't any. We concluded that the past, when people could simply let go and pass away when their time came, was far better. And it's true, when the time comes, just dying, without prolonging suffering, that's the merciful path.

While we were caring for our patient, the patient in the neighboring room passed away. After ensuring the stability of our patient, who had woken from anesthesia, and handing them over to the assigned nurse, I left the ICU. Outside, the family of the deceased stood silently weeping. One man was banging his head against the wall in anguish. Unable to simply walk past, I gently patted his shoulder.

Before I know it, I'm at the hospital parking lot, pulled from my thoughts. My heart feels heavy. The constant on-call shifts and callbacks throughout the week have left me physically and mentally drained. Just the other day, I couldn't refuse the blood donation bus that had come to the parking lot, so I used my lunch break to donate 350 ml. Almost immediately after, I started feeling unwell, with a headache setting in. Despite this, I stayed at the hospital until 3 a.m. that night. When I finally made it home, I collapsed straight into bed. The next morning, I received a call from the hospital saying no one else was available to work. Unable to say no, I went in at 9 a.m. and ended up staying until 9 p.m., battling a headache and low-grade fever the entire time. Why couldn't I say no? Why couldn't I just admit I was too sick to work? Why am I so foolishly stubborn?

A friend, hearing that I was unwell from overexertion, remarked, "Writers consider dying young a badge of honor, which is why they neglect their health." Oh my, how embarrassing. I'm already past the age to die young, aren't I? Having missed the chance for an early death, I want to go out gracefully, or at least well; like a true human being or a proper writer. Then they added another biting comment: "If you keep wearing yourself out like this, you won't die well when the time comes." "Oh, give me a break. What do you expect me to do? I'll just live my way and go when it's time. It's not like I get to decide how I die anyway."

That's absolutely true. The thought of entrusting my soul to God, surrounded by loved ones on a beach with a beautiful sunset, may sound lovely, but it's nothing more than a wishful fantasy. Hoping to maintain dignity while ensuring that the process of one's death doesn't cause pain or trauma to loved ones is, in truth, an unreasonable demand, an illusion born from ignorance, as if one could play God.

At 2 a.m., the surgeon finally arrived. After transferring the patient to the operating room, I assisted the OR nurse and technician by gathering the necessary supplies. I stayed for a while, ensuring everything was running smoothly, and once the atmosphere felt stable, I returned to the recovery room.

I open S's poetry collection and find myself unable to take my eyes off a particular verse: "…endless wandering, weary despair, worn-out sighs, heavy solitude… unresolved longing, unspent pain…" Oh my, so that's how it was. You must have spent countless nights awake. You must have suffered so much. Because of your gentle smile and generous nature, I never saw the depths within you.

Why am I always so slow to understand? I should have realized it long ago, when I first received this book of poems. I should have paid closer attention to the lines describing you as "an utterly honest man, incapable of compromise—achingly sincere, never letting go of his sharp-edged stubbornness." I should have seen his pain, his tears, and his solitude. If I had understood what kind of person he was back then, I could have embraced him with warmer understanding. Now, it hurts. I wish I had treated him better when he was near. But now, he's in a distant place, and I can no longer see him as often.

A patient was brought into the recovery room. A robust 21-year-old young man, who couldn't let go of his mother's hand and had tears in his eyes as he was wheeled into surgery, called for her the moment he woke up from anesthesia. "Mommy, Mommy, Mommy...."

It's fascinating. Even when young patients, dazed by anesthesia and unable to open their eyes, have wildly unstable vital signs, hearing their mother's voice instantly calms them. A mother's voice is medicine. The love Latin American mothers have for their children is especially profound, it moves anyone watching to tears. The way they gently stroke their children's hair and whisper softly in Spanish is so warm and tender, like a lullaby. Sitting beside them, I find myself repeating the phrases I hear the mothers say to their children: "Voy a quedar contigo" (I'll stay with you). "Te amo" (I love you). "Tú eres mi bebé" (You are my baby). Your mom is here. I'll never leave you. My sweet baby. My beautiful baby.

The patient, now somewhat conscious, squints and asks, "Did I really have the surgery? I don't remember a thing." "Of course," I reply. "You were in a deep sleep." "You people are amazing. Thank you, all of you." I call over Dr. Quijada, who is dictating notes in a corner of the recovery room. "Dr. Quijada, the patient says you did an excellent job and is very impressed." He gives a warm smile, his kind nature shining through.

The patient awakened fully from anesthesia and regained a stable rhythm. After transferring him to the general ward and tidying up, I finally stepped out of the hospital. It was 4:30 a.m. Technician Mary Ann stretched out on the break room sofa, saying she couldn't drive because she was too sleepy. She had to be back at the hospital by 6:30 a.m.

After returning home, I took a shower and prepared three lunchboxes. By the time I finished, it was already time to leave for work. I arrived at the hospital at 7:20 a.m., 20 minutes late. The morning passed in a flurry of activity, but as the afternoon slowed down with only a few surgery cases. A sudden wave of exhaustion set in. I finished my shift on time and headed home, only for my car to seem intent on changing lanes on its own, stubbornly resisting me. The freeway felt unusually long as I drove. Once home, I went out to the backyard and crouched by the vegetable garden, gazing endlessly at the tiny new sprouts pushing through the soil to reach the surface. If these little things can break through the heavy ground to grow, how could I, living above the earth, fail to handle my daily life? With renewed determination, I prepared dinner for my youngest son, who had just returned from a basketball game.

After taking a shower, with my hair still damp, I collapsed onto the bed. It was 9 p.m. At 10:20, a friend called, and we talked for 30 minutes. At 11:10, my daughter called from her college dorm. We chatted for 15 minutes. After that, my memory fades into a soft blur. I must have slipped into a deep sleep, the weight of the day finally pulling me under. Perhaps I dreamed, I can't quite recall. Maybe I floated through the universe, adrift in a quiet, endless expanse or perhaps I was talking to the stars. The gentle hum of conversation, the lingering warmth of connection, and the hush of the night all wove together, carrying me into the embrace of sleep. I vaguely recall hearing a song: "Love is lovely."

Chapter 1

Chapter 2

Conversations with Dr. Collins

Mama Estrella Valdez

Ivan

Memories of Julia

The Blossoms of Connection

Three Days of Togetherness

La Vida es Hermosa (Life is Beautiful)

The Last Romance

Touching

Jane Ha

Conversations with Dr. Collins

Dr. Collins is a seasoned anesthesiologist with 30 years of experience. For over 20 years, he dedicated three to six months each year for missionary work, traveling to countries with limited medical care, offering his services. Now, this seasoned warrior has finally settled down.

When he is in the operating room, no matter how complex or challenging the surgery, our OR team feels at ease, knowing the patient is in capable hands. His extensive knowledge and exceptional skill in managing surgical patients are unmatched. With a calm and gentle voice, he brings a sense of reassurance, making even the most difficult situations easier to accept with a nod and some quiet peace.

Dr. Collins has led a rich and dynamic life. He has journeyed through the mountain valleys of Peru and the Himalayas countless times, learning to love God, humanity, and nature. Listening to his stories, woven from the tapestry of the world, seen through the eyes of a doctor, it feels like stepping into a dream. You find yourself wishing to meet the unknown people he has encountered, to wave at them, to embrace them, and to share in the beauty of their existence.

Hearing his stories of operating rooms in underdeveloped countries brings both joy and sorrow. He recalls performing surgery while adjusting the number of incandescent light bulbs hanging from the ceiling like clusters of grapes as an improvised method to regulate the patient's body

temperature. Then, there was the heartbreaking story of a mother sobbing as she clutched the lifeless body of a 12-year-old girl who succumbed to an acute blood infection, one that could have been easily treated if only antibiotics had been available.

I asked him, "Now that you've returned from your long journeys, is there anything you'd like to share with your neighbors and friends?"

Without hesitation, he replied, "Slow down and smell the roses." Then, after a brief pause, he added with a knowing smile, "The walls have ears." I took it to heart. It was a maxim Dr. Collins had distilled from his 60 years of life—words shaped by experience, wisdom, and the countless lives he had touched along the way.

He's right. When life gets too busy, it's easy to overlook the precious elements of living. There's no room to gather and savor life's meaning. No one wants to let cherished relationships slip away simply because they're preoccupied. And how compelling and practical is the reminder that walls have ears? There is a phrase that captures the idea perfectly, "There is always a space that bridges the daytime words overheard by birds and the nighttime whispers caught by mice."

For true human existence, walls are essential. It wouldn't be an exaggeration to say that our lives are surrounded by walls. Being mindful of our words, wherever we are, could help us avoid many of life's storms.

Perhaps Dr. Collins meant more than just caution in speech. Maybe he was suggesting something deeper, a reminder to live with greater attentiveness. To slow down. To be present. To not only mind our words but to truly listen to the voices around us.

I thoroughly enjoyed my conversations with him. His deep understanding of life, coupled with reflections shaped by wisdom across cultures and eras, reinforced a simple yet profound truth that no matter the space or time, we humans are ultimately one. Our exchanges of proverbs and philosophies transcended boundaries, reminding me of our shared human essence. I felt deeply grateful to have him as my neighbor. He was someone who so beautifully balances warm compassion for humanity and unwavering professionalism.

He shared a phrase he turns to when his body and mind grow weary:

"I am wounded today, but I am not dead as yet.

So let me lay down and bleed awhile.

Tomorrow I will rise and fight again."

Yes, even those who seem boundless in strength and wisdom carry unseen burdens. The realization that someone so composed and capable also faces exhaustion and struggle brings an unexpected kind of comfort. It doesn't diminish their strength but rather deepens my respect for them.

Resilience isn't about being unshaken. It is about recognizing our wounds, allowing ourselves the space to heal and rest, and then rising again. The image of him "bleeding for a while" is striking. It becomes a powerful metaphor—not as a symbol of weakness, but of endurance. It is comforting because it validates our own struggles. That if, even someone with such patience and energy must pause to gather himself, then surely we too are allowed moments of stillness before continuing forward.

True resilience isn't just about standing tall at all times; it's about knowing when to rest, when to acknowledge pain, and when to gather the strength to rise again. The thought of someone so steadfast allowing themselves a moment of vulnerability, feels movingly human. In that, we find reassurance. If even the strongest among us need time to heal, then we can grant ourselves the same grace as well.

He said, "We cannot breathe all at once. Everything in existence has its own rhythm. Let's live as if dancing to that rhythm." It is a beautiful philosophy, one that acknowledges the natural cadence of life. We cannot rush breath, just as we cannot rush healing, love, or understanding. Everything unfolds in its own time, in its own rhythm. To live as if dancing to that rhythm means embracing both the pauses and the movements, the moments of stillness and the bursts of energy. It's a reminder to trust life's flow rather than resist it. Just like a dance, life isn't meant to be controlled rigidly; it's meant to be felt, experienced, and moved through with grace. Perhaps that's the secret to true resilience, not forcing things before their time but learning to move in harmony with life's natural rhythm.

I saw it. Beyond Dr. Collins' glasses, beyond the wind threading through the branches outside the window, the silent depth of years gone by. A quiet testament to a life fully lived. A fervent gesture toward existence itself. Love and grace unfurling like a flag in the breeze. For a fleeting moment, it felt as though the intricate code of life had been deciphered.

Yes, that's how it should be. I should live slowly, savoring each moment, fully feeling and cherishing the beauty that surrounds me. Keeping my ears open to others, listening carefully, while choosing my words with care.

Jane Ha

Mama Estella Valdez

Mama Estella is 97 years old, a Mexican grandmother with perfectly round eyes, as if drawn with a compass. She strikes up conversations with anyone she meets, and her eyes grow even wider when she emphasizes words with her spirited pronunciation. When I first heard about her two nights ago during a handover report from the night-shift nurse, I felt uneasy. They described her as someone very difficult. She kept removing her IV, refused her medications, and didn't want to eat, making things challenging for everyone.

What made it even more challenging was her confusion and repeated attempts to climb out of bed. Although the doctor had finally ordered her wrists to be restrained, she thrashed so violently that half her body often ended up hanging off the side. Every twenty minutes, the nursing staff had to reposition her, carefully lifting her back onto the mattress, adjusting the sheets, and smoothing down the pillows. Yet, as soon as they turned away, the cycle began again. It was as if her body held a memory of movement too strong to surrender.

But when I finally met her in person, she was nothing like the disruptive patient I had imagined. Her warm, expressive eyes and the gentle way she spoke to everyone around her immediately softened my initial apprehension. Yes, she was strong-willed, but there was something undeniably endearing about her—something that made it impossible to view her as just a "troublemaker." Her refusal to take medication and eat wasn't mere defiance; it felt more like an unspoken protest, a quiet resistance born from something deeper. Was it fear? Exhaustion? Or perhaps a lifetime of unwavering independence that made surrendering to hospital routines so unbearable?

By the way, the restraints were meant for her safety, but they seemed almost cruel. A stark contrast to the independence she had likely lived with for nearly a century. Despite them, she still fought, her body restless and determined, as if resisting not just the hospital bed but something far greater.

The language barrier added to the challenge, as Mama Estella didn't speak a word of English, requiring a translator for every interaction. Moreover, her two daughters took turns staying at her bedside, and their constant interventions and exacting demands made even the doctors hesitant to assert themselves. Her daughters, hovering with a fierce protectiveness, scrutinized every action taken by the medical team. Their concern was understandable, but their intense watching created an uncomfortable and tense atmosphere. No decision could be made without their approval, and no step taken without their questioning.

Mama Estella's greatest battle, however, wasn't with her caregivers or her daughters, but was with her refusal to eat. Each meal tray was met with the same resistance. She would turn her head away, press her lips together, and shake her head with a quiet but resolute finality. No pleading, no coaxing, no well-intended persuasion could move her.

Ultimately, she could not be discharged due to her complete refusal to eat. According to hospital policy, patients who refuse all food fall into a special category requiring essential care for sustaining life, making discharge impossible. Despite her advanced age, she had no significant underlying illnesses. The doctor diagnosed her condition as a sodium deficiency caused by dehydration. Although, the latest lab results indicated that her sodium levels were approaching normal.

The human body is astonishingly delicate. A slight imbalance in chemical composition or ratios can cause mental confusion. A small drop in oxygen, or a minor fluctuation in potassium, whether slightly too high or too low, can lead to critical conditions or even death. No matter how much we try to glorify human existence with refined words like elegance, dignity, or sophistication, it is ultimately a futile endeavor. While humans are metaphysical beings, their survival is grounded in the physical.

Can we live without eating? Without eliminating waste? Without sleep for days? These basic functions, so often taken for granted, are the very foundation of life.

Every morning, as I receive the lab reports detailing patients' test results, I practice humility. Just look at these tiny numbers—values that, at a glance, seem so insignificant. Yet, a mere 0.1 difference can be enough to trigger an emergency, requiring immediate intervention. It is a sobering reminder of how fragile we truly are.

As soon as I stepped into her room, Mama Estella wasted no time in scolding me. With a stern expression, she demanded to know why an ordinary housewife was wandering about so early in the morning. Shouldn't I be home doing laundry, cooking, and cleaning? Her daughter, clearly embarrassed, translated every word faithfully.

But instead of feeling offended, I found her endearing. Her wide, round eyes sparkled with conviction, and her words carried the weight of a time-honored tradition. Wasn't her reaction simply a reflection of the values deeply ingrained in the elders of our culture? After all, in the past, what housewife from a respectable family would be at a hospital at 7 a.m., tending to strangers of all ages and genders, all in the name of work?

I liked her immediately. Gently, I removed the restraints from her wrists and began massaging them. For patients with restrained wrists or ankles, protocol requires they be released for ten minutes every two hours, with their skin condition carefully monitored. Sitting by her bedside, I patted the back of her hand and made a request.

"Let's have a good day, okay? No pulling out IV needles, no removing the heart monitor, and no trying to climb out of bed. If you can promise me that, I'll do everything I can to help you get home."

She looked at me with a radiant smile, so warm, so full of life, that I couldn't resist pressing a kiss to the hand I was holding. Her face, slightly sunken from not wearing her dentures, only made her smile all the more angelic. Looking into my eyes, she said, "When I'm discharged, I'll make you Comida Pollo. You have to come to my house.""

I couldn't understand why the night-shift nurse had found her so difficult. To me, Mama Estella was nothing but kind. Every time I visited her, she showered me with compliments, her daughter eagerly translating with visible excitement. The tension I'd felt, expecting a demanding, stubborn patient, now seemed like a distant dream.

Even without translation, I understood her completely, her animated expressions spoke louder than words. She held my hands, shaking them enthusiastically, side to side, up and down, as if she were pouring all her affection into that simple gesture. Watching her, I couldn't help but think how wonderful it would be to grow old with such joyful innocence.

By the afternoon, her memory had improved so much that I no longer needed to restrain her wrists. She had regained full clarity and was completely cooperative. The next day, she was even able to sit up in a chair. With her long, white hair neatly braided into a single plait, she looked more lively than ever.

I playfully reminded her of the chicken dish she had promised to make, urging her to get well soon. Her round eyes sparkled as she nodded eagerly, fully agreeing. With newfound determination, she took her medications and finished every meal I handed her—diligent, as if preparing for the day she would cook for me.

The next day, Mama Estella was finally discharged. She clutched my hands tightly, showering me with all kinds of blessings. Her small, frail frame—worn down by time—was carefully settled into a wheelchair, and I escorted her to the hospital's front entrance.

Before leaving, she insisted that I must visit her home. She spoke excitedly about her grandson, who worked in Washington state, and promised to introduce me to him when he came to California on vacation. She also encouraged me to learn Spanish, her round eyes widening with enthusiasm. I barely managed to suppress my laughter as I nodded along, promising I would. It was endearing how she simply assumed I was single.

About an hour after I returned to the ward, two large, round plastic gift boxes were delivered in my name. They were from Mama Estella's daughter. Inside, I found beautifully decorated Mexican castellas in vibrant colors, each one a work of art. Nestled among them was a handwritten note:

"Thank you for making my mother so happy." As I held the note, I felt a warmth spread through me. Despite the long hours and challenges, moments like these reminded me why I do what I do.

Mama Estella must be happy. Speaking her mind freely, her lovely round eyes sparkling as she talks endlessly, she lives peacefully in her own world, untouched by worry. She will likely keep repeating, over and over again, "I need to make chicken for Jane. To do that, I have to get home soon."

Perhaps, in her heart, cooking for me is her way of showing gratitude—a gesture of warmth, a symbol of affection in the language she knows best. And though she may not remember everything clearly, the feeling of kindness shared between us lingers, etched into her heart in a way words never could.

The past three days with her brought me so much happiness. Starting tomorrow, I have four days off—time to step out of my role as a nurse and simply exist as an ordinary person. Yet, as I stand in the now-empty room where Mama Estella had stayed, I already feel the ache of her absence.

I picture her lively eyes, the way she animatedly repeated the same phrases, her stubborn yet endearing presence. The room feels too quiet without her. It's strange how some patients leave a mark, not just in the hospital but in the heart.

Ivan

Ivan had been absent from work for two weeks. On his way home from meeting a friend at a local coffee shop, he was ambushed by gang members—mistaken for someone from a rival crew. They stabbed him in the left chest and beat him mercilessly with a baseball bat, leaving him unconscious in the street. He was rushed to the nearest ER, barely clinging to life. But he survived.

Today, Ivan returned to the unit. The moment he stepped in, we—his OR family—embraced him, overcome with emotion. We had held our breath, hoping and praying for his return. And now, seeing him standing before us, alive, the relief had us broken down in tears.

Ivan is a 28-year-old technician in the gastrointestinal lab—a well-built, strikingly handsome man with a quiet demeanor. He and his girlfriend are raising a one-year-old daughter. Among all the people I've met, Ivan stands out as one of the kindest souls I've ever known. His gentle spirit and remarkable patience are truly rare. In the past ten years, I cannot recall a single moment when he raised his voice, sulked, or even hinted at frustration.

The sound of people calling for Ivan often fills the unit like a chorus. I have never heard him say, "No" or "I can't." Refusal simply isn't in his nature. Whenever patients weighing 300 pounds or more needs to be moved, either from a gurney to the operating table, from the table back

to the gurney, or from PACU to their room, nothing moves without his help. Moving a 350-pound Cesarean-section patient who has yet to recover from lower-body anesthesia is a task fraught with risk. Without Ivan's strength and steady presence, injuries—both to the patient and the staff—become a real possibility. After surgeries, it's also his job to clean the blood-soaked operating room floors and dispose of all the trash. The OR staff seem to unload all the unpleasant, messy, and undesirable tasks onto him. He's also the one who takes everyone's finicky lunch orders, often driving to multiple restaurants just to accommodate our colleagues' diverse tastes. On hot summer days, he goes the extra mile by packing a plastic tub full of ice to keep ice cream orders from melting before delivering them.

One afternoon, after a relentless morning of back-to-back surgeries, exhaustion weighed heavily on all of us. By 2 p.m. we finally stole a brief, much-needed break in the nurses' lounge, sipping tea in weary silence. We knew we had to eat something before the next case began, even though the thought of moving felt like an impossible challenge. Michelle, the head nurse, urgently paged Ivan. When he came running, she patted him on the back and shoved some cash into his hand. "Brother, go to the cafeteria and grab every kind of cookie they've got. All of them." I was stunned. "Michelle, you paged Ivan just for that?" My mouth hung open in disbelief.

As Ivan replied with a simple "Okay..." and turned to leave, Rose suddenly gave him a firm kick in the rear. Shocked, I turned to look at her, but she just shrugged and said matter-of-factly, "It's fine. No matter what you do, he never gets angry."

The OR staff all wear standardized uniforms, laundered with a special detergent, and creates a sense of unity. Yet, in spite the identical attire, their roles, ranks, and incomes vary widely. Surgeons, anesthesiologists, interns, residents, nurses, technicians, surgical instrument and supply managers, custodians, and transporters all perform vastly different duties, each carrying its own level of responsibility and compensation. The disparity is stark, but in the OR, we all move as one team.

When the OR is packed with surgical cases, the nurses, technicians, and housekeepers work together to clean the OR. Given the strict infection control regulations (maintaining low temperatures, ensuring proper sterilization, and preventing contamination) the process of cleaning is meticulous and time-consuming. When nurses are preoccupied with patient care, the responsibility of cleaning often falls on the technicians. Of the many technicians on staff, it is usually Ivan who handles most of the cleaning alone.

Ivan takes on all the unpleasant tasks willingly, never voicing a single complaint. He's the kind of person who, on a female colleague's birthday, thoughtfully selects a luxurious perfume from a high-end department store. On mornings when the OR schedule is packed, he anticipates that his coworkers might skip breakfast, so he picks up a box of donuts on his way to work. Come lunchtime on those very same days, he sits quietly in the corner, eating a 25-cent Cup O' Noodles, soaked in hot water. The donuts we devour without a second thought, often without even a proper thank-you, are likely paid for with the lunch money his girlfriend gave him.

When surgical cases are light and the recovery room is empty, the three male staff members in the OR push a gurney to the corner, turn on rock music, and break into impromptu hip-hop dances. Watching Ivan attempt a one-arm balance only to crash spectacularly, or misalign his hands while trying to lift his hips and toppling over, never fails to send me into a fit of laughter. Then there's his uncanny impression of nurse Ethan's crawling bug routine, so hilariously spot-on that I end up laughing until my stomach hurts.

Ivan, noticing my laughter, grins and says, "It's nice to see Jane laugh. It's my duty to make Jane happy." Then, with exaggerated determination, he repeats the move again and again, each time ending up flat on the floor, sending me uncontrollable bursts of laughter, until tears start rolling down my cheeks. One time, while attempting a handstand, Ivan miscalculated his kick and struck the fluorescent light fixture on the ceiling with his sneaker. We all gasped, clutching our chests in relief when it miraculously didn't shatter. Another time, their impromptu dance session was interrupted by an unexpected visit from the supervisor, who caught the trio mid-move and delivered a stern scolding. Even as they stood at attention, pretending to be remorseful, I struggled to suppress my laughter. The sheer absurdity of the moment, watching the OR's legendary trio get caught red-handed, made it all the more unforgettable.

One afternoon, we had a rare lull in cases and a brief moment of peace. I sat in a corner of the recovery room, sipping tea, when Ivan walked in. There was something different in his demeanor, quieter, more solemn. He hesitated for a moment before saying, "I want only you to see this." Then, slowly, he unbuttoned his shirt. What I saw left me breathless. I had never seen bruises so deep, wide, and brutally severe. It spread across his torso in ominous shades of purple and black, marking every place the bat had struck. It was nothing short of a miracle that his heart and other vital organs had been spared from critical damage. My body reacted before my mind could process it. I instinctively squeezed my eyes shut, unable to bear the sight for too long.

Ivan, however, tried to comfort me instead. With his usual gentle smile, he said he would heal soon and that I shouldn't worry. His resilience was astounding—he spoke as if his injuries were nothing more than minor scrapes, as if the brutal attack had been just an unfortunate inconvenience rather than a brush with death. Then, in a quick, almost detached tone, he said, "Jane, do you know who I thought of while groaning in pain? It was you. I kept thinking that if Jane were there, she would take good care of me."

The words landed softly yet heavily, sinking into the space between us. He didn't elaborate, didn't wait for a response. Without offering any further explanation, he simply turned and walked away. I remained rooted to the spot, stunned, my heart caught in the unexpected weight of his words.

A loud bang went off in my head, leaving me momentarily paralyzed. I couldn't move, couldn't think. When I finally regained my composure, an overwhelming wave of emotion washed over me. My chest swelled with a quiet yet profound happiness—one that brimmed with warmth, gratitude, and something deeper, something almost sacred. Tears welled up in my eyes at the thought that, in a moment of pain and fear, the person Ivan thought of was me. Me. Not a family member, not a childhood friend, not even a doctor—but me, Jane. The weight of that realization settled over me like a warm embrace. Ivan, someone as kind and pure as an angel, had reached for me in his thoughts when his life hung in the balance. And that simple truth struck me with an undeniable clarity. Isn't this why I became a nurse? To hold even one person's trust so deeply? To be the one they think of when they need comfort? To hear words like this, even just once?

Memories of Julia

Julia is a 24-year-old woman who has been paralyzed from the waist down since a car accident eight years ago, leaving her in a constant cycle of hospital stays. Despite her age, her mental and emotional development remains that of a teenager. With long blonde hair streaked in red and blue, and piercings adorning her tongue and lips, she embraces self-expression with a bold and youthful spirit. However, beneath her vibrant exterior lies a body that has endured relentless suffering. She has no sensation below her waist, and her feet are slowly deteriorating. The deep, hollow wounds on both hips—each the size of palm—are remnants of the accident, now chronic and resistant to treatment. Despite the strongest antibiotics, the infections persist, making her battle for healing an ongoing and painful struggle. For years, her wounds have continuously oozed pus and blood, refusing to heal. She endures relentless pain in her lower back, often crying out for narcotic medication, anxiously counting down the seconds until her next dose. Her life revolves around managing pain, and the hospital has become a second home—she is admitted every few weeks or months for surgical debridement of her necrotic skin and intensive antibiotic treatments. Yet, despite these interventions, the cycle of infection and suffering never truly ends.

Each morning, when the nurses see Julia's name on their assignment list, they can't help but let out a quiet sigh. Her

demanding nature and difficult temperament, often treating nurses more like personal attendants than caregivers, require immense patience and mental preparation. She insists on having everything done her way, often snapping or throwing tantrums when things don't go exactly as she wishes. Because of this, an unspoken rule has developed among the staff: whenever Julia is admitted, they take turns caring for her, rotating the responsibility day by day to share the emotional burden.

For three consecutive days, I was assigned to care for Julia. The head nurse must have felt relieved, thinking at last someone had stepped up to manage such a troublesome patient without protest. But what she didn't know was that I had come with a quiet resolve. I had made up my mind: this time, I would not let her slip by untouched. I couldn't bear to see her remain walled in by loneliness, exiled by a temperament she couldn't seem to master. More than sympathy, what stirred me was a sense of responsibility, a quiet duty to reach her, to help her grow. She needed to mature, to find a way back to people, to connect, instead of always driving others away.

It was a miscalculation on my part—arrogance, even. Julia was unyielding. My lofty goals had to be abandoned early on. Her constant whining and calling for the nurse every ten minutes completely wore me out. How can one person truly change another? Transformation doesn't happen through sheer will or external effort. It must come from within, sparked by an awakening of consciousness, a moment of realization that allows a person to confront their own reality. I already knew this truth well, yet I had charged in with misguided passion, believing I could somehow break through. How foolish of me as a nurse.

It was the afternoon of my third day caring for Julia. While I was on the phone, receiving orders for a newly admitted patient from the patient's attending physician, I was momentarily delayed in responding to Julia's call. Somehow, in that brief time, she had already complained over the phone, and soon after, I found myself being reprimanded—not just by her attending physician but also by the supervisor. They knew her behavior well. Yet, without hesitation, they scolded me as if I had truly neglected my duty. I was utterly stunned. The genuine effort I had poured into her care over the past few days felt completely disregarded—trampled upon, as if it had meant nothing. A boiling mix of anger and frustration surged within me. I could not contain the deep sense of injustice I felt.

Nurses are professionals when it comes to masking their emotions in front of patients. After taking a deep breath to steady myself, I stepped into Julia's room. She was waiting—her glare defiant, daring me to react. I met her stare, unblinking. A silent battle of wills had begun. Perhaps sensing the shift in my demeanor, she lashed out first, her voice rising to a piercing scream. "Jane, what have you even done for me these past few days?" What followed was a flood of profanities, so vile it was hard to believe they came from the same girl. Her once bright green eyes, clear and full of life, had darkened, turning cold and gray in an instant. It was fascinating how human emotions could so visibly alter the warmth in someone's gaze.

Without meaning to, a surge of anger welled up inside me. For a fleeting moment, I had the urge to shout back at her, matching her volume and intensity. The thought of how she had refused the care of nursing assistants for even the most intimate tasks—demanding that only nurses tend to her, insisting I be the one to clean her, to wash her hair—and now repaid those efforts with such venomous ingratitude, made my chest tighten with bitterness. The resentment felt unbearable. Afraid that it would show in my eyes, that my frustration might seep into my words and wound her just as she had wounded me, I shut my eyes tightly. I pressed my lips together, terrified that if I let even a single word escape, it might be something I could never take back.

I'm not sure how much time had passed, but her once-agitated voice began to quiet. Her breathing was ragged, her words trembling. "This pain—how could you ever understand it, Jane?" she gasped.

Something in her voice cracked open a space inside me. Without thinking, I stepped forward and wrapped my arms around her, pulling her into a fierce embrace. She was both infuriating and unbearably fragile. Her body stiffened in shock, unaccustomed to touch, unprepared for the weight of my arms around her. But I didn't let go. I held her even tighter, as if trying to press out every ounce of frustration, every unspoken word, every wound between us. She cried out, "It hurts, it hurts!" but she didn't push me away.

When I finally released her, her face was streaked with tears. She whispered, almost in disbelief, that since her accident, no one had held her like that. Her words shattered me. Overcome with guilt for the resentment I had harbored, for the anger I had let build, I felt my own tears rise. They spilled over uncontrollably, blurring the edges of the moment, dissolving the lines between anger and sorrow, between caregiver and patient, between two human beings simply trying to hold on.

A month later, she was admitted again. Naturally, she was assigned to me. By then, something between us had softened. We never spoke about what had happened, but the shift was undeniable. The battle lines had blurred, replaced by something quieter, an unspoken understanding. Only now did I truly see the truth behind her difficult behavior. She had not felt love from others. Every sharp word, every impossible demand, every outburst wasn't just defiance. They were the desperate cries of a girl drowning in despair. I had failed to recognize it before. Her wounds were not just on her body; her heart bore scars just as deep. The nursing theories I studied in school offered no solutions for this. They were meant to prepare us, to equip us with protocols and knowledge, but in moments like this, they only served to dull our sensitivity to suffering. They provided no guidance on how to reach a patient like Julia, whose pain ran deeper than medicine could touch. What truly mattered was not a set of professional principles or carefully studied techniques. What mattered was simply this: seeing her, understanding her, and meeting her in her pain. Not as a nurse, but as another human being.

Being assigned to her in the morning is no longer a burden. Instead, it feels peaceful. The weight of dread that once came with her name on my patient list has lifted. She no longer intimidates me, and I no longer brace myself before stepping into her room. In fact, I now find myself visiting her even when there's no pressing need.

Often, I find her crying, and I let her. No interruptions, no words—just quiet presence. I've learned that some pain doesn't need fixing; it just needs space to exist. When we talk, I look deeply into her eyes, and each time, a fresh wave of affection for her wells up within me. She is no longer just a difficult patient—she is Julia, a young woman who has known more suffering than most.

Today, she said thank you more times than I could count. And for the first time, the relentless call light that once dictated every hour has fallen silent for long stretches. She doesn't call for a nurse as often anymore. Maybe, just maybe, she's learning that care is not something she has to demand, that it is something that can be freely given.

A few days later, when I returned to the ward, she was gone. I was told she had been discharged, and to my surprise, I felt a twinge of sadness. I hope that the next time we meet, both of us will have grown into more mature versions of ourselves.

The Blossoms of Connection

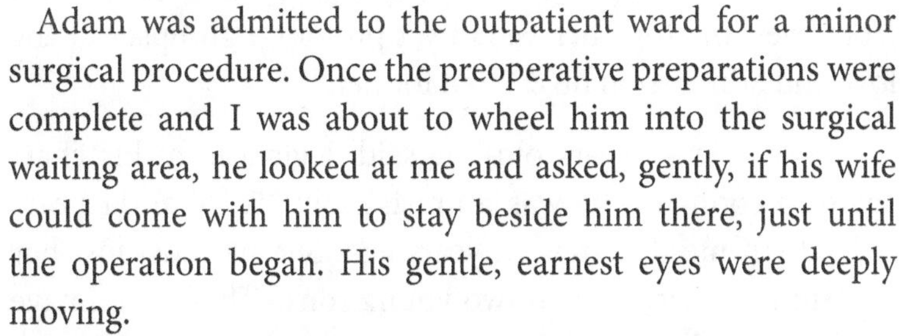

Adam was admitted to the outpatient ward for a minor surgical procedure. Once the preoperative preparations were complete and I was about to wheel him into the surgical waiting area, he looked at me and asked, gently, if his wife could come with him to stay beside him there, just until the operation began. His gentle, earnest eyes were deeply moving.

Of course, a guardian can accompany a patient in certain situations—when the patient is a minor, too elderly to be fully conscious, unable to sign necessary documents for various reasons, or requires a translator. However, it was unusual for a healthy, articulate 35-year-old man with no communication issues to specifically ask for his wife.

His request stirred curious intrigue within me. What made her presence so essential to him at this moment? Was it comfort, reassurance, or something deeper—an unspoken connection that only she could provide?

While waiting for the surgeon, the couple sat in a corner of the waiting area, holding hands and whispering to each other with such tenderness. The soft murmur of their Spanish sounded like music. Noticing that I was paying attention, Adam looked at me and asked with a smile, "Isn't my wife very beautiful?"

I glanced at her again. She was an utterly ordinary middle-aged Latina woman, not someone you would describe as particularly pretty or striking. When I asked what made her so beautiful, Adam answered without hesitation. "Everything. There isn't a woman in this world as beautiful as my wife. We've been married for 11 years, and not once has she ever disappointed me." With that, his words began to flow effortlessly, as if he had been waiting for someone to ask. Without any prompting, he eagerly shared stories, moments from their life together. Small yet profound glimpses of the love and admiration he carried for her.

"My wife is 46 years old," he said. I glanced at his chart again to confirm—he was unmistakably 35. "She's 11 years older than me. We met 12 years ago. She had just lost her husband and was raising two young sons." That would have made him only 23 at the time.

He said he fell in love with his wife because of the way she loved her children. He had decided not to have children of his own, as they already had two boys and didn't need anyone else to complete their family. As an electrical technician, he worked hard to ensure his wife could stay home and focus entirely on the household. He sent both boys to private schools and helped raise them to be remarkable individuals. With quiet pride, he added that the two sons love and respect him even more than they would a biological father.

He said that meeting his wife taught him the true meaning of life. His wife and her children desperately needed a home, and he found fulfillment in being their protector. However, marrying her came at a cost. He lost the support of his own family, relatives, and friends, who refused to accept her as one of their own. Although this loss brought him deep sadness, he has never once regretted his decision. With solemn conviction, he swore that he has never, not even in thought, betrayed his wife to this very day.

My throat tightened with emotion. It felt as if the landscapes of pain and trials his soul had traversed over the past 12 years unfolded vividly before me. In this day and age, few speak of purity in heart and mind. How many couples around us grow to love and cherish each other more deeply as time goes on? His unwavering devotion felt almost otherworldly—an unshaken testament to love that defied the erosion of time and hardship.

After his surgery, once he had awakened from anesthesia and stabilized, we transferred him to the ward. As I was about to leave, I made a simple request: to never lose the feelings he had when he first met his wife, to treasure the love he holds now forever. His eyes quickly welled up, glistening with tears. In that moment, I saw a love so deep and unwavering that even time and hardship could not diminish it.

The next day, I dropped by Adam's room after transferring a post-operative patient from the recovery room to the medical-surgical unit where he was staying. I should not have gone. I should have left his beautiful love story as a cherished memory, unspoiled to the end. I should have been content with the uplifting feeling of yesterday, believing the world is still a place worth living in. I should not have ventured beyond the joy of yesterday, where the modern-day tale of pure devotion had filled me with warmth. Some stories are meant to be preserved in their perfect glow, untouched by the reality that often follows.

He was quiet, almost somber. As he gazed toward the door, he mentioned that his wife had stepped out for a while and wouldn't return until evening. "I already miss her," he admitted with a soft sigh. When I asked how he was feeling, he shifted uncomfortably and spoke of the persistent back pain that had plagued him for years. For the past seven years, he had undergone procedures every four to five months to manage it, yet he couldn't pinpoint a specific injury that had caused it. The unrelenting pain, he confessed, left him feeling both guilty toward his wife and frustrated with himself.

I sat by his bedside, quietly watching him, sensing the weight of something unspoken pressing down on him. Then, suddenly, he broke. His composure crumbled, and the emotions he had kept locked away for years spilled out. He admitted that the past years had been unbearably hard and lonely. That, despite the love and warmth he shared with his wife and stepsons, there was an ache inside him that never faded—the pain of missing his family. He had not seen them in over a decade, and he couldn't understand how people who had once embraced him with warmth could turn so cold. As he spoke, his voice wavered, and then, unable to hold it in any longer, he sobbed uncontrollably.

I let him cry. I didn't try to console him with words, nor did I tell him to be strong. Instead, I sat in quiet presence, giving him the space to release everything he had buried for so long. Sometimes, the best care a nurse can provide isn't in a procedure or medication—it's in allowing someone to feel, to grieve, and to find their own way back to calm.

Once he had composed himself, I spoke, gently breaking the heavy silence. "You must have endured so much all these years." Then, after a pause, I asked directly, "What is it that you truly want right now? Follow where your heart leads you. If you miss your family, reach out to them. Holding back out of fear that the pain might deepen is not necessarily the best choice. What could possibly be worse than living as you are now, disconnected from them? For all you know, your family might be missing you just as much at this moment. Perhaps they are waiting with open arms, hoping you will come back to them." His eyes flickered with something—hesitation, longing, maybe even hope. The words hung between us, heavy with the weight of possibilities yet unknown.

I told him that perhaps it would be beneficial if his love for his wife loosened just a little. I explained that by keeping multiple doors in his heart closed—revealing only the refined, polished emotions that filter through—he might be limiting the true depth of his feelings. Instead, he might consider allowing his love to flow more freely, so that his wife could experience the full spectrum of his genuine emotions.

I told him that honestly expressing his emotions could, in some ways, be a greater form of love. I encouraged him to speak up if he was struggling, admit when he disliked something, and express himself when he was in pain. I explained that holding in that tension isn't good for either of them. I asked if his wife might be living as if she were walking on thin ice or carrying feelings of guilt, and whether she had ever opened up to him about such things. Had he ever truly listened to her deeply? I reassured him that if he became more honest about his emotions, his wife might also feel more at ease and be able to love even more deeply. When I mentioned that unexplained back pain is often caused by mental stress, he seemed visibly surprised. His life, full of enduring and suppressing his feelings, seemed so pitiful to me.

As I left his room, I questioned myself—was the advice I gave him appropriate? Why had I poured out so many words in front of someone already hurting? For a moment, regret washed over me. But then I reminded myself that this was a mountain he would have to climb eventually, and perhaps I had simply given him a nudge to begin the journey.

People shed their skins, too. Shedding comes with pain and risk, but it's a necessary process for growth and maturity. Without it, like a snake unable to shed its skin, one can die, not just physically, but emotionally and spiritually. Adam and his wife will undoubtedly face many challenges ahead. Greater love and sacrifice will be required of them than ever before. But Adam is a mature adult, and I believe he has the strength to confront the truth, to face his pain, and to navigate the complexities of his heart. What I said may have unsettled him, but I trust that he will recognize its intent—not to wound, but to open a door. Whether he chooses to walk through it is entirely up to him.

The flower of connection. What could be more beautiful and bittersweet in this world than the meeting of two people? Some connections bloom effortlessly, while others are forged through trials and time. Yet each holds its own weight, its own meaning. Dreaming of a world where harmony is possible, where relationships are nurtured with patience and love, I step out of the ward once again today—carrying with me the echoes of stories, the weight of unspoken emotions, and the quiet hope that, in some way, I have helped a connection bloom.

Chapter 2

Three Days of Togetherness

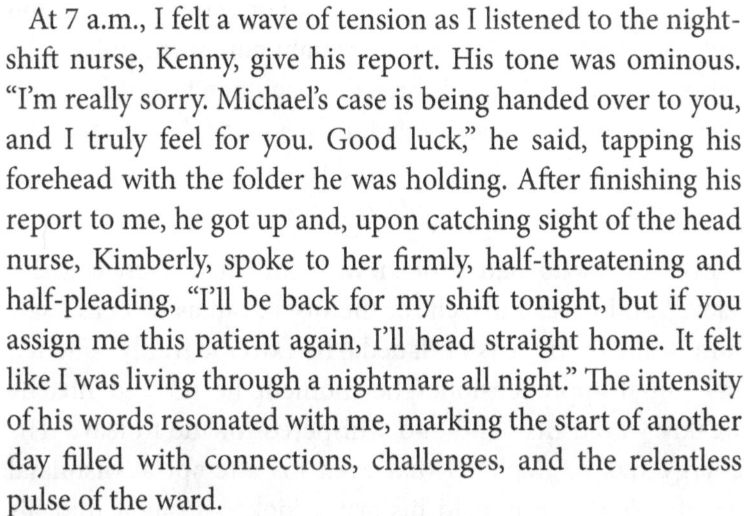

At 7 a.m., I felt a wave of tension as I listened to the night-shift nurse, Kenny, give his report. His tone was ominous. “I’m really sorry. Michael’s case is being handed over to you, and I truly feel for you. Good luck,” he said, tapping his forehead with the folder he was holding. After finishing his report to me, he got up and, upon catching sight of the head nurse, Kimberly, spoke to her firmly, half-threatening and half-pleading, “I’ll be back for my shift tonight, but if you assign me this patient again, I’ll head straight home. It felt like I was living through a nightmare all night.” The intensity of his words resonated with me, marking the start of another day filled with connections, challenges, and the relentless pulse of the ward.

Getting assigned difficult patients early in the morning can be draining. Patients who try to jump out of bed, pull out essential medical lines and devices, or refuse medications are still manageable. Even those carrying resistant bacteria or contagious diseases that require donning gloves, gowns, and special masks every time you enter their room are not the worst. The real challenge comes with patients who rely on machines to breathe, needing frequent suctioning and constant checks every ten minutes, or those with severe mental illnesses who lash out with verbal abuse. Patients involved with multiple attending physicians, requiring numerous tests and frequent trips in and out of the ward, or those set for discharge or transfer to another hospital, make for an exhausting day. But beyond these, there are patients so complex and challenging that they defy description. Michael was one of those.

When I entered Room 47, located close to the nurses' station, I was met with the piercing gaze of a gaunt 21-year-old Caucasian man. Sitting hunched in his wheelchair, he had pulled his hospital gown up to cover his nose. He believed the room was filled with poisonous gas, released by people trying to kill him. Convinced that not only the hospital food but even the meals his father brought contained poison, he refused to eat. Admitted three days ago due to severe blood composition imbalances, mental illness, and dehydration, he had rejected all medical tests and treatments, resisting every attempt to stabilize his condition.

Everyone who had spoken with him had been called a "devil," so I braced myself for the worst. But as soon as I saw him, some of my tension faded. His extreme frailty softened my initial apprehension. The moment he noticed me, he weakly waved his hand and whispered for me to leave. His energy was so depleted that even his attempt at dismissal was feeble. I gently held his arms, looked straight into his eyes, and said firmly, "I'm your nurse. I'm not here to hurt you. You can trust me."

He struggled and pulled his arms free, then raked his nails across my forearm with all his might. The scratches stung, and small spots of blood began to surface where bits of skin had been scraped off. Strangely, I found myself smiling. Instead of slapping or punching, he had used his nails, and something about the gesture seemed almost endearing in its innocence. His father, meanwhile, was beside himself with guilt, apologizing profusely.

Pretending as if nothing had happened, I spoke in a firmer tone. "There's no poison gas in this room. If there were,

covering your nose like that wouldn't make any difference. Look at me—I'm not covering my nose, and I'm perfectly fine." Of course, I knew my words alone wouldn't change his perception. But regardless of a patient's state, a nurse's duty is to gently guide them toward reality, offering stability and reassurance wherever possible.

He raised his middle finger and thrust it in front of my face. Calmly, I took his hand, lowered it, and gently placed it on his knee. Speaking slowly and deliberately, I said, "I want to help you. Sincerely, I do." As I left the room, I could hear him complaining to his father, "She's the devil. Don't talk to her."

He had been sitting in his wheelchair for over eight hours—since 11 p.m. the night before. He defecated and urinated in his chair, refusing to be cleaned, violently lashing out at anyone who tried. His outbursts came with a torrent of insults, each one more vicious than the last. Over the past two days, he had torn out his IV lines seven times. He rejected medications, blood draws, X-rays—every essential diagnostic test meant for his care. Doctors, nurses, and case managers were at their wits' end, struggling to manage him.

A bone marrow biopsy had been scheduled for the morning. The doctor and two OR nurses came to his room, spending a long time trying to persuade him, only to leave in frustration, hands thrown up in surrender. It was a difficult situation. There was no valid reason for him to remain in the hospital, yet hospital policy prohibited discharging him without proof of stability. His refusal to eat or take in any food was considered an emergency. Thus, the first day passed. Perhaps because I had mentally braced myself so thoroughly, I didn't feel burdened or overwhelmed by him at all.

The next day, as I entered the ward, I saw his name on my patient list again. He had reportedly stayed in his wheelchair the entire night. His swollen feet were icy cold to the touch. I folded a warm blanket and laid it on the floor, suggesting he rest his feet on it. As I knelt in front of his wheelchair to arrange the blanket, my face suddenly ended up buried between his thighs. He had punched the top of my head with all his strength. Perhaps because I was caught off guard, it hurt less than I expected. Instead, I found myself worrying about his frail hand bones—how could they endure such force? He weighed only 82 pounds, having barely eaten all week. Meanwhile, a lump quickly began to rise on my scalp.

Stories of colleagues who lost their lives in the line of duty came to mind, nurses who fell victim to patient violence. If that isn't martyrdom, what is? Martyrdom doesn't always come with grandeur. It happens quietly, unnoticed by the world, in places like this.

Without saying a word, I held his frail hands tightly. His wasted youth weighed heavy on my heart. Michael, what has left your body and soul in such ruin? You're struggling, but believe me, the tears of pain I've shed through my own hardships haven't been few. Neither of us had any rehearsal before being thrown into this life. Isn't that the reality of existence? You don't need to hate. You can shout, curse, and reject this cruel world. At least you have the courage to do that. Me? I, lacking even that courage, am a coward. Why do I feel such pity for you? Perhaps because you are measured by the merciless standards of this world, judged and cast aside. And that feels incredibly unjust. But what can we do? Unless you conform, you will always remain an outsider.

On the third morning, his name was on my patient list once again. He was in his wheelchair, still using his hospital gown to cover his nose. I pulled out a disposable mask I had prepared and waved it in front of him. For a fleeting moment, a glimmer of light flashed in his eyes. My heart raced. This is it. Seizing the opportunity, I said in an upbeat tone, "This is a special mask. Want it? It'll keep you safe from what you're worried about. You won't need to cover your nose with your gown anymore. Plus, wearing this will free up your hands." I demonstrated by pretending to put on the mask. He quickly reached out for it, and I helped him put it on.

And then, something remarkable happened. For the first time, he gave me a warm, sincere look and said, "Thank you." No suspicion or fear, but with kindness. That moment, voices echoed from the hallway. Instantly, he pressed a finger to his lips, whispering, "Shh! You and I are safe now, right? It's our secret." There was something heartbreakingly pure about him. In that moment, we weren't nurse and patient. We were just two children, giggling over a shared secret, hands clasped together in a fleeting moment of trust.

From that moment on, he became a completely different person. The trust that had begun to take root blossomed into a series of remarkable changes. For the first time in a week since his admission a week ago, he ordered hospital food—mashed potatoes without gravy and a side of peas—for dinner. It was a small step, but it felt monumental. He promised not to refuse any of the medical tests the hospital needed. At lunchtime, he devoured the fried chicken, French fries, and chicken sandwich his father had brought, as if making up for lost time. Later, without a word, he stood up from his wheelchair and calmly walked to the restroom to handle his "functions" on his own. The transformation was nothing short of extraordinary.

News of Michael eating food spread through the ward like wildfire. The case manager immediately began the discharge process for him. She called each of the three doctors overseeing his care, informing them of the progress and canceling all the scheduled tests. The necessary steps to transfer him back to his primary care physician were quickly finalized. What had seemed impossible just days ago was now unfolding seamlessly.

As I wheeled him out of the ward, I felt a pang of sadness. While his father went to get the car, I asked him, "Do you like music?" "Yeah." "You should try listening to classical music, it can really calm your mind. How about Beethoven or Chopin? They're my favorite composers." He promised to give them a try. After a pause, he asked, "Can I still listen to rock sometimes?" I couldn't help but smile at how endearing he was. "Of course. Do you want to learn an instrument?" "Saxophone," he replied. "Then start lessons right away. And stay healthy," I urged. "Why bother being healthy?" he asked. "Think about your father, who's been through so much for you. If you're healthy and happy, he'll be happy too. You're only 21 years old. The world is beautiful, and there's so much for you to do. To travel where you want and do the things you love, you need to be healthy." He nodded thoughtfully. "Do you have a girlfriend?" "No," he said. "Once you get healthy, you'll find one. Do you realize how handsome you are?" At that, he lowered his head shyly, and I couldn't help but feel a surge of hope for him.

With his father's support, he climbed into the car with some difficulty, pulling his hat low over his face. His profile looked so forlorn, so fragile, that it tugged at my heart. As the car began to pull away, he reached his hand out the window and waved, though his head remained bowed, unable to lift it to look back at me. I tilted my head upward, looking at the sky. It wasn't tears from my eyes, but rather the sky itself seemed to release millions of raindrops, cascading down in a quiet farewell. The small, worn car carrying him moved slowly through the hospital parking lot, then disappeared into the vast world beyond.

A pain stirred deep in the pit of my stomach. It had been a brief connection, just three days. It was barely enough time to truly know someone, yet just enough to leave an indelible imprint on my heart.

Jane Ha

La Vida es Hermosa (Life is Beautiful)

Caring for Mr. Ramos over the past two days brought me joy. He always greeted me with a smiling face, not looking at all like a man burdened by illness. He had been battling a recurrence of lung cancer from ten years ago, with fluid filling his lungs and making it difficult to breathe. His abdomen is also swollen with fluid, resembling late-stage pregnancy. Even taking a single step must have been a tremendous challenge and agony for him, yet he obediently followed the instructions of nurses and physical therapists, struggling valiantly to walk down the hallway.

Dealing with patients or families who treat nurses as personal servants, I often find myself muttering "Good grief!" under my breath countless times a day. Yet, every time I entered Mr. Ramos's room, a different feeling washed over me, one of quiet happiness. "Thank you for taking the time to care for someone like me, even when you're so busy." "May God bless you." "You must be having such a hard time." "I'm sorry for the trouble; I take so many medications that it must be a hassle for you to check them all." His sincerity shone through every word. From him, I learned just how many ways there are to express humility and thankfulness.

I respond with genuine sincerity, saying, "I am here for you today. If you need anything at all, do not hesitate to press this call light button. Whenever you call, I will drop everything and come running."

He never calls for me—not even when it's past time for his pain medication. When I find time to check on him and ask if he needs anything, he simply says, "Now that you're here, everything is fine. I even prayed to God, hoping you might stop by, if even by chance."

He tries to teach me Spanish, lighting up with joy when I manage to get it right: Señor (gentleman), Señora (lady), Señorita (young lady), Comida (food), Niña (girl), Niño (boy), Contigo (with you), Amor (love)… Each word feels like a small bridge connecting our worlds.

As I wheeled him down the hallway on my last shift of the week, he turned to me with a curious smile and asked about my favorite Mexican food. I told him that while I enjoyed tacos and burritos, tamales were my favorite. His eyes sparkled with delight, and without hesitation, he promised, several times, that he would make some for me and bring them back. His sincerity was so heartfelt, so genuine, that I couldn't help but believe him.

His sudden urgency made me pause. Just before exiting through the front door, he exclaimed, "Wait!" I turned to him, expecting he had forgotten something. "No," he said, shaking his head. "I just want you to look at me." I stopped the wheelchair and stood before him. He held my gaze, his eyes filled with warmth. Then, with a slow, deliberate smile, he declared, "La vida es hermosa! Life is beautiful! Jane, you already know this, don't you?"

Suddenly, my throat tightened. It wasn't just the words, it was the weight behind them. A 78-year-old man, who had endured countless illnesses, lived with unrelenting pain, and had already signed the papers to donate his body to medical research after his death, was the one declaring, "Life is beautiful."

For a moment, I stood still, absorbing the depth of his conviction. His frail body, marked by years of suffering, carried no trace of bitterness—only gratitude. How could someone who had faced so much still see life as something beautiful?

I nodded, unable to speak, but he understood. His eyes twinkled with wisdom, as if he had just handed me a priceless secret—one that only those who have truly lived could share.

Chapter 2

The Last Romance

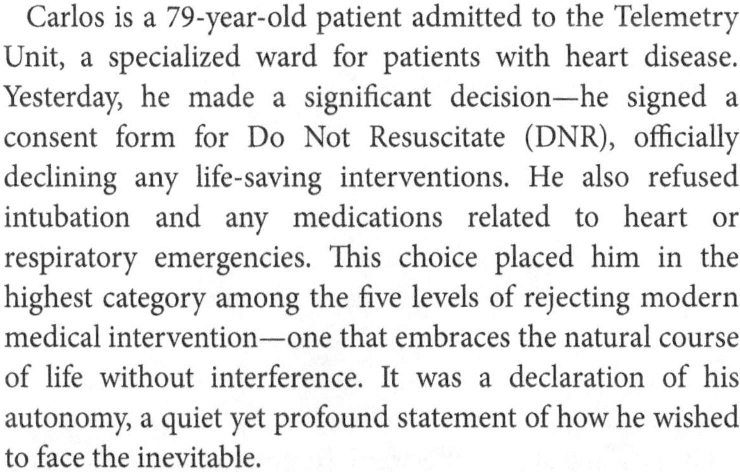

Carlos is a 79-year-old patient admitted to the Telemetry Unit, a specialized ward for patients with heart disease. Yesterday, he made a significant decision—he signed a consent form for Do Not Resuscitate (DNR), officially declining any life-saving interventions. He also refused intubation and any medications related to heart or respiratory emergencies. This choice placed him in the highest category among the five levels of rejecting modern medical intervention—one that embraces the natural course of life without interference. It was a declaration of his autonomy, a quiet yet profound statement of how he wished to face the inevitable.

DNR forms are typically signed by a family member, especially when the patient is elderly, suffering from an incurable illness, or experiencing dementia or severe mental confusion. The decision is usually made after a doctor's recommendation and a family meeting to designate a representative. It's a sorrowful process—while it reflects a resolve to stop prolonging futile suffering, it must also feel like a final farewell, as though they are, in some way, letting go of someone they love. The American healthcare system's emphasis on honoring a patient's wishes is commendable. Yet, witnessing someone like Carlos personally sign the highest-level DNR form stirs a complex mix of emotions—a deep sense of respect, intertwined with a quiet sadness.

Carlos is a clear-minded adult who has the right to choose or refuse medical treatment concerning his own life. With no family or relatives nearby, he had been living alone in an apartment until recently, when he moved into a nursing home. Over the past few days, he faced a life-or-death crisis due to septic shock caused by a blood infection. As soon as he regained consciousness yesterday, he signed the DNR form. A decision made entirely on his own. Watching him navigate these choices alone was heartbreaking. I hoped he could overcome this crisis and be granted some time to put his life in order, even just a little.

Yesterday was a critical day for Carlos. Everyone expected it to be his last. Knowing this, I paid him extra attention, tending to him with deliberate care. To manage his persistent high fever, which wouldn't subside even with antipyretics, I used ice water to cool his body. I thought it was better to clean a living body than a lifeless one—it felt like the right thing to do for both of us. I convinced Lupe, the aide, to help me, and together we carefully washed every inch of his body. Looking at him afterward, freshly cleaned and resting comfortably, I felt as if I had been the one to bathe—I was refreshed and uplifted.

When I arrived at the ward this morning, I saw Carlos on my patient list again. Typically, critical patients like him are rotated among nurses, but with his death seemingly imminent, it was clear no one wanted to take him on. Managing the procedures and paperwork following a patient's death is no small task. The night-shift head nurse, Amy, must have thought assigning him to Jane—the stubborn nurse who believes she must see her duties through no matter what—would spare her from early-morning complaints about switching patients and other troublesome issues. Considering the stress she must already be under, I found myself unable to refuse.

Seeing Carlos's delighted face, I felt more relieved than troubled—grateful that he was still alive. Although he had spent much of the previous night in a near-comatose state, his mind was clear throughout the morning. I made frequent visits to his room, doing my best to meet his needs, ensuring that each moment counted in whatever time he had left.

Sometimes he would drift off into a weak sleep, other times he would simply stare quietly at the ceiling. Each time I asked if he needed anything or if he was in pain, he would respond in his warm voice, "I'm fine, thank you," repeating it countless times. I felt a deep sense of pity and sorrow for him. That morning, the IV site on his paper-thin, fragile skin had deteriorated, so I placed a new line in his other arm and half-locked so it could be used immediately. As I worked, he gave a wistful smile and said, "I might leave this world before the next IV line is needed. If that happens, Jane, it'll make things easier for you, wouldn't it?" A tightness formed in my throat. How could he think that his absence would make things easier for anyone?

In the afternoon, I entered his room to find him asleep. While connecting the IV antibiotic that he was receiving every six hours, he suddenly woke up. As he lifted his head slightly, he reached out and grabbed the pocket of my uniform with surprising strength, pulling me down. In an instant, I found myself sitting on the edge of his bed. It was astonishing. Just that morning, he had been too weak to swallow a pill, so I had crushed it into powder, mixed it with water, and held his head up to feed it to him.

"Let's run away together." I blinked, convinced I must have misheard him. "Pardon me? What did you just say?" He repeated himself, his voice steady, his gaze unwavering. "Jane, I came all this way, from that distant country, just to meet you. Only you. You and I were destined for each other long before time began. I've loved you even before you were born, and I've waited all this time for you. I'll make you happy." For a moment, I considered the possibility that he was delirious, or that perhaps he was reciting poetry.

"I want to have sex with you. I'm ready. Don't you want to touch me?" My goodness! He suddenly lifted his gown and, before I could react, grabbed my hand and pulled it toward his lower middle area. A jolt of shock coursed through me. My mind barely had time to process what had just happened. Quickly, I pulled my hand away and stood up, my body rigid with disbelief. Just yesterday, I had struggled to insert a urinary catheter for him—his body too weak, unresponsive. At that moment, it had been nothing more than a clinical procedure, devoid of any emotional weight. But now, this—this was entirely different. Against my will, the sensation of my hand touching such an intimate part at his forceful insistence was deeply unsettling and horrifying.

A deep sense of unease and revulsion settled in my chest. My instinct was to flee the room, but I forced myself to stay composed. Taking a step back, I spoke slowly, keeping my voice low but resolute despite the turmoil inside me. "Carlos, that is not appropriate. I am your nurse, and I am here to care for you. I need you to respect that. Let go of my hand immediately, or I will call the supervisor and security." Perhaps startled by the firmness in my voice, he loosened his grip on my hand." His expression flickered—perhaps a hint of regret, or maybe just frustration. Perhaps startled by the firmness in my voice, he loosened his grip on my hand. I turned and left the room, my hands clenched into fists, my pulse still pounding in my ears.

Back at the nurses' station, I shook my hands vigorously, unable to stop myself from letting out faint groans of "Oh my! Oh my!" I paced quickly around the cramped station, even shaking my head as I moved. The charge nurse, Chloe, pulled me into the dictation room and slammed the door shut. I could only shake my head, unable to form any words.

Chloe sighed deeply, crossing her arms as she leaned against the desk. "Jane, you need to toughen up. This happens more often than you think. When patients are nearing the end of their lives, their minds can take them to strange places—memories, desires, hallucinations. It's not personal."

I swallowed hard, still feeling unsettled. "But it felt so real," I muttered. "Of course, it did," she replied, her tone softer now. "But it wasn't about you. He could've been seeing someone from his past, someone he loved, or someone he longed for but never had the chance to be with. Delirium, medications, hypoxia—they all mess with a person's mind. If you react like this every time, you'll burn out fast."

I exhaled sharply. I knew she was right. I had seen patients in altered states before, confused and lost in fragments of their past. But this? This had been different. The physicality of it, the way he grabbed me, had left a mark that logic alone couldn't erase.

After a while, she asked, "So, what are you going to do now? Do you want me to switch patients for you, or are you going to stick it out with him to the end? This is a great chance to toughen up. But if you keep making a big deal out of it like this, you'll make yourself an easy target for other nurses." When I expressed uncertainty about how the patient might react, she patted me on the shoulder and encouraged me to give it another shot. "Go on. Try again."

After Chloe delivered a stern lecture to him, she took over, skillfully infusing the antibiotics into his IV line without hesitation. Soon after, he fell asleep. At lunchtime, the nursing aide Rosa informed me that he had refused to eat even a single spoonful of liquid food. Concerned, I went into his room. He stared at me for a moment without saying a word, then shifted his gaze to the ceiling. I asked gently, "How are you feeling?" He nodded and replied that he was fine.

Around 4 p.m., his fever began to spike again. Rosa and I used towels soaked in ice water to cool his body. He started crying silently, and the tears just wouldn't stop. His vital signs were alarmingly irregular. When I held his hand, he gripped it tightly and wouldn't let go. I sat in the chair beside his bed, gently caressing his head.

Chloe summoned me. "I've assigned that patient to Jasmin. Don't go into his room again. I'm not letting him die of cardiac arrest on my watch." Her tone was cold as she brushed past me without so much as a second glance. She didn't even allow me to give a direct report to Jasmin. Apparently, while I was in his room, his heart monitor readings displayed on the station had been so unstable that the staff became alarmed. As Chloe handed off the patient to Jasmin, I left the area feeling as though I had been chased away.

Jasmin, a stocky nurse with striking, protruding eyes, called me over from the nursing station and gave me a long, critical look. "You need to be tougher. Patients test their boundaries based on who they're dealing with. Don't go thinking he acted that way because you're pretty, alright? Look around—there are plenty of young, kind, and attractive nurses here, and none of them have had to deal with that nonsense. Do you know how compliant that patient is with me? Ugh, Jane, you're giving me a headache. I honestly don't know how long you'll last in this field." She rattled off her thoughts rapidly, then brushed past me, leaving a cold breeze in her wake.

Oh, my goodness! I'm seriously tempted to quit this nursing job right now. No, that's not it. Next time something like this happens, I need to remain composed and not make a fuss. Over time, as I become a veteran nurse, I'll learn how to handle any situation calmly. Sigh, this is so hard. How did I end up becoming a nurse in the first place?

Two hours later, I heard that his fever had spiked again. Despite administering antipyretics, placing ice packs under his arms and on his forehead, and wiping him down with cold towels, there was no improvement. When I went into his room, he appeared unconscious, muttering strange words over and over. Jasmin told me it was his native language. She explained that patients often revert to their mother tongue when in a delirious state. The language sounded like music, or perhaps poetry, though I couldn't understand a single word. When I held his hands, there was no energy, no life left in his touch. By the time my shift ended, there was still no change. Leaving him in his unresponsive state, I walked away from the ward with a heavy heart.

When I returned to the ward after five days, his name was no longer on the patient list. I asked the charge nurse, Chloe, what had happened to him, and she told me he had passed away, right after I finished my shift and left the ward, and had left his room for good. Ah, such a heavy feeling. So bittersweet.

Jane Ha

Touching

Lorraine is a 77-year-old Caucasian woman who receives nutrition through a gastric tube running from her nose to her stomach. She repeatedly pulls out her IV lines and tugs at her urinary catheter, so her wrists are secured to the bed rails on both sides with sturdy restraints, and thick gloves cover her hands. When I arrived at the ward in the morning, the night-shift nurse, May, warned me during the handover. "You'll have a tough time with this one," she said. "No matter what you do, she won't respond."

She had an utterly expressionless face, unresponsive no matter how many times I called her name. Her tangled hair resembled a bird's nest, and her face glistened with dried mucus. When I removed her gloves to check the skin on her wrists, I noticed her long fingernails were caked with dirt, their tips blackened. I couldn't focus on anything else. I set aside all other tasks and, with the help of nursing aide Katrina, gave her a thorough cleaning. We washed her hair and combed it neatly, replacing all her bedding with fresh sheets and blankets. Seeing her lying there, clean and tidy, filled me with an immense sense of relief and satisfaction.

I gently stroked her hair and face for a long while. About an hour later, I went back and stroked her hair again. When she opened her eyes wide, I exclaimed, "Wow, you have such beautiful eyes, ma'am!" At this, she gave me a faint smile. "You're even more beautiful when you smile," I added, and this time, she broke into a radiant grin. When I showed her a mirror, she beamed brightly, her smile as full as a harvest moon. Whenever I had a moment, I would stop by her room and gently stroke her hair again.

By the afternoon, she began to speak, though her words were difficult to understand. The attending doctor, making his rounds, was surprised by her sudden improvement and immediately ordered her restraints to be removed. He also instructed that she be seated in a chair every two hours. Every time she saw me, she held out her hands, asking me to take them. When I clasped her hands and gave them a good shake, she would beam like a child. Once she held onto my hands, she refused to let go, gripping them tightly with a radiant smile.

In the afternoon, her gastric tube was removed. A nutritionist came to assess whether Lorraine could swallow food through her esophagus. A speech therapist also conducted various tests to evaluate her pronunciation. Both were pleased with the results, noting that Lorraine's cooperation made the procedures highly effective.

In the evening, she ate a bowl of thin porridge. I was quite worried she might vomit or struggle with indigestion, but she handled it well. A procedure to insert a feeding tube through her abdominal wall to her stomach had been scheduled for the next day, but the doctor canceled it. No one could explain why her condition had improved so suddenly. I was just as amazed as everyone else.

On my way home after a 12-hour shift, a thought struck me. Perhaps Lorraine had finally uncovered her will to live, hidden deep in her subconscious, and decided to embrace it today. Could the clean scent of soap have brought back memories of the past, giving her strength? Maybe it was

Katrina's and my warm, gentle touches that made the difference.

Could that really be it?

Chapter 3

In the Gastrointestinal (GI) Lab

A World Learned on Bended Knee

Reflections on Broken English

Beauty and Ugliness

A Nurse's Tears

The Face of Silence and Tranquility

Deliberation at Year's End

The Art of a Wonderful Relationship

The Story of My Big Hands

Jane Ha

In the Gastrointestinal (GI) Lab

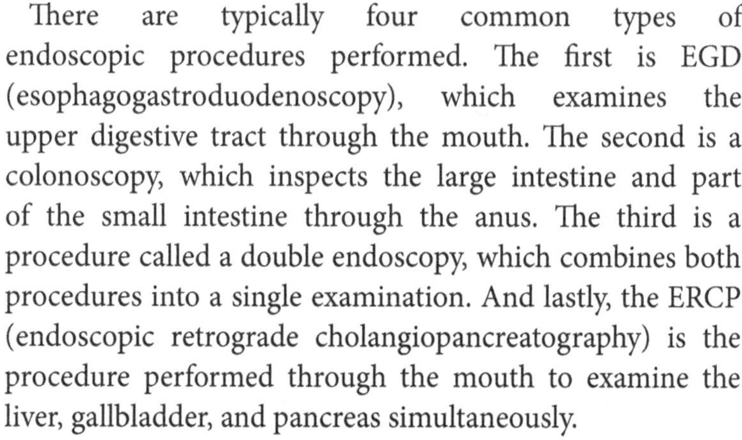

There are typically four common types of endoscopic procedures performed. The first is EGD (esophagogastroduodenoscopy), which examines the upper digestive tract through the mouth. The second is a colonoscopy, which inspects the large intestine and part of the small intestine through the anus. The third is a procedure called a double endoscopy, which combines both procedures into a single examination. And lastly, the ERCP (endoscopic retrograde cholangiopancreatography) is the procedure performed through the mouth to examine the liver, gallbladder, and pancreas simultaneously.

Working alongside a gastroenterologist who examines and treats the intestines through endoscopy always provokes deep reflection. Watching the interior of the intestines clearly displayed on the screen feels like exploring an uncharted world. Though the procedures and anatomy are consistent, each patient presents a uniquely different impression and experience.

Typically, two or three types of medications are used during the procedure. A sedative and a painkiller are standard, with stronger sedatives and antihistamines added depending on the patient's needs. If excessive peristalsis makes diagnosis difficult, or when the doctor needs to closely examine a specific area, a medication to temporarily halt intestinal movement may be administered.

Gastroenterology procedures require a team composed of a doctor, a technician, and a nurse. When examining the liver or gallbladder, a specialized X-ray device called a C-arm is used, operated by a trained technician. Additionally, all team members in the room must wear lead aprons to shield against radiation and badges to monitor their exposure levels.

Patients are given a choice: endure the discomfort and pain while remaining fully conscious during the procedure or opt for partial sedation. Most patients, even in a semi-conscious state, prefer to watch their internal organs on the detection monitor known as the "tower." Physicians also have differing preferences when it comes to sedation. Some dislike patients complaining of pain or moving around during the procedure, as it disrupts the examination. Others are more patient, taking the time to communicate thoroughly and explain each step in detail.

Meanwhile, some doctors, naturally impatient, complete the procedure in no time and leave the ward quickly. I sometimes wonder how such fast-paced examinations can accurately detect abnormalities in the intestines. Yet, these doctors rarely miss abnormal cells or other issues. I am constantly amazed by their skilled hands and profound expertise.

Even seemingly minor abnormalities can sometimes indicate cancer, while severe-looking gastric erosion might not pose significant danger. Small polyps in the stomach are temporarily inflated and tied off with rubber bands to cut off their blood supply, causing them to detach naturally. What is fascinating is that even a tiny polyp can cause noticeable symptoms. It is fortunate when symptoms appear before the issue becomes serious. Detecting problems at an advanced stage makes treatment challenging and worsens the prognosis. Patients who come in deeply worried about serious conditions, only to be diagnosed with simple gastritis or enteritis, or those who undergo minor polyp removal leave their consultations with joy, and audible sighs of reassurance.

Our internal organs are delicate and fragile, and there is not a single one that is unimportant. Every time I work in gastroenterology, I am reminded of the beauty in humanity. While our outer skin weathers harsh conditions, wrinkles, ages, and dries out, our organs deteriorate for entirely different reasons. They are not harmed by external factors but endure ferocity from their own host. Without the powerful ability to heal themselves, our organs would quickly succumb to serious illness and fail to endure for long.

Every time I see a patient's stomachs displayed on the screen, I feel a deep sense of pity. If we could regularly see the insides of our own bodies—those delicate, soft, and sensitive organs—I believe we would treat them with greater care. We might think twice before pouring strong alcohol into empty stomachs or mindlessly consuming excessively spicy, salty, and coarse foods.

Though composed of delicate cells, the stomach and intestines possess remarkable self-healing abilities. No matter how much abuse their owner inflicts, they work tirelessly to restore themselves. But when they can no longer endure, they cry out through pain, vomiting, constipation, and diarrhea—a desperate plea that says, "Help me! I want to keep you alive." If these cries go unanswered, the cells become eroded, inflamed, swollen, bleeding, or obstructed. These symptoms are not mere malfunctions but a last-ditch effort to protect the life the body holds.

Long ago, a precursor who had extensively studied food advised against consuming more than four types of food in a single meal. She warned that the chemical interactions between different foods could place significant strain on the stomach. She believed that the key to a healthy stomach was simple, well-prepared meals eaten in small portions, slowly, and with gratitude.

Our organs are highly sensitive to mental and emotional states. When we are sad or depressed, the stomach slackens; when we are angry, it is said to turn red. Eating in these states can lead to indigestion or illness. Peristaltic movement slows significantly, or even becomes sluggish, prolonging digestion time and placing a heavy burden on the gastrointestinal system.

The body is not truly ours. To believe it belongs to us is to justify treating it however we please, but this is not so. The body is a gift from Heaven, passed down to us through our parents. After marriage, it becomes a shelter for one's spouse and children. How, then, can we treat our bodies so carelessly? Can we even control a single breath by our own will?

What we eat and what we think, these are matters that deserve careful reflection.

Jane Ha

A World Learned on Bended Knee

Dr. Channell is a delightful person; a General Orthopedic Surgeon with a remarkable talent for whistling. He's also a gastroenterologist, someone who could likely navigate the human body's internal organs with his eyes closed.

Hel had just finished a surgery and entered the recovery room. While waiting for the patient to wake up and be transferred from the operating table, he began dictating notes and issuing prescriptions. During this time, medical student C, who had observed the surgery, asked him a question. As Dr. Channell explained, the student sat nearby, determined not to miss a single word. He even slid off his chair and knelt on the floor to get closer, hanging on to every detail with unwavering focus.

Dr. Channell was teaching how to suture a surgical incision. Using imaginary needles and thread, both of them bent and flexed their fingers repeatedly, practicing the same motions over and over. As Dr. Channell explained the technique, his hands moved deftly demonstrating each step. "No, no, don't do it like that—bend your index finger like this," he instructed. Even after Dr. Channell finished his explanation, C continued practicing diligently on his own.

It was a beautiful sight: kneeling on the floor, the student was completely absorbed in replicating the doctor's technique. His focus was so intense that it felt almost reverent. Even after Dr. Channell left, the student remained kneeling in the same spot, continuing to practice. So engrossed was he in his efforts that he seemed unaware of his posture. It was possibly the first time in his life he had ever knelt like that.

When I told him his suturing looked beautiful, he smiled brightly. Yet, tilting his head repeatedly, he insisted it wasn't going well. Then, his face lit up as he shared that yesterday, under Dr. Elias's supervision, he had sutured the incision for an appendectomy himself. I urged him never to lose his beginner's mindset. He nodded enthusiastically, indicating he understood.

The sight of him humbly kneeling to achieve his goal was admirable. His eagerness to learn carried a certain fragrance of sincerity. His determination, constantly seeking to observe more closely, to work faster, to perfect his technique, was refreshing and inspiring to see.

Wouldn't it be wonderful to approach every moment of life with the humility of a kneeling posture? In that lowly, humble state, we could let go of greed. And when greed disappears, peace can take its place. With a calm heart, we could see others more clearly, allowing love and trust to grow. Then, I, my neighbors, and this world would be filled with humility and become a better place.

We must not forget the countless moments we have knelt in humility. The act of kneeling must remain a part of our lives. Those who kneel often recognize one another instantly. There is a distinct aura about them. They understand that the more they kneel, the deeper their understanding of the world becomes.

Jane Ha

Reflections on Broken English

A Hispanic patient, fresh out of surgery, was brought into the recovery room. Speaking with her in broken Spanish, I didn't feel the least bit self-conscious. Was it a sense of camaraderie, knowing that English isn't a native language for either of us? It's strange—broken Spanish doesn't trouble me in the slightest, but my imperfect English fills me with agony. Why? Because of the countless humiliations I've endured over 24 years of living in an English-speaking world. English, English, English. The language I will likely die speaking. The language that would remain cold and indifferent, even if I died trying to pronounce it perfectly.

I recall an incident long ago with my 19-year-old daughter. I was talking to her about work when, suddenly, she turned serious and asked me to repeat the doctor's name I had just mentioned. Dr. Wood. Shaking her head, she said, "No, Mom, that's not it. Try again." Even after carefully repeating it three or four times, it seemed to still fall short of her expectations. Finally, with a deep sigh, she said:

"Mom, you should have spoken to us in Korean from the start. Then you wouldn't have to struggle to communicate with us in English, and we'd now be fluent in both languages. I feel so ashamed that I can't speak Korean."

"Oh, my goodness, you're right. I felt a wave of guilt. I'm sorry. But even if I had spoken Korean to you, Dr. Wood would still have to be pronounced in English, wouldn't it?

What do you expect me to do about it now? I deeply regret not teaching you Korean more diligently. But I wish you could also understand my feelings. I wanted you to fully grasp the meaning of what I was trying to say. My English pronunciation isn't perfect, but I thought it would ensure my intentions came through clearly. In any case, haven't we always shared everything openly, without barriers?"

I suddenly remembered a moment from my daughter's high school graduation party, a video interview. The host had asked her, "Who's your best friend in the world?" Without hesitation, she answered, "My mom. I can tell her everything without hiding a single emotion. She knows me better than anyone else on this planet. She's my best friend." I was so moved I could hardly swallow a bite of food.

I recalled that moment and said, "Maybe it's thanks to my broken English that we became friends?" My daughter shook her head. "Mom, it's not because of the language. It's because we trust each other. Language is secondary." "No," I replied. "Language is culture. The way we think changes depending on the language we use."

My daughter continued, "When I was little, I used to feel frustrated whenever you spoke in English because I couldn't see your intelligence shine through."

A brief silence filled the car. I was driving when suddenly, the windshield of the car ahead started to blur. A chill ran down my neck, and my collar kept grew damp. Without realizing it, tears were streaming uncontrollably down my face. It wasn't intentional, it just happened. Then sobs began to escape, deep, guttural cries. A flood of memories, painful stories and wounds tied to English, rose up all at once, tearing at my heart. It was like pouring hot oil onto a burn, a searing agony I couldn't contain.

When my daughter was six, we were drawing pictures on a sheet of paper. I picked up a purple crayon and said, "Purple." She immediately corrected me, her face serious. "No, that's wrong. It's 'pur-ple.' Say it: pur-ple." "Puh-ple," I repeated. "No, that's not it, Mom! Say it like me." She demonstrated the shape of her lips and tongue, urging me to imitate her. In the end, she shook her head in frustration, left to right, over and over, before bursting into tears, crying, "Mom doesn't even know the word for purple!"

I was taken aback but couldn't think of a way to turn the situation around. To my young daughter, a mispronounced English word meant I didn't even know its meaning.

Still, I tried to explain, whether she could understand or not. "Sweetheart, my tongue grew up with Korean. So even if I know what some words mean, it's still hard for me to pronounce them." As she grew older, she stopped criticizing my English pronunciation. Instead, she encouraged me. "You're doing great, Mom. It's fine. I understand everything you're saying."

When I was a rookie nurse, I noticed a patient's blood pressure had dropped drastically to 82/45, with a pulse of 42. His baseline blood pressure was in the 120s. I measured his blood pressure in three different positions, lying down, sitting, and standing. Each time confirming the unmistakable signs of hypotension. Following standard measurement guidelines for nurses in cases of low blood pressure, I ensured readings were taken at regular intervals. Although the patient was asymptomatic, his blood pressure was low enough to be a cause for concern.

As I headed to the nursing station to call the doctor, I found his cardiologist, Dr. Y, already there, seated at the desk.

Feeling relieved to see him, I eagerly reported the patient's condition. He looked puzzled and asked, "What? Purse? Are you talking about a wallet?" Then, he pulled his wallet out of his pants pocket and waved it in front of me. For a moment, my mind went completely blank. "Doctor, you're this patient's cardiologist. Even if my pronunciation isn't perfect, I believe you understood what I meant." "No," he replied, his eyes widening. "I have no idea what you're talking about. What's this about a wallet?"

I stood there helplessly, listening to his mocking tone. Ariel, the case manager sitting nearby, turned red with anger and shouted, "Dr. Y, you're unbelievable. You're a terrible person. The only one here who can't understand what Jane is saying is you, the cardiologist! You're trapped in your own arrogance."

My heart pounded with anxiety, fearing that my shortcomings might lead to a full-blown argument between the two. Dr. Y said nothing in response to Ariel and abruptly stormed off toward the patient's room. Ariel exhaled sharply, then turned to me and said, "Jane, from now on, don't use the word pulse with that guy—just say heart rate. I guess complicated medical terms like pulse are beyond him."

I pulled myself together, and the situation became clearer. If he were truly a doctor who had taken the Hippocratic Oath, he would have rushed to the patient immediately instead of wasting time criticizing a nurse's pronunciation. That day, I gained a crystal-clear understanding of how a professional should, and should not, conduct themselves.

The pain I've endured because of English doesn't end there. There were countless embarrassing and agonizing moments, but nothing cut as deeply or felt as sorrowful as hearing my own child say, "Mom, when you speak English, I can't sense your intelligence at all." That pain stemmed from a retroactive shame. The crushing realization that, for the past 24 years, I may have left the same impression on others. What made it even more heartbreaking was the lack of any guarantee that things would improve in the future. After all, my clumsy English pronunciation wasn't going to suddenly transform into fluent, native-like speech overnight.

My child's words kept echoing in my mind, relentless and unshakable. Once the tears began to flow, they wouldn't stop. A flood of long-buried sorrow burst forth uncontrollably. Seeing this, my daughter, startled and overwhelmed, began to cry as well. "Mom, I'm so sorry. Please forgive me. I shouldn't have said that. I'm so proud of you." She sobbed uncontrollably, as if she couldn't bear the fact that her words had hurt me so deeply.

I didn't try to explain myself to my daughter. I didn't tell her that despite starting nursing school later in life, I never had to retake even the most challenging courses. I didn't mention that while young people born and raised here, with advanced education and straight A's in general courses, often dropped out of nursing programs, I never failed a single subject.

I didn't say that during an 18 weeks, I simultaneously studied anatomy, microbiology, and college-level English, completing 17 essays and seminar reports. I didn't remind her that I earned an A in my communication class or that, while my study group peers struggled to pass their nursing licensure exams, some failing even on their second attempts, I passed on my first try.

I didn't point out that I work in a high-tech ward, rarely missing instructions mumbled by masked doctors in operating rooms or labs. I didn't mention that over the years, I've trained more than ten new nurses at the hospital.

Nor did I tell her that I recently received the "Excellence in Patient Care" award.

As soon as we arrived home, my daughter rushed over to me as I got out of the driver's seat and hugged me tightly. However, I comforted her instead. "It's okay. Thank you for telling me a hard truth. It only shows how much you love me. Right now, it stings a little, but in the long run, it will be good medicine for me. And you know, even though living in America comes with so many challenges and limitations, I'm still happy."

Snapping out of my reverie, I found the patient on the bed staring at me intently. "Frio? Are you cold?" She nodded. I took a warm blanket from the blanket oven and gently placed it over her, then wrapped my arms around my own shoulders. Had autumn already arrived? The once-lush leaves beyond the hospital window were now sparse and bare.

I still can't properly pronounce words like pulse, wood, purple, and countless others. These days, I've found ways to work around it, I spell out the letters to preempt any confusion: "'W' as in 'world', 'O' as in 'orange', 'D' as in 'dog'..." Or I simply admit upfront, "I don't pronounce this word well, so don't stress over my accent or intonation." Sometimes I even joke, "Why don't you try learning Korean? I bet your Korean would sound just as fluent as my English." People chuckle in disbelief, amused. And yet, I am still happy.

Jane Ha

Beauty and Ugliness

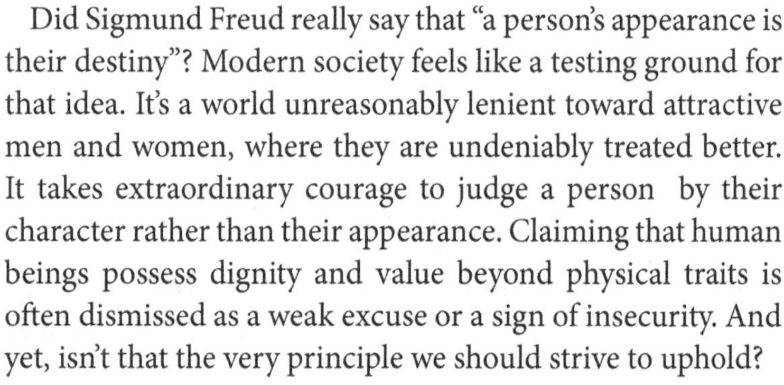

Did Sigmund Freud really say that "a person's appearance is their destiny"? Modern society feels like a testing ground for that idea. It's a world unreasonably lenient toward attractive men and women, where they are undeniably treated better. It takes extraordinary courage to judge a person by their character rather than their appearance. Claiming that human beings possess dignity and value beyond physical traits is often dismissed as a weak excuse or a sign of insecurity. And yet, isn't that the very principle we should strive to uphold?

The ancient Greek poet Sappho's belief that "What is beautiful is good, and the good become beautiful" remains an unshakable bastion in modern times. There is a compelling logic, now almost an undeniable code, that physical beauty and charm increase one's chances of leading a happier life. After all, those who are perceived as attractive may experience the world with fewer distortions, encountering less resistance and bias than those without such attributes.

Not long ago, two universities published intriguing research findings. At Spain's University of Valencia, a research team tested the quality of men's sperm and then asked women to rank the attractiveness of the sperm donors. The results showed that men with handsome features tended to have higher-quality sperm. Meanwhile, at the University of Nottingham in the UK, male participants listened to recordings of 30 women and ranked their voices based on

attractiveness. They were then shown photos of the same women and asked to rate their facial features. The findings revealed a striking correlation; women with melodious voices often also had attractive faces.

Anyone who has studied science understands that forming a hypothesis and testing its validity is often fraught with errors. Experimental conditions can significantly influence the results, sometimes leading to misleading conclusions. Thus, selecting appropriate methods is just as critical as the findings themselves. This responsibility goes beyond basic courtesy, it is an obligation to both the scientific community and the broader public. Moreover, there is no doubt that scientific research must always be grounded in ethics and humanism.

Judging sperm quality based solely on motility, while ignoring genetic factors or the presence of diseases, is a precarious oversimplification. While it is a logical assumption that healthy sperm exhibit higher motility, this reasoning is far too fragile to account for numerous latent factors that remain unexamined. Similarly, linking women's physical appearance and voice through experiments relying on photographs and recordings raises serious questions about the rigor and validity of such research. Furthermore, relying on a sample size of just 30 participants severely undermines the reliability and credibility of the findings, making them vulnerable to critique. Additionally, the study's integrity is further called into question by the lack of transparency regarding the qualifications and characteristics of both the participants and the sample group. Without such disclosures, the research remains open to significant skepticism.

No matter how noble the motivations behind these studies may have been, their crude execution raises serious doubts about whether they truly belong in the academic realm. It is troubling to think that such work could be publicly presented as legitimate research in today's world—and even more concerning to imagine a society that accepts these findings without critical scrutiny. This research feels less like a genuine academic inquiry and more like a reflection of the commercialization of humanity by industrialism, leaving an unsettling impression.

These research teams should exercise greater caution before announcing such black-and-white conclusions. For instance, does the sperm quality of a man who becomes handsome through plastic surgery also improve? Does a woman who achieves beauty through procedures like cheekbone reduction, double eyelid surgery, nose augmentation, and jaw narrowing also find her voice becoming more attractive? Are women with unconventional appearances inevitably cursed with unpleasant voices? What exactly defines the standards of beauty and ugliness? These questions must also be addressed.

Physical beauty and high-quality sperm cannot be the ultimate measures of value. The greater goal is to create an environment where high-quality sperm can develop into a well-rounded individual, a person of integrity and character. For beauty and a pleasant voice to hold true meaning and value, they must serve a purpose beyond personal vanity. Their value lies in contributing to the welfare and harmony of society, not merely in fulfilling selfish desires.

Beauty is a gift, and appearance matters. It is undeniable that physical looks influence a person's autonomy and opportunities in life. However, relying solely on beauty while looking down on the world leads to a lonely and thorny path. This world is not so easily navigated with a beautiful face alone.

When a society begins to establish value standards based on beauty and ugliness, it inevitably descends into superficiality. Treating handsome men and beautiful women as mere commodities because of their appearance is a sorrowful reality. If society is to be captivated by beauty, let it be drawn to a deeper beauty that is intrinsic, essential, and lasting, rather than one that is confined to external appearances.

Jane Ha

A Nurse's Tears

In the end, I couldn't hold back my tears. Looking down at the front of my uniform, now soaked, I felt an overwhelming sense of defeat. Tears that flow against your will when you don't want to cry are truly bewildering. What's worse is that in such moments, they become uncontrollable. When suppressed emotions finally break free, their force is immense. It's no wonder they are often compared to a bursting dam.

Hannah, who was ten weeks pregnant, went for her routine check-up at the doctor's office, only to receive devastating news: her baby had died. She was immediately admitted to the hospital. Due to various hospital circumstances, she endured an exhausting day of waiting and was only able to enter the operating room late in the evening.

I was on call that day. When the hospital called about a surgical case, frustration welled up inside me. It was the weekend, and I had been enjoying a rare evening with delightful company over dinner. This wasn't an emergency. She wasn't bleeding heavily or in pain. It was a case that could have been handled during regular hours in the morning. A creeping sense of resentment arose—why did this surgery have to be done so late at night?

She lay in silence on the bed in the waiting area. Beside her were her husband and 13-year-old son, following her like shadows. Their heads were bowed low, and their faces were tight with tension, as if they might burst into tears at any moment. I wanted to ask them to step out, but that wasn't an option. Since this wasn't a regular case, there were no other patients around, and the doctor had instructed that they stay with the patient, as the procedure wouldn't take long.

I felt uneasy. The instinct to distance myself from people steeped in tension, fear, and sorrow was a form of self-preservation. There's a reason why comforting those in deep emotional distress is so difficult, no words can truly console them. You cannot tell them to find joy in the midst of their pain; such advice is meaningless. In such moments, the best approach is simply to let them feel, to allow their emotions to run their course without interference.

Caring for patients' families can often feel like an added burden. Their nerves are frayed with worry, and at times, their frustration manifests as unwarranted anger—almost as if blaming the medical staff for their loved one's illness. Some see their rudeness or demanding behavior toward healthcare professionals as an expression of love and concern. Yet, the outlandish requests and questions born from ignorance can be more exhausting than attending to the patient itself. Calming anxious family members during a surgery is no small task—especially when the patient is a child. In such cases, managing parents in emotional shock can be one of the greatest challenges of all.

After Hannah's surgery, she returned to my care, appearing calmer than I had anticipated. I sighed in relief, thinking everything was under control. But within moments, she began to cry. Her pale face, still groggy from anesthesia, shattered the fragile calm. Then, as if on cue, her two companions joined in—a silent chorus of grief. Her teenage son, his reddened eyes cast downward, sat with slumped shoulders. Her husband stood by the bedside, tears falling freely. I gently urged him to sit, but he refused, steadfast in his sorrow. The sight of this large man clutching his wife's small handbag, weeping silently, was profoundly heartbreaking.

I placed a hand on his shoulder in a quiet attempt to comfort him. But unable to bear the sadness, he turned and walked out of the recovery room, his son following closely behind. I turned to the doctor who was dictating and questioned him. "I don't have the capacity to care for the patient's family as well. And the son is a minor. I fail to understand why you insisted on keeping them in this room from start to finish." The older doctor simply offered a faint smile, saying nothing. Then, without a word, he disappeared.

Left alone with the patient, I found myself at a loss for words. I couldn't tell her that this was simply as far as fate allowed this time, or that accepting things as they might bring her peace. Nor could I say there was no need to unravel the inscrutable plans of a higher power or urge her to be strong and move forward. I couldn't bring myself to mention that, at 35 years old, she was considered of advanced maternal age and that such losses were not uncommon. In the end, I decided to give up trying to comfort her as she cried inconsolably. Whether she wept or not, I left her to it and resolved to focus on my work.

Glancing toward the door, I noticed the two men hadn't left after all. Instead, they were leaning against the wall, their faces buried in it, quietly crying. It was quite a sight.

I called them back in and had them sit down. Then, I shifted my gaze between the three of them, caught somewhere between exasperation and pity.

But then, to my surprise, a wave of emotion welled up within me. I realized just how desperately they must have waited for this baby over the past ten years, how deep their pain of loss truly was. Their emotions seeped into me, raw and unfiltered. It was overwhelming. "Ugh, what is this strange feeling?" I thought. "I was already frustrated about losing my weekend rest, and now my heart feels like it's crumbling. Why is this happening?" A mix of emotions churned inside me—frustration, sorrow, and something else I couldn't quite name. And to my own dismay, I found myself upset with myself for feeling this way.

I am a bold nurse. In my everyday life, I struggle to voice my opinions or step out of the shadows—but once I don my scrubs, I transform. I come alive when teaching patients. "If your husband doesn't follow my instructions, call me," I say with a grin. "I'll kick his butt for you." Even with topics most nurses avoid out of embarrassment or discomfort, I tackle them head-on. Subjects that would make even the most seasoned nurses blush, I address them without hesitation. When it comes to teenage girls, I sit them down with their boyfriends and, like a mother or aunt, candidly remind them to take responsibility for what needs to be done while they're young.

Starting an IV line for a new patient can be a real challenge for a nurse. Factors like the patient's illness, age, and dehydration from fasting can make finding a suitable vein incredibly challenging. Sometimes, I've had to rely on the tiniest veins in the knuckle of the pinky finger or the delicate ones running over the ankle bone. For patients with a history of drug abuse, finding a healthy vein is nearly impossible. African American patients with kidney issues often present an additional layer of difficulty. By the time multiple people have prodded their veins, causing them to retreat deeper into the skin, frustration sets in. It's not uncommon for a patient to finally declare, "No one is touching me anymore!" That's when the floor nurses call me in. I actually enjoy the challenge of stepping up, sometimes in front of a whole crowd of family members, to confidently place the IV line. Even if I make a mistake, I remain calm and collected. There is something about putting on my uniform that fills me with a courage I don't usually have in my daily life.

Perhaps it's because I exhausted all my tears long ago; nothing brings a single drop to my eyes anymore. Not when a patient I just cared for let's go of their lifeline. Not when someone who was laughing cheerfully before surgery ends up in a coma afterward. Not even when comforting a mother sobbing as she holds her stillborn baby. My eyes remain dry. It's not because I lack a personal connection to these patients, nor is it entirely due to the rigorous training that demands acceptance of medical realities. It's not even just the result of my own self-conditioning to never cry at the hospital. The truth is, I learned long ago that the matters of life and death lie far beyond human control. Even if sorrow wells up, I've learned to mourn silently, inwardly, even when sadness comes. For this reason, the death of a formless, unseen fetus, a mere clump of blood, was not a significant trauma for me.

As I was entering the patient's vital signs into the computer, suddenly; oh my, what was this? Droplets of water began falling onto the front of my uniform. Tears.

Had I been infected by the sight of the entire family crying together? I hadn't intended to cry, yet the tears came unbidden. Once the tears found their way out, they flowed without restraint. I let go completely, and to my surprise, releasing that tension felt liberating. The four of us cried freely, uninterrupted by anyone. There wasn't a single sound, no sobbing, no sniffles. Just quiet immersion in shared grief, a release that felt oddly comforting.

Deeply buried emotions surged to the surface all at once. Long ago, I had been in the same situation as her. I could vividly see myself lying in a hospital bed after losing a 12-week-old fetus. I had gone in for a routine checkup, unaware of what was to come. As the technician conducted the ultrasound, she suddenly abandoned the machine and left to fetch the doctor. On the screen, my baby drifted aimlessly in the amniotic fluid, weightless, without tension or resistance, gently pushed back and forth.

The doctor confirmed that the baby had died but couldn't explain why. There was no bleeding or no pain, so I was advised to go home, rest, and return if bleeding started or if I experienced abdominal pain. But I couldn't do that. I couldn't eat, sleep, or rest while carrying my lifeless baby inside me. I insisted on staying. Right then and there, I was admitted to the hospital and underwent a dilation and curettage procedure.

The tears I shed carried a multitude of meanings. There was sorrow for how easily I had forgotten my own painful past. Grief over how dry and barren my emotions had become. Mourning for a life that vanished before it ever had the chance to see the light. And the profound weight of witnessing the deep bond of a family.

All these feelings intertwined, a tangled knot of emotions. But what surprised me most was how I had let my own history slip away; how I had come to see her as merely a case, a simple presence, rather than someone living through what I once endured.

Before transferring Hannah to the ward, I took two warm blankets from the warmer and gently wrapped them around her shoulders and feet. In that moment, a memory resurfaced—of my own shoulders and feet, unbearably cold as I lay on a makeshift bed long ago.

Jane Ha

The Face of Silence and Tranquility

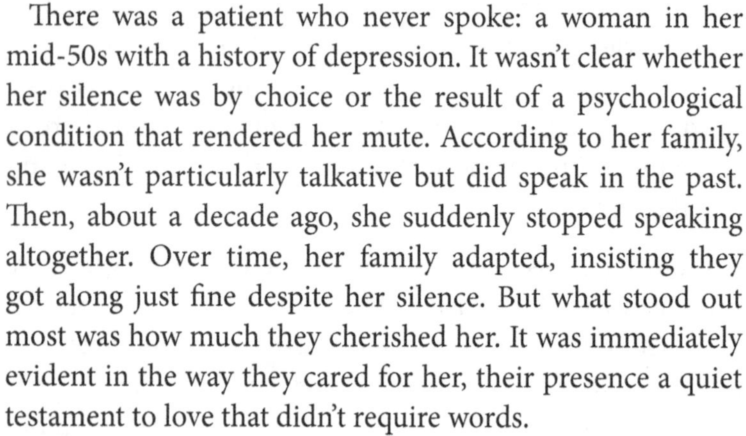

There was a patient who never spoke: a woman in her mid-50s with a history of depression. It wasn't clear whether her silence was by choice or the result of a psychological condition that rendered her mute. According to her family, she wasn't particularly talkative but did speak in the past. Then, about a decade ago, she suddenly stopped speaking altogether. Over time, her family adapted, insisting they got along just fine despite her silence. But what stood out most was how much they cherished her. It was immediately evident in the way they cared for her, their presence a quiet testament to love that didn't require words.

Communication was enough. I adjusted all my questions to be closed-ended, allowing her to respond with gestures or nods. There was no need to raise my voice or embellish my words. I spoke only what was essential, in a soft and gentle tone. The peace emanating from her silence and stillness was unexpectedly profound.

Maintaining eye contact with her was essential. The usual method of glancing at the patient while working on the computer, asking and answering questions in a hurried manner, couldn't be applied to her. It was unfamiliar yet refreshing.

I found myself wondering, when was the last time I had looked so deeply into someone's eyes? I had long forgotten

that a person's gaze could hold such depth, that it was possible to see something beyond words.

Being able to look into someone's eyes is a privilege. One granted only when they allow you to see into their gaze. At the same time, it requires me to open my own heart to them. The expression in one's eyes cannot be fabricated is both an advantage and a vulnerability. The meeting of gazes is an exchange that requires permission and acceptance. Through this singular window, we glimpse the otherwise hidden depths of each other's hearts; a moment of unspoken sincerity, carrying its own quiet gravity.

The tranquility of her presence as she lay in bed seemed to wash over me, as gentle as the look in her eyes. There was a quiet joy in reading the neutral stillness, devoid of desire or will. I felt as though I had discovered why her family loved her so deeply.

Her aphasia might medically be classified as an illness, but on the other hand, it could also be a deliberate choice. Perhaps she is someone who fully understands that she is the master of her own life. The absence of any psychological symptoms commonly linked to aphasia suggests this possibility. What kind of mystery might she be experiencing within the world of silence she has crafted by her own will?

Several days passed, yet she lingered in my thoughts. In the midst of chaos, I found myself thinking of her even more. There was something unresolved within me, something I needed to confront. I couldn't shake the feeling that it was tied to her image.

I deliberately set aside a day to experience silence and stillness. Speaking too much stirs greed and thinking too much awakens desires. So, I chose to move as little as possible limiting myself to only essential words and thoughts. I resolved to remain silent, like one who cannot speak, and feign ignorance, like one who cannot hear. I turned away from newspapers and computers, put my phone aside, and shielded myself from the words I neither wanted to say nor hear. How often do speaking and listening themselves become sources of disorientation and unease?

I was unsuccessful. How difficult it is to refrain from speaking and listening. The more I became aware of it, the more despair consumed me. I wanted to turn inward, but it was impossible. My mind was a muddied pool, so murky that I couldn't even begin to guess what thoughts might be swirling within it.

Long ago, when I first arrived in America, I was quiet. Not knowing English and with no one to speak to in Korean, I would sit beneath the shade of a towering sycamore in the middle of the yard, idly plucking at the grass. On weekends, I would go to Santa Monica Beach, sinking into the white sand, or sit by the shore of Silver Lake, gazing endlessly at the waves as they crashed and receded, again and again.

These days, I am anything but quiet. I juggle precariously between my clumsy English, which never seems to improve, and my half-baked Korean, fossilized 25 years ago. I am constantly caught between the temperaments of these two vastly different languages, trying in vain to appease them both. Overwhelmed by a flood of miscellaneous information, my eyes and ears scream in protest, yet I am helpless.

Why is there so much "essential" information and "necessary" conversation? Could it be that my need to absorb the world's noise is rooted in an obsession with myself? Am I too fixated on how others perceive me? Me, me, me. How long will I remain trapped within the confines of "myself"?

Words are merely a means to justify myself to others, a superficial strategy for seeking approval and understanding. If one's inner self were truly strong and whole, would the opinions of others matter so much? No matter how hard I try, I cannot change how others perceive or judge me. Considering that my existence is not a perfectly rounded sphere but rather a multifaceted entity, is it really the end of the world if they view one of my sides through the lens of their own biases?

I want to refrain from using words to assert or justify myself. Instead, I should speak up for those trapped in darkness. I must train myself to close the gates of my ears to unwelcome noise, while keeping them wide open to warm, kind, and heartfelt stories.

Eventually, the tangled threads of consciousness will be unraveled and put in order. Beautiful thoughts will flow like a gentle current over the calm, clear waters of the mind's river. In that stillness, I will finally understand the messages that silence has been waiting to reveal.

Jane Ha

Deliberation at Year's End

The end of the year is near—my mind is restless. It's hard to stay composed. So many places to be, so many things to manage. Why am I like this? Why am I even here? I ask myself over and over, yet no clear answers emerge. I'm not making meaningful memories with those I care about, yet I feel breathless, chasing something I can't even name. That's it, I'm merely reacting, helplessly responding to whatever conditions and stimuli arise. As the holiday whirlwind pulls me in, I am swept along; dizzy, unmoored, unable to find my footing.

How much calmer will I become later to be fluttering about like this now? How deeply will I settle one day to be drifting so aimlessly today? How long has it been since I sat at the kitchen table, sharing a quiet meal with my family? When will I finally meet an old friend, sit across from them with a cup of tea, and share a warm, heartfelt moment?

Last week, I went back and forth to downtown LA no less than four times. Returning home at 11 p.m. sometimes even midnight, I found myself asking, What is the essence of life? I'm certain I asked myself this very same question and had the same thoughts 10, maybe even 20 years ago.

Why do I feel so uneasy? Amid the beautiful interior decorations, the elegant table settings, the delightful laughter of radiant women, and the warm hospitality and smiles of charming gentlemen, why does it all feel so unfamiliar? Why do I leave myself abandoned in such a lonely place?

Why must we compress all the love we failed to show, the affection we left unspoken, and the gratitude we never expressed into this one fleeting season? When is there ever time to reflect on the past and dream of tomorrow? If the time granted to us as humans is meant for awakening and wisdom, wouldn't it make more sense to spend this season in silence and introspection, as if retreating into solitude for self-reflection?

And why is it that, despite my long-held desire to escape, to either soar into the sky or sink into the earth, hide, and then return, I have yet to act on it?

Last evening, I attended my hospital's employee Christmas party. Just hours earlier, we had all been colleagues in our daily uniforms, barely distinguishable from one another. Perhaps it's the hospital environment, where individuality is best subdued for the sake of professionalism. But under dazzling lights, my coworkers transformed. They wore spaghetti-strapped dresses that revealed shoulders and décolletage, their hair voluminous and their striking makeup. We patted each other on the back, exchanging excited chatter and showering compliments like, "Amazing!" "Gorgeous!" "So chic!" Amid the flurry of words, one phrase stood out, settling firmly in my ears as the truest, most ripened remark: "Oh my, you've got a surprisingly fit body!"

The drive home felt unusually lonely. Maybe it was because I had laughed too much, eaten too much, and talked too much. My heart felt cold, like an empty shell. I bit my lip and vowed never to attend another year-end party. But no, I know I'll do the same thing again next year.

The house felt cozy as I stepped inside. Though it was late, I put water to boil, then poured it into a mug, dropping a few green tea leaves on top. Suddenly, Jules Supervielle's poem "The Secret Sea" came to mind; the one about the sea as it exists for itself when no one is watching. Not the one known to people when no one is watching.

Literary critic Shin Hyung-chul once said, "The sea we know is merely the sea we've seen. The sea that exists when we aren't watching—when it is solely for itself—is an entirely different sea."

The sea that moves and inspires us is not the sea that exists solely for itself. I understand, of course, that this is not the whole meaning—but still, I feel a bit petulant. What significance does a sea entirely different from the one we know have for us? If the sea wears two faces, then it ceases to be the sea. Essence, essence—let's not insist that only essence holds value. I am who I am. Whether I flutter about or sink into stillness, it is all me, all my essence.

Isn't it the same with the seasons? Whether nature or people, everything exists along the continuum of time. When something leaves, we let it go; when it arrives, we welcome it. There is no obligation to feel or express anything special just because it's year's end. Silence is perfectly fine. By this time next year, I'll probably be caught up in the same thoughts, feeling restless, only to regret it once again.

The green tea has cooled; the teacup sits cold. How did time slip away so quickly?

The Art of a Wonderful Relationship

What truly defines a meaningful connection?

I once learned that it is "a bond that brings strength and meaning to someone, inspires dreams, fosters growth, and quenches thirst like a drop of dew." Yet, this definition feels so metaphysical that forming such a bond seems almost impossible.

A meaningful connection does not happen by chance; it is cultivated through effort and intention. Even when a relationship begins on a positive note, complacency and neglect can easily cause it to fall apart. How, then, can we build meaningful connections and nurture them to last overtime?

The most fundamental and primary aspect is of any connection communication. Through conversation, we understand the other person's feelings, convey our own emotions, and foster mutual understanding.

I recalled RESPECT, introduced by Mrs. Ford, a nursing professor, on the first day of class. It struck me as a practical and detailed explanation of the Korean proverb, "A single kind word can repay a thousand debts." It serves as a communication guideline for nurses, who must build strong relationships with patients and their families while collaborating closely with colleagues due to the nature of their work. But beyond nursing, it is a golden rule for anyone seeking to form meaningful human connections. A benchmark for evaluating the quality of their communication.

Recognize your communication style.

Empathize with the experience of others.

Speak from your own experience.

Participate in the process by listening as well as speaking.

Examine your own assumptions and perceptions.

Commitment to maintaining confidentiality.

Take responsibility for yourself and what you say.

I have come to understand <RESPECT> in my own way. To me, it means being mindful of the tone and manner of my speech, embracing others' circumstances with deep compassion and understanding, and expressing my thoughts with honesty and humility. It is about listening with genuine attention and care, examining myself to ensure that I do not view others through the lens of prejudice or bias, and respecting their secrets and privacy.

It also involves recognizing and responding to others' emotions with maturity and thoughtfulness, while taking full responsibility for my own words.

When we truly practice <RESPECT>, we can sustain meaningful and positive relationships, even with those who may seem difficult to approach.

I was also reminded of the Ten Commandments for Making Good Friends.

"Take good care of yourself first. Try to understand others' perspectives. Be polite, especially to those closest to you. Let go of your pride and love sincerely. Speak less, listen more, and avoid unnecessary nagging. Keep your words and actions consistent. Be humble, yet express your thoughts clearly. Strive to be honest rather than perfect. Praise others for their strengths. And do not force yourself to befriend those who do not wish to be close."

Both <RESPECT> and these commandments share a simple but powerful truth: genuine relationships begin with self-awareness, empathy, and sincerity. When we learn to respect others as well as ourselves, friendship ceases to be an effort—it becomes a natural expression of kindness and humanity.

Within these commandments lies the wisdom of those who understand that truth will always reveal itself, and the composed spirit of those confident enough to live without pandering to societal expectations. The phrase "Don't force friendships" resonates deeply with me. What is happiness? Perhaps it is found in spending beautiful moments with people you cherish, valuing one another, and fully experiencing both the love you give and the love you receive.

To avoid loneliness, one must reflect on their language habits. Even if others withhold praise, neglect to give, or even criticize and slander you, it is essential to remain thoughtful and vigilant—always striving to avoid causing harm. Through self-reflection and awareness, meaningful and lasting relationships can be built.

This morning, I find myself longing, more than usual, to meet people with beautiful hearts, and to become one myself.

Jane Ha

The Story of My Big Hands

My hands are big. Even if hands are big, they can still be considered attractive if they have slender bones and long, elegant fingers. But my hands are not just large—their knuckles are thick, and my palms are broad and sturdy, resembling the hands of a seasoned laborer. As a teenager, I believed my large hands would doom me to a life without marriage. And if a partner failed to notice them at first and married me anyway, I feared he would eventually lead to divorce.

The size of my hands can be attributed to genetics, as I inherited them from my father. But I place more weight on environmental factors. From a young age, my hands became accustomed to enduring strenuous labor. Growing up in the countryside, I worked tirelessly in rice fields, vegetable plots, and orchards, never hesitating, never holding back.

During my elementary school years, it was a daily routine to pull weeds in the garden with my grandmother or climb the hill behind our house to gather pine branches, carrying them back on my head. In the freezing winter, I scrubbed laundry against cold rocks in an icy stream as I had to without a second thought. My hands were constantly cracked and bleeding, regardless of the season. Over time, the wounds on my hands eventually hardened into calluses.

When I lived in the hillside neighborhood, I was in third or fourth grade. The only access to running water was over

a steep hill. I would collect the trickling water from a spigot into buckets, hang them on a shoulder yoke, and make the arduous trek back home. Though I gripped the buckets tightly with both hands to prevent spillage, by the time I poured the remaining water into the jar at home, barely half remained.

When I was in my first year of middle school, my father decided to return to our rural hometown. Both he and my mother were educators, but they also took up farming.

He cultivated about one acre of rice fields and an orchard, using them as educational tools for his one son and four daughters.

People often say that farming is a seasonal task, but in reality, it demands constant attention year-round. After the autumn harvest, we would scatter compost from the outhouse over the fields multiple times.

My father stored sacks of rice seeds at the mill until they were processed. When our household ran out of rice, I was tasked with pulling a handcart to the mill and bring back freshly milled white rice. The cart, weighed down by the heavy rice sacks, was nearly impossible for my young strength to control. The handles felt as if they were glued to my hands as I gripped them tightly, struggling to move forward under the sheer weight.

Orchard farming was even more demanding. During droughts, we spent entire nights watering the thirsty fruit trees. Lighting fires to lift the dew, picking and washing grape clusters, wrapping apples, peaches, and pears in protective bags, and carefully handling the harvest — every step required immense labor.

Often, neighbors were called upon to help with the work. As a child, I wasn't of much help, but after school, whether it was day or night, I often stayed in the orchard with my father, working alongside the laborers. I loved listening to my father, always in awe of the wisdom, knowledge, and insight woven into his words.

Even now, when our gardener comes to mow the lawn or technicians arrive to repair broken equipment, I make an effort to stay with them while they work. This habit likely stems from the unspoken lesson I learned back then—that such actions are a gesture of respect and courtesy. I remember my father saying that workers tend to be more diligent when the master is present.

I've found that being a conversation partner helps keep them engaged while they work. It also allows me to respond immediately to their questions or needs. Beyond that, it's a great opportunity to learn from their specialized knowledge and expertise.

After each autumn harvest, a familiar task awaited me—delivering freshly harvested rice to my eldest aunt's house in Seoul, a five-hour bus ride away. My father likely never imagined that a young girl like me could single-handedly carry a 20-kilogram sack of rice all the way to her home. At every step of the way, there was always someone who offered a helping hand. I knew my father was giving me the opportunity to learn a valuable life lesson: no one can navigate life without the kindness and help of others.

When I was in eighth grade, my father designed and built a house himself. After school, I would return home and help with small tasks, such as carrying bricks. One time, when the cement ran low, my father bypassed the workers and send me on the errand instead.

On a sweltering summer day, I pull a cart into town to buy two bags of cement. The load was so heavy and difficult

to manage that I would break into a sweat just trying to maneuver the cart.

Once the house was completed, my father began crafting a garden using sand and stones from the nearby river. Though he assured me this was a strenuous task, even for men, and that I didn't need to assist, I refused to sit idly by. On freezing winter days, I followed him to the riverside. I can still vividly recall the icy sting of the stones in my hands, a memory that remains etched in my mind.

After graduating high school, I enrolled in a university located an hour away by intercity bus. I lived on my own but returned to my rural home every weekend to be with my parents.

During school breaks, I worked alongside my mother preparing meals for the laborers. We loaded the food onto large trays, balanced them on our heads, and carried them to the fields. The trays were so heavy it felt as if my neck might shrink, but I gritted my teeth and carefully navigated the slippery paths through the rice paddies.

After graduating from university and moving to Seoul, I worked in the editorial department of a publishing company that produced monthly magazines, often working late into the night, racing against deadlines to edit manuscripts. My hands became indispensable; reading, writing, and organizing articles, they carried the weight of my work.

One of my acquaintances owned a seaweed-roasting factory and often needed extra hands when short-staffed. Although machines handle much of the cutting, roasting, and packaging of seaweed, many steps still require human intervention. After finishing my editorial work, I would take a bus to the factory and spend the night packaging roasted seaweed. The work involved both a conveyor belt and manual labor. Keeping up with the relentless, unyielding pace of the machines required quick and precise hand movements. When I left the factory at dawn, the world outside was always shrouded in mist. It wasn't until much later that I realized the "mist" was just my exhaustion clouding my vision.

My father firmly believed that being a girl was no reason to be excluded from labor. I, too, held the conviction that work shapes humanity. Labor was never something to be ashamed of. At night, my father and I often discussed Kierkegaard and Tolstoy, bound by a shared understanding that philosophy without action is meaningless. I never wanted to betray his trust, and, truthfully, I never even considered the work burdensome. A girl in a skirt hauling sacks of rice and cement on a cart, or handling the foul-smelling task of spreading manure, naturally drew sympathetic glances from others. But for me, who lived in a reality where ideals and everyday life were seamlessly intertwined, those pitying looks held no significance whatsoever.

When I entered university, I often had the opportunity to shake hands with male students. It was rare to encounter hands rougher or larger than mine. Even men with larger hands couldn't fully envelop mine, yet my hand wasn't particularly larger than theirs either. This always led to an awkward handshake, lacking the typical dynamic between men and women. In truth, a more accurate description would be that these men, grasping my hand without a second thought, were startled by its size and let go in surprised confusion.

After every handshake, I would always feel awkward and embarrassed. The person I shook hands with would inevitably glance back at my face, as if trying to reconcile the disparity. In cases where the interaction was lighthearted, they would often exclaim, "Wow, your hand is really big!"

For those too sheepish to comment, I would break the tension by joking, "My hands are pretty big, aren't they?" This usually eased the awkwardness, prompting a bashful laugh in response. Occasionally, someone would ask to shake hands again, insisting they confirm whether they had imagined the size difference or not.

At some point, I began avoiding handshakes altogether. Mischievous male peers in my college club made a game of betting on which man might dare to shake hands with me and when. To this day, handshakes still make me uncomfortable. In unavoidable situations, I would offer only half of my palm to the other person's hand. However, after an elder scolded me for giving a halfhearted handshake, I began bowing as a substitute or outright avoiding situations that might require shaking hands.

My husband, who has broad palms and plump fingers but short knuckles, an unfortunate trait that led him to abandon his love for playing the guitar. He has always felt self-conscious about his hands. Yet, he takes immense pride in my large hands. All three of our children inherited my long fingers and wide palms, making them naturally suited for any musical instrument: piano, violin, clarinet, or guitar. Their music teachers often praised their large hands, remarking that they would face fewer hurdles mastering complex techniques. "Thank your mother for those hands," my husband would urge the children, and I couldn't help but smile with satisfaction.

There's a Korean proverb that says, "Even a rat hole gets a chance to see the sun." What was once a weakness and a source of insecurity has become a strength and a point of pride. A complex, you say? That feels like ancient history. Now, I go one step further, declaring my large hands to be treasures.

Becoming a wife and a mother expanded the roles of my hands in ways I could never have imagined. Raising children, cooking, fixing things, and cleaning became endless tasks. At night, once my family was asleep, my hands turned to writing. Translating the thoughts trapped in my mind throughout the day into words on paper. Even when reading, my habit of underlining passages and jotting down notes kept my hands perpetually busy.

Becoming a nurse made my hands even more active. Large hands are an asset in this profession, especially when washing or moving patients. In the ward, no one mocks or criticizes the size of my hands. On the contrary, my colleagues say my hands make my work look efficient and impressive.

Handling patients with varying conditions and severities often leaves my heart tangled in emotion, shifting with each situation. Yet my hands remain steady, unaffected by such emotional turbulence, always gentle and agile.

My hands are the primary tool in opening the hearts of patients who are both physically and emotionally in pain. While listening to their words, my hands are always at work—holding theirs, patting their shoulders, or firmly clasping toes wrapped in a blanket. Rarely are they idle or hanging uselessly without purpose.

Among the writings of essayist "J," one piece stands out, titled The Prayer of Hands. The passage, "Hands that can touch the foreheads of those in pain, hands that reach out to those groaning in darkness and suffering," made me reflect on the hands of a nurse. I found it a guidepost for the path my hands should follow. Like in his writing, I hope to cleanse my heart and soul every time I wash my hands.

I look at my large hands. They are a nurse's hands, rough and dry from being washed dozens of times a day. They are no longer defined by words like beautiful or unsightly, large or small. These hands have carried out diverse and complex tasks over a long span of years. They have been worker's hands, a mother's hands, writer's hands, and ultimately, a nurse's hands. These hands have wiped away countless sorrowful tears and cleaned up countless messes. What challenges might await them in the future? Perhaps the reason I do not fear new endeavors lies within these large hands.

I am finally proud of my large hands—hands that know labor, hands that understand pain. My hands are far more diligent and steadfast than my heart, which often feels lost and empty, wandering without a clear path.

Chapter 4

Tears of an American

Nightingale's Dream

Once I Wished to be a Man

A Ten-Minute Journey Together

Eyes of Understanding

The Razor Blade of My Heart

A Mother and Her Two Sons

Muscles of the Heart

Modern-Day Tears of the Amazon

Jane Ha

Tears of an American

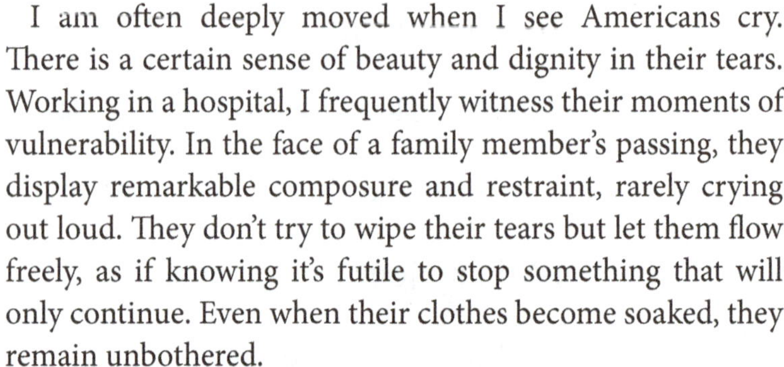

I am often deeply moved when I see Americans cry. There is a certain sense of beauty and dignity in their tears. Working in a hospital, I frequently witness their moments of vulnerability. In the face of a family member's passing, they display remarkable composure and restraint, rarely crying out loud. They don't try to wipe their tears but let them flow freely, as if knowing it's futile to stop something that will only continue. Even when their clothes become soaked, they remain unbothered.

When family members rush in after hearing that their loved one is nearing the end or has passed away, they are often the quietest of visitors. Six or so people might sit in the room for hours, enveloped in a solemn silence perhaps out of respect for the dying.

They remain calm, holding each other's hands and staying by their precious one's side. When they leave the ward, they never fail to thank the hospital staff for taking care of their beloved in their final moments. In their tear-filled eyes, one can sense a sorrow too deep for words.

I remember a patient who shed endless tears that were invisible to the eye. He was a doctor who had devoted his life to healing others, now facing his own imminent death from cancer. As he lay in his hospital bed, he watched his wife beside him, weeping uncontrollably. With quiet composure, he pressed his index finger to his lips in a silent "shhh,"

gently comforting her even as his own time was running out. His eyes: clear, deep, peaceful, intellectual, and sorrowful, left an indelible impression. Even in his final moments, he remained fully conscious. When I face challenges, I often think of his eyes.

A man who had been playing ball with his young granddaughters in the park collapsed from a heart attack and was rushed to the ER. When the doctor announced that resuscitation was unlikely, his wife sat beside him, stroking his lifeless hands, and spoke gently: "You have been a good husband to me. I was happy to have met you. Thank you for loving me and respecting me all this time. I hope to see your bright smile again. Do not worry about anything and rest peacefully, my love. We're just parting for a little while, and we'll be together when Jesus comes again."

She spoke softly, her voice low and measured. Her large, beautiful eyes overflowed with a steady stream of tears, yet she made no attempt to wipe away. Nor did she let out a single sob. If your eyes were closed or if you weren't looking at her, you would never have known she was crying. Her quiet, graceful weeping lingers in my memory.

There was a gentleman who could only watch helplessly as his wife succumbed to septic shock. In the three hours spent in the emergency room, it seemed he shed more tears than in his entire lifetime. He cradled her face in his hands, showering her eyes, forehead, and lips with endless kisses. Then, he would turn away to wipe his tears before returning to her side. He cried so much, yet so quietly. Even in his grief, he remained composed and rational when speaking to the hospital staff. I often wonder how he's doing these days.

When I see people cry, I feel the urge to cry with them. I want to gently pat their shoulders and say, "We are the same."

For this moment, I want to comfort them as a brother, sister, or family member.

Tears seem to be a privilege granted to humanity. What if we couldn't cry? Wouldn't the world feel even more barren and desolate? Perhaps it would threaten the very essence of human existence. Those who have much to cry about know this well—tears are a natural purifier. After crying, the mind often becomes clearer, and a renewed sense of energy and love wells up within.

To those who believe that tears deepen life's richness and maturity, cry often. If you are going to cry, do so meaningfully, gracefully, and wholeheartedly. Cry until all the dust accumulated within is washed away.

Nightingale's Dream

Bella, a surgical technician, was injured after mistiming the handoff of a scalpel to the surgeon, resulting in a deep cut on her finger. How sharp and precise these surgical blades are! The stress intensified because the scalpel was contaminated, It had been used on the wound of a young male patient with multiple severe illnesses. While comforting and assisting her as she rushed between the emergency room and various tests, I was flooded with memories of my time in the Telemetry Unit long ago.

At the time, I was administering an insulin injection to a woman in her early 50s. She suffered from a psychiatric condition, and I had endured her verbal abuse throughout the day. She preferred subcutaneous injections in the back of her upper arm. But just as I was withdrawing the syringe, she suddenly pressed her heavy arm downward, driving the needle deep into my index finger at a right angle.

I turned on the sink and firmly massaged the area from my palm below the wrist down towards my fingertips, pushing hard to encourage blood flow. Afterward, I cleaned the area with an alcohol pad. She, however, offered no apology. Instead, she sneered and said, "You know I have Hepatitis C, right? I got it from my husband. Who knows, I might even have AIDS. Well, lucky us. Looks like we'll get a proper AIDS test this time." She was already aware that both, she and I would have to undergo various blood tests together.

I traveled back and forth to a distant hospital for an extended period, undergoing various tests while taking multiple strong medications as a preventive measure. Weakened by the medication and unable to work for several days, I struggled to hold onto the belief that her actions had not been intentional.

During the tests, I discovered something surprising: while working on the ward, I had unknowingly developed immunity to a couple of types of hepatitis. I had never feared caring for patients with contagious diseases like tuberculosis or shingles, nor those carrying rare pathogens. But this time, I was momentarily shaken.

An incident from the past comes to mind. I was establishing an IV line for a 37-year-old male patient. Just as I was about to secure the Angio Catheter with tape, he suddenly grabbed the short IV tubing connected to the needle and yanked it out. In an instant, blood splattered across my face and eyes, as if someone had sprayed paint all over me.

As I washed my eyes and face under running water, Renele, a male nurse who had heard what happened, rushed over. His presence was reassuring and comforting. Without hesitation, he questioned the patient in ways I would never have dared: "Are you sexually active? How many sexual partners do you have? Have you ever been tested for HIV antibodies? Was there a specific reason or any symptoms that prompted the test? If you have any noticeable symptoms, what are they?"

Working in the ward often comes with difficult and dangerous moments. What's truly remarkable is that no matter how inhumane a patient's behavior be, it never seems to leave emotional scars on my heart. When someone approaches me as a patient, everything somehow becomes forgivable. Even more intriguing is that the moment I step into the ward, the ordinarily indecisive version of myself transforms into someone with a clear sense of purpose. No matter how difficult the situation, I remain steady and resolute, never wavering. The vigilance required of those who step onto the battlefield against unseen pathogens keeps me firmly grounded.

I do not take the act of touching another person's body lightly. Each time I care for a patient, I practice gentleness and patience. They are mirrors reflecting me. In them I see, like the two faces of Janus, good and evil, beauty and ugliness, coexisting in harmony.

Today, as I care for my patients, I learn once again about the profound intricacies of human nature. Through their words and actions, I reflect on my own emotions and motivations. I approach cheerful patients with respect and somber ones with patience and understanding, drawing valuable lessons from each interaction.

I hope that the broken and distorted thoughts buried deep within me will fade, making way for brighter and more uplifting ones to take their place. This is my simple dream as a nurse.

Jane Ha

Once I Wished to Be a Man

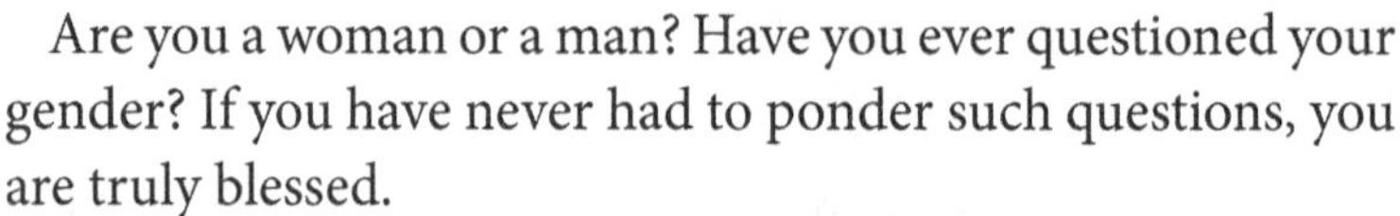

Are you a woman or a man? Have you ever questioned your gender? If you have never had to ponder such questions, you are truly blessed.

A man in his early fifties was brought into the pre-surgery waiting room on a gurney. This is where patients reconfirm their surgical procedure and prognosis discussed with doctors in the general ward while receiving reassurance and encouragement. It's also the perfect opportunity for a recovery room nurse to introduce themselves to patients, as the information gathered here is invaluable for post-operative care. When the patient arrived, I could only offer him a distant nod of acknowledgment, as I was tending to another post-operative patient.

After the surgery, he was brought into the recovery room with an oral airway and nasal trumpets inserted in both nostrils. While connecting the monitor lines, I noticed he was still under the influence of anesthesia, barely responding when I called his name. While receiving a report from the OR nurse on the surgery's progress, I checked the surgical site on the lower abdomen and was shocked. The patient was not a "he" but a "she." The gently rounded breasts, unmistakable markers of female anatomy, momentarily left me confused.

I looked at the patient's face again; thick, dark hair covered the face and limbs. The patient was unmistakably male.

How fortunate it was that she was under the influence of anesthesia when I called out "Señor." Years ago, due to a sudden hormonal imbalance, she had become intersex, neither fully male nor female.

A story from a fellow nurse in the emergency room comes to mind. His patient was a young and beautiful woman; silky, long hair, clean and delicate facial features, and notably full breasts, but she was suffering from a severe heart condition. As her blood pressure and heart rate plummeted, he prepared to insert a urinary catheter as per the doctor's order. That is when she spoke up, saying, "Don't be surprised. I am not a woman." It turned out that she was, in fact, biologically male.

There was a time when I wished to be a man. It happened one night in my early twenties—I realized I couldn't even lift one of my father's legs as he lay sprawled across the doorstep, drunk. I resented the frailty of being a woman. In the summer, I despised myself for being unable to protect my father from the relentless mosquitoes; in the winter, from the bitter, biting winds. As I went next door to ask my uncle for help, I couldn't shake the fervent wish I was a man.

During my middle and high school years, I often wished I was a man as I followed my father's strict rule that all the women in the household must return home before sunset. I used to dream of a world where all the wicked men who harm women would simply disappear.

Once, an acquaintance of mine, who had lived as a kind husband, a wonderful father, and a successful pastor said to me, "If I had been born a woman, I think I would have felt far less lonely." His words left me quietly shaken. Yet, in that moment, I found myself accepting and even taking pride in my identity as a woman, and it was a peculiar feeling.

There is beauty in women embracing their femininity and men, their masculinity. It is sorrowful when one's gender identity becomes clouded and complicated.

We cannot know the circumstances that have shaped those who stand before us. How can we fully grasp the pain of those whose bodies are female, yet whose consciousness feels male? Or those whose bodies are male yet carry a femininity deeper than any woman's? We must strive to see with eyes of tolerance and to understand and embrace them, even if only a little.

They endured such profound suffering to become women or men, yet I became a woman without paying any price. How grateful I am for this. From now on, I will fully embrace and cherish the blessings and pride that come with being a woman.

A Ten-Minute Journey Together

On my way back from the Human Resources office, located in a different building from the ward, I met an elderly Hispanic man, likely in his late seventies, walking slowly with a cane. As I hurried past him, he called out to me. Seeing someone in a hospital uniform, he said, brought him relief. He needed to get a blood test but could not find the location.

The hospital where I work has so many doctors' offices attached as annex buildings that it easily be nicknamed "the Doctor's Hospital." The man said he did not know the name of the doctor. I asked if he had any paperwork, and he pulled a single sheet from inside his jacket. It turned out he needed to go to the hospital's lab, not a specific doctor's office. I told him to follow me and began walking ahead. Nurses walk quickly by nature, and I soon noticed him struggling to keep up, breathing heavily as he tried not to lose sight of me.

Professional instinct kicked in. I immediately slowed my pace. If he were to fall, it would be a serious problem. I could find myself in a difficult situation, potentially leading to counseling on basic medical ethics or even being called as a witness—an ordeal no one wants.

I had forgotten that he was a person with dignity. Instead of worrying about how painful and difficult a fall would be for him, I was solely concerned about my own inconvenience. I despised myself for such selfish thoughts.

I came to a full stop and waited for him. At that moment, I heard a crashing sound within me, as if something had collapsed. I felt like a Sherpa in the mountains near Mount Everest—one who, after walking for a time, stops and waits, unbothered by the mountaineers' urgency, to ensure no soul is left behind.

As he hobbled along with his cane, his precarious steps overlapped with the image of my own soul. An aged, frail, and tattered soul. His labored sighs echoed like the quiet sobs of my own exhausted spirit, struggling to keep up. In that moment, I realized how I had been living, rushing forward without a thought for my own well-being. Days spent as an empty shell, devoid of substance. The hollowness and loneliness in my daily life had been inevitable all along.

He arrived, and in that moment, it felt as if I had finally come face-to-face with the image of my own soul. I began to walk in step with his pace. When was the last time I walked this slowly? It felt as if it were the first time since I had learned to walk as a child. Overcome with emotion, I found myself on the verge of tears. My eyelids stung, forcing me to blink repeatedly. Meanwhile, an elderly man, oblivious to my inner turmoil, wore a serene expression on his face.

He repeatedly apologized, explaining that he could not walk quickly because of his arthritis. His slippers were so worn that his toes peeked through the holes in his threadbare socks. Both feet were so severely deformed that he couldn't even wear closed-toe shoes. When I mentioned that it must be painful, he nodded quietly. He said it had taken him a long time to walk from the bus stop in front of the hospital to here. The calmness in his voice only made it more heartbreaking.

Sensing his unsteadiness, I reached out to support him by the arm. He rested his left arm on my right, using it as a brace, and his face lit up with a bright yet shy expression. Perhaps it had been a long time since he had allowed himself to lean on anyone like this.

As I guided him to the reception desk and turned to leave, he thanked me. I gently patted the back of his hand, the one gripping the cane. His eyes reddened almost instantly. Exiting through the front door and rounding the corner of the building, I suddenly stopped. An impulse surged within me. I turned back and ran inside. I wanted to thank him for allowing me to meet my own soul. But he was already gone, swallowed into the depths of the room.

I returned to the ward, walking in step with my soul. It suddenly occurred to me that perhaps he was an angel sent to deliver a message: to slow down, to move through life with greater ease and gentleness.

Jane Ha

Eyes of Understanding

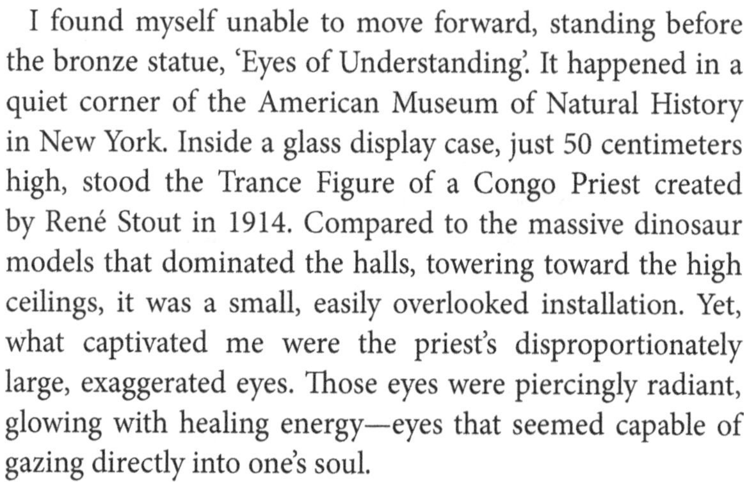

I found myself unable to move forward, standing before the bronze statue, 'Eyes of Understanding'. It happened in a quiet corner of the American Museum of Natural History in New York. Inside a glass display case, just 50 centimeters high, stood the Trance Figure of a Congo Priest created by René Stout in 1914. Compared to the massive dinosaur models that dominated the halls, towering toward the high ceilings, it was a small, easily overlooked installation. Yet, what captivated me were the priest's disproportionately large, exaggerated eyes. Those eyes were piercingly radiant, glowing with healing energy—eyes that seemed capable of gazing directly into one's soul.

What a great blessing it must be to have eyes that truly understand people and things as they are. The more we understand, the more at ease, compassionate, and joyful we become. How wonderful it would be to read another's spirit, not through words or gestures, but through the eyes of the soul. Then, we could love more deeply.

Long ago, my heart pounded as I stood before my preceptor, Nurse Amber, wearing my Registered Nurse's badge on my uniform for the first time in the Telemetry Unit. Without saying much, she led me to a patient. Standing outside the room, she said, "Jane, you have three minutes. Observe as much as you can."

After we left the room, she turned to me and said, "Tell me everything you saw." Oh my, what had I seen? A man with thinning, graying hair, vacant eyes filled with despair, fingernails stained and misshapen, a cup of water on the bedside table, its rim marked with food residue, and an unpleasant smell lingering in the air.

Amber let out a deep sigh of exasperation, clearly disappointed. She began firing questions at me: What was the condition of the patient's skin? How was the quality of his breathing? Where was the IV needle inserted? What type of IV fluid was being administered? At what rate? What was the name and dosage of the medication in the piggyback IV? What was its running speed? Did you see the sign on the bed instructing not to take blood pressure on the right arm? Why was that? How many side rails were raised? Did you notice the blanket covering the rails? Why was that? Did you see the bandage on the right side of his neck? What was its condition? What about the catheter? What was the quantity and color of the urine? I stared at her, wide eyed, realizing I couldn't confidently answer a single one of her questions.

From that moment on, Amber's rigorous training began. Her mission was to transform my overly sentimental eyes into ones that were sharp, precise, and practical. The most challenging and demanding patients were always assigned to me. Every time I stepped onto the ward; she shared her personal techniques and insights with me. Through her, I inherited the habits and virtues essential to becoming a good nurse.

Now, when I step into a patient's room, I can absorb a wealth of information at a glance. I have come to understand even more than what Amber initially expected of me. I can spot faint, barely visible veins that others might miss, and even when they are not visible, I can find them by touch alone. This has made me an expert in establishing IV lines for patients. I became someone who was frequently called to other departments— ambulatory, the GI lab, the operating room—and even by other wards through internal calls or pages. These skills were not gained easily. They were acquired through countless tears, mistakes, and moments of despair.

Working in the ward has taught me that people often see only what they want to see and hear only what they want to hear. Sometimes, this desire is so strong that they distort reality to fit their expectations, rather than perceiving things as they truly are. The saying "seeing is believing" holds little credibility. Human history has been shaped, often tragically, by the phrase, "I saw it with my own eyes."

The ultimate eyes of understanding are surely the eyes of Jesus. The merciful eyes that looked upon Judas with compassion that night in the upper room. The forgiving eyes that met Peter's, warmly and unwavering, after he had denied Him three times at dawn.

How wide and deep are the eyes of my heart? Am I judging the world through the narrow and limited perspective of a short-sighted nurse? Have I been complacent, assuming that wisdom and insight will come naturally with age?

I must not turn away from what is unpleasant. I must not close my ears to unkind words. No, rather than avoiding them, I should accept and embrace them with grace, allowing beauty to take root within me. I must strive to cultivate and expand the eyes of understanding, so that, ultimately, I may live a life where few words are needed.

I dream that the eyes of understanding will become the most defining part of my face and being.

The Razor Blade of My Heart

I was assigned to the team conducting a gastric examination on a female prisoner who had swallowed a razor blade. Following the gastroenterologist's instructions, I administered an IV sedative and pain reliever. The patient's vital signs remained stable.

As the room lights dimmed, the endoscopic imaging tower's monitor glowed brightly. Thus began the journey through her upper gastrointestinal tract—esophagus, stomach, and duodenum, the first part of the small intestine—as the endoscope entered through her mouth.

The stomach, glowing in a healthy pink hue, was clean and unblemished. There were no signs of damage or discoloration. Had I expected to find lesions, ulcers, or inflammation? Had I assumed that her digestive system would be as battered and scarred as her skin, marred with sores and the marks of self-harm? A pang of remorse struck me for the assumption.

Astonishingly, the razor blade slipped through the narrow esophagus without leaving a trace of injury. It came to rest upside down, perfectly horizontal, against the stomach wall. Using a specialized retrieval basket attached to the end of the endoscope, the doctor carefully maneuvered the instrument. After several attempts, he successfully extracted the blade. As soon as the blade was extracted, bleeding began. The procedure was swiftly completed with laser cauterization.

From tracking the razor's position via X-ray to its removal, the entire process took no more than a couple of hours.

In the recovery room, I asked her nothing. I did not question why, at such a young age, she was living a life with her freedom taken away. I was not curious about what had driven her to swallow the razor blade. I did not assume she lacked responsibility for her own life, nor did I believe she had done it out of mere anger. Nor did I think she had swallowed it out of mere anger. Without a word, I simply patted the back of her hand.

She must have endured years of pain and agony. Whatever crime she committed, it is not unfamiliar in the context of the modern age. Anyone could find themselves in her position—judgment is simplistic and narrow-minded. Perhaps she was even a victim herself. I felt a deep, unshakable sense of compassion for her.

My colleagues shook their heads in horror at the thought of swallowing a razor blade, calling it dreadful. I said nothing. I understood. I did not judge her—I simply accepted her actions. When you lay your life on the line, everything in this world holds beauty. I, who have never risked my life for love, nor dared to challenge the world with everything at stake, felt only shame and bitterness. I envied her fierce passion, her relentless energy for life. Her illness, though severe, carried a kind of innocence; simple, straightforward to treat. But someone like me, tangled in the endless complexities of my own mind, is beyond saving — even if others want to help.

There is a razor blade within me too. My sorrow lies in the fact that I cannot scream out that a razor blade resides in my heart—that it hurts. The blades embedded in the veins of my soul are invisible, undetectable by even the most advanced X-ray technology. They drift along with my blood, lodging themselves at random, cutting deep without warning, causing pain at unpredictable moments. It's not as if I can tear my body apart to search for their elusive hiding places. How could anyone comb through 60,000 miles of blood vessels, traversing every organ, to find countless blades? How much time would that take? Any doctor would surely give up. And even if the blades were found, removing them all at once would be dangerous. It would cause massive bleeding.

I close my eyes. Ah, I see the razor blade. The cold, lonely childhood. The anguish of youth, swayed by delusion and confusion. The despair of middle age, like a three-legged race gone awry. The unbridgeable gap between dreams and reality that has shadowed my life. The countless razor blades I have swallowed in the folds of time. Their shards remain scattered within me.

It is time to stop swallowing razor blades. From this point on, I must turn to gathering, mending, and healing. I wish I could thread an endoscope through every vein, every delicate capillary of my heart, in search of the razor blade fragments buried deep within. I want to collect their remains in the basket and finally lay them to rest. I ache to break free from the chronic pain woven into the fabric of my being—to taste, at last, a joy untouched by shadows.

Jane Ha

A Mother and Her Two Sons

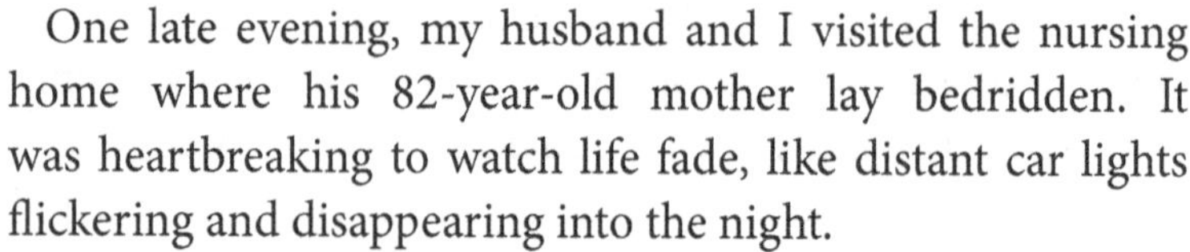

One late evening, my husband and I visited the nursing home where his 82-year-old mother lay bedridden. It was heartbreaking to watch life fade, like distant car lights flickering and disappearing into the night.

She struggles to breathe, her lungs heavy with fluid. Her eyes, always open, are perpetually bloodshot. Who is she waiting for? "Mom," my husband calls softly as he steps into the room, his eyes brimming with tears. His hands, constantly stroking her frail shoulders, face, head, back, and hands, are filled with sorrow.

"Mom, your eyes are so red. Please close them. I am here, so you can sleep peacefully," my husband said as he gently stroked her eyelids. It felt unsettling. It felt unsettling, as though his words were a metaphor. "Mom, it's time to let go of your weary body. It's painful to watch you suffer."

A little later, my brother-in-law came in. He, too, gently stroked his mother's back with his large hands. On either side of the bed, the two men stood, their hands moving endlessly caressing their small, frail mother with quiet, aching devotion.

Their mother, now wordless, remains indifferent to any stimulus. How could she understand the turbulent emotions of these two men, who are struggling to contain their grief after reluctantly agreeing to hospice care? Watching the three of them from the sidelines, an indescribable sadness wells up within me. These strong men were conceived and born from this small body. Someday, they too, like their mother, will fall, and so will I.

It was heartbreaking. I could not share the quiet, unspoken emotions my husband and brother-in-law exchanged as they reminisced together. I was absent from the memories they held close. My husband once told me how, as evening fell, he would crouch by the roadside, waiting for his mother to return from selling aluminum dishes. He took the heavy load from her, carried it inside and served her the rice he had kept warm—a quiet gesture of devotion. Meanwhile, as I looked at my brother-in-law, I recalled a story my mother-in-law once shared about his childhood. On a blazing summer day, she carried him on her back and balanced a heavy sack of rice on her head as she traveled from the mainland to a far-off island to sell it. On one of those journeys, while riding a small ferry, an elderly man remarked, "The son on your back will grow into a fine man one day. Endure these hardships, and better days will come." Those simple words became a wellspring of strength, sustaining her through a lifetime of poverty and hardship.

Neither of them let go of their Hands touching from their mother's body, even for a moment, until they left the room. Do they know the incredible healing power of touch? Though she can no longer express herself with words, their mother surely felt the warmth of her sons' loving hands. For a brief moment, she must have forgotten her pain, loneliness, and fear.

I suddenly recalled my yoga teacher's words: "Before touching someone, you must first compose your heart." The yoga principle of avoiding physical contact with others during practice struck me with a new interpretation. I now understood it not just as a rule, but as a wisdom; an acknowledgment that touch is more than physical. If two people are not centered, they might unknowingly absorb each other's negative energy, causing harm instead of healing.

Doesn't that mean that a touch, when given with a gentle, warm, and calm heart, carries profound healing power? Perhaps it is the paradox that only when the energy within me is bright, warm, and healthy can it truly comfort others and convey love.

How precious are these touches? A mother's hand gently patting her sick baby's back or soothing an aching belly. A mother dog tenderly licking her injured pup. A quiet hand of encouragement placed on a colleague's shoulder after a mistake. The tender gaze of a husband as he embraces his wife after a long, weary day.

I thought about the touch of a nurse and a wave of regret washed over me. From now on, I resolve to touch each patient with a prayerful heart, hoping that my hands will bring warmth and comfort rather than harm.

It was not easy to leave the room, knowing my mother-in-law quietly staring blankly at us. Outside, the sky was scattered with countless stars. Life is precious and beautiful because we are born, and we die. The world is beautiful because things come into being and eventually fade away. Even if we, too, disappear one day, the fact that we are living in this moment makes it all the more beautiful.

Chapter 4

Muscles of the Heart

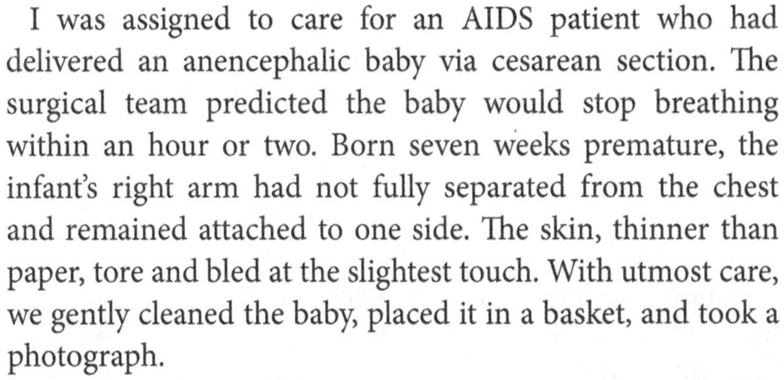

I was assigned to care for an AIDS patient who had delivered an anencephalic baby via cesarean section. The surgical team predicted the baby would stop breathing within an hour or two. Born seven weeks premature, the infant's right arm had not fully separated from the chest and remained attached to one side. The skin, thinner than paper, tore and bled at the slightest touch. With utmost care, we gently cleaned the baby, placed it in a basket, and took a photograph.

The mother held the baby, whose breathing was irregular, and wept endlessly. If there was a face that embodied the deepest sorrow in this world, it would be hers—a grief so profound that no words of comfort could ever truly console. She pressed her forehead against her husband's, who bore the same illness, and together, they sobbed in quiet devastation. There was nothing to say. All I could do was stand there, silently watching, swallowed by despair.

The baby's breathing gradually faded. Deprived of oxygen, its tiny body turned patchy blue. How desperately it must have wanted to breathe. And yet, we, blessed with functioning brains, burdened by endless thoughts—so often find ourselves wishing not to live.

Suicides are on the rise. Those who take their own lives do not do so because they want to die, but because they see no way to live as they long to. They believe death will bring peace. But that is a misconception. In death, nothing can be perceived. Only the living can truly understand what peace is.

Humans, more than anything, desire to live rather than die. At their core, they are born with a deep love for life. But life itself is delicate, so gentle that even the slightest wound can cause deep pain. Why does the mind feel confused? Because it is searching for a way to live well. Why do we suffer? Because life does not unfold as we expected. How can we live well? By training the heart; by strengthening and developing the muscles of our hearts.

People strive for well-defined, sculpted muscles, free of excess fat or flab. The ultimate mark of physical fitness is the Chinese character for "king" etched on the abdomen, commonly known as the six-pack. These muscles are not built in a day nor are they the result of casual exercise. The abdomen, broad and naturally soft, is one of the most difficult areas to tone. A six-pack is more than just a sign of strength; it is a badge of honor earned through self-discipline, perseverance, and unwavering restraint.

The heart, too, has its own muscles and, like the body, consists of many chambers. These do not strengthen overnight; they are the result of patience, discipline, and refinement. What we choose to fill these chambers with shapes our lives and character. Love, joy, hope, gratitude, peace, gentleness, kindness, and harmony...

When the muscles of the heart are well-developed, navigating life becomes smoother. There is no need to pretend to be strong. You will learn to let things go with grace to act as if you did not see or know, even when you did. Criticism will no longer wound you. Most importantly, you will stop hating yourself. You will find the strength to forgive your own moments of weakness, to accept the times you resisted but faltered. You will no longer resent the world. Instead, you will face reality as it is—with clarity, acceptance, and peace.

You and I, we have each walked countless rough and lonely paths, often unknown to others. There were moments when we felt utterly alone, convinced we were unloved. The tears we shed in secret, wondering, "Why me?" The sorrows we buried so deeply, even from ourselves. The countless times we wished our breath would simply stop... And yet, despite it all, here we are, alive in this very moment.

We must believe that being alive is proof that we are loved. The lonelier we feel, the stronger we must become. We need to learn how to love ourselves, for in moments of solitude, our only true companion is ourselves. Those who can befriend themselves are the ones best equipped to overcome loneliness.

When will that day finally come to me? Ah, it is time to strengthen the muscles of the heart.

Jane Ha

Modern-Day Tears of the Amazon

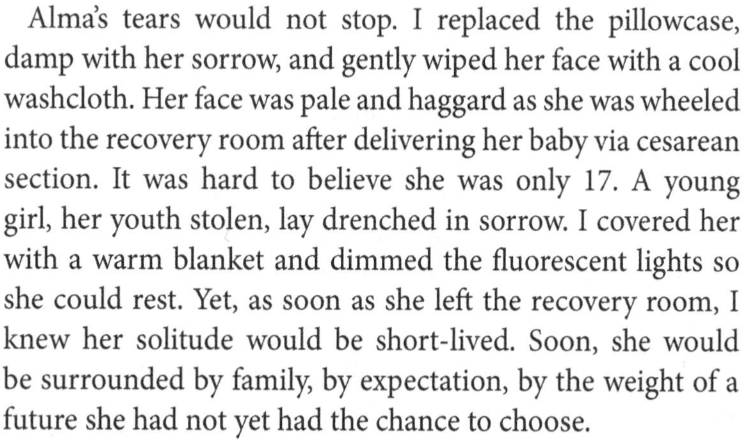

Alma's tears would not stop. I replaced the pillowcase, damp with her sorrow, and gently wiped her face with a cool washcloth. Her face was pale and haggard as she was wheeled into the recovery room after delivering her baby via cesarean section. It was hard to believe she was only 17. A young girl, her youth stolen, lay drenched in sorrow. I covered her with a warm blanket and dimmed the fluorescent lights so she could rest. Yet, as soon as she left the recovery room, I knew her solitude would be short-lived. Soon, she would be surrounded by family, by expectation, by the weight of a future she had not yet had the chance to choose.

Just when I thought she had fallen asleep, she began to sob again. She must feel lost, overwhelmed by the thought of raising a baby on her own. Her heart is likely shattered by the betrayal of her boyfriend, just a boy himself, who had abandoned her during her pregnancy.

As I stroked her trembling shoulders, I thought of The Tears of the Amazon. A story of indigenous people living as one with nature in the Amazon Basin, untouched by the relentless digital tide of the 21st century, where text messages and video calls dominate communication. A docudrama capturing the burning, deforestation, and destruction of Earth's last treasure, the Amazon, sacrificed to the greed and selfishness of modern civilization.

Among them is the life of the indigenous Waurá women. When a Waurá girl experiences her first menstruation, she is secluded from her family for an entire year. Alone in a hut, she learns self-reliance and independence. During this period, she is reborn into a true woman. It is a time of transformation, a time to cultivate the strength to rise again, even after being trampled upon and broken by the world and humanity. A strength that ultimately allows her to nurture and sustain life.

Once the isolation period ends, the girl earns the right to have a boyfriend, entering a free union beyond parental interference. The rules of marriage are simple: sleep with her boyfriend four times or conceive a child. As she steps into adulthood, she adopts an ancestral ritual using a knife made of fish teeth to scrape her thighs and calves two to three times a week, drawing blood. This practice serves as a profound reminder that love and pain are inseparable, that life and suffering coexist. The sight of her enduring the pain, tears brimming in her eyes, is considered an expression of strength—one of raw and haunting beauty.

In some ways, the challenges faced by modern youth are even harsher than those of the Waurá tribe. How many young men and women sacrifice love in the pursuit of wealth, status, and luxury? How many relationships are strained or broken under the weight of family interference? Unlike the Waurá, where love is embraced despite its hardships, modern youth often choose to forgo love altogether rather than endure its pain.

What if we applied the Waurá tribe's tradition of isolation to the modern world? Imagine if every adult had the right or even the obligation to retreat into solitude at regular intervals, much like a vacation or a business trip. This designated period of self-reflection and renewal would allow people to return to their lives with renewed strength and a refreshed spirit. They could embrace the people and things they cherish with even greater passion and depth. It would be an opportunity not to escape from relationships, but to enrich them; to nurture love, deepen understanding, and cultivate a more profound appreciation for the connections they have built.

I snapped back to reality. Gently, I suggested to Alma, who was still crying, that once her body recovered, she should consider stepping away from her family for a little while to rest. I encouraged her to take time for herself to reflect, to gather her thoughts, and to envision the life she wanted to create. A moment of solitude could offer her the clarity and strength she needed to start anew.

I repeatedly reminded her that as a mother, she needed to be healthy. As a mother, she needed to be strong. I told her that she must never allow anyone to wound her soul. Her large, tear-filled eyes met mine, and she nodded in silent understanding. It was the modern-day Tears of the Amazon.

Even now, somewhere in this land, countless Almas are crying. To wipe away their tears, this world must change. It must grow kinder, warmer, and gentler; day by day, even if only by a little. Because this is the world my daughter must navigate, the world my sons must endure, and the space where those I love must live.

Chapter 5

Jane Ha

Love

It's the season of love. The Surgery Unit is filled with the Valentine's Day spirit. Colorful jelly stickers with phrases like "Hug me" and "Be my valentine" are shamelessly plastered on every window. Hearts in warm hues sway gently in every corner. Darlene, giggling as she prepares to send a photo to her boyfriend, puckers her lips beside a "Kiss me" sticker and takes a selfie.

I thought of my husband, John. He is training intensely, running 21 miles a day in preparation for the Huntington Beach Marathon, now just a week away. This morning, he ran 9 miles from our house to the hospital where I work. Even during the few minutes we spent together in the hospital courtyard, he jogged in place, afraid that his muscles would stiffen and disrupt his rhythm. When I scolded him for coming all this way, he playfully replied, "Thinking about seeing you made it easy." As I saw him off, he teased, "What if someone steals my beautiful wife?" Waving me back inside, he kept turning around to look at me, again and again. Standing in the hospital courtyard, I watched the worn, unassuming figure of a middle-aged man running away, unable to take my eyes off him.

In my single days, I was always in love with someone. The object of my affection would change, but not a single day passed when I was free from the fever of love. How many times did I feel that I could throw myself entirely into someone's arms? Sadly, it was always unrequited. I would fall into love awkwardly, only to sink into hopeless despair and eventually turn away. The other person remained unaware, while I loved alone, grieved alone, and then, all by myself, suddenly stopped loving.

I was afraid. When the person I loved finally extended a trembling hand, I could not bring myself to take it. I lacked the confidence to deepen the connection into something more meaningful. And yet, I felt lonely and hurt. I could not understand why, despite the passion in my heart, my words and actions in front of them came across as cold and detached. Night after night, turbulent emotions swirled within me. Lingering, inexplicable regrets refused to leave my mind. I would create endless questions and answers about them, replaying scenarios in my head over and over. Ah, who could ever understand: the loneliness, the anguish of such love? Because of love, my broken heart lay bleeding silently.

A few days ago, I heard a gentleman's confession. "I now truly understand the essence of love. My wife has been a strict vegetarian her entire life. If a dish so much as touched fish, she would shatter the dish on the spot. But now, she buys fish herself, scrapes off the scales, cuts off the fins, and endures the awful smell as she grills it in a frying pan. She blows on the fish to cool it, picks out the bones, and feeds it to our grandchildren."

Tears spilled over from my eyes. I thought of my youngest aunt. She was a devoted member of Won-Buddhism, living as a celibate woman of faith. A strict vegetarian, she believed that even eating vegetables involved taking life, and so she lived with extraordinary modesty and restraint.

One day in late autumn, during a time when I was lost in a desolate period of my life, I went to see her. I was in tears.

She did not ask a single question. After hours on a long, slow train ride from the countryside to Seoul just to see her, she simply stayed by my side all night long.

At dawn, I dozed off briefly and woke to the smell of fish filling the entire house. When I went to the kitchen, my aunt greeted me with a bright smile and a warm good morning. She was ladling soup from a pot and tasting it. "This is the first time I've ever made fish soup. I wonder if it will taste any good?" To this day, I cannot forget the pollock soup my aunt carefully prepared and cooked for me that morning.

As I gaze at the heart decorations on the windows in the OR nursing lounge, I think of my aunt. I think of the woman picking fish bones for her grandchildren. When will my own love mature, like the love of these two women, to the point where I can completely let go of myself? I feel ashamed to even look at the red hearts hanging on the window.

True love transcends the systems of the world. It is powerful enough to forsake one's own benefit. Love is stronger than religion. In life, there are often moments without answers, times when we cannot discern God's will. Yet, even in those moments, what remains is love.

One day, even for 27-year-old Darlene, the time will come when she understands the profound and unfathomable depths of love. When love is no longer about fleeting passion or grand gestures, but about quiet sacrifices, enduring patience, and the willingness to put others' needs before her own.

A Lament for Aborted Babies

A pregnant woman at 38 weeks was rushed into the operating room with a uterine rupture. Her life was fragile, like a candle flickering in the wind, after losing more than 3,000 mL of blood. The doctors managed to save the mother, but they could not save the baby. The newborn girl, with delicate and lovely features, was now a lifeless form cradled silently in her mother's arms. The mother, who had prayed only for her baby's safety, sobbed uncontrollably before falling into a stupor. The baby, suddenly deprived of oxygen, must have endured unimaginable suffering. The once warm, soft, and dim amniotic world where she lived serenely before must have turned into a hell of agony in an instant.

Yesterday, I cared for a mother who delivered a stillborn baby at 39 weeks. She had slipped in the kitchen, hitting her swollen belly against the floor, and when she woke the next morning, she realized there was no fetal movement. The accident had occurred just two days before her scheduled cesarean delivery.

I couldn't scold her, sobbing as she was, for not coming to the hospital immediately. After moving her to the ward, I went to the room where the baby had been placed. I unwrapped the swaddling cloth and held the baby's already cold hands and feet for a long time. The CT scan showed no signs of broken limbs or brain injury. The baby had simply stopped breathing. Though I have seen countless stillbirths, witnessing the tragedy of such young lives two days in a row left my heart in utter despair.

I've had the painful experience of losing the life of my second child. The baby was 22 to 23 weeks along. After three days of severe bleeding, I went to the hospital, where they told me that part of the placenta had detached. Following an amniocentesis, the doctor, with 13 years of experience, seemed uncertain and hesitant. She recommended an abortion, explaining that a healthy baby could not be guaranteed due to the lack of sufficient oxygen and nutrients.

I decided to let go of the baby. My husband had a sibling with hearing loss, and I, too, had a sibling who had struggled with a disability since birth. I was terrified of a future with a baby who might be born with an unforeseen disability, and I lacked the courage to face it. The procedure revealed that the pregnancy was further along than initially thought, so instead of a simple minor procedure, dilation and curettage, it required a two-day delivery process. Outside the surgical center, a silent protest was taking place. Protesters wore white masks and carried white crosses with signs that read, "Baby killers to hell!" I felt faint and staggered under the weight of it all.

A week after the procedure, I received the results of the amniocentesis. They congratulated me, saying it was an extremely healthy baby boy. The brownish tint of the amniotic fluid was due to bleeding and was no longer a concern. The placenta was stable as well. This notification was a clear mistake caused by a communication failure between the hospital and the lab, as the matter had already been resolved. And yet, I could not dismiss it as mere coincidence. Instead, it felt like a punishment, a reckoning that would remain with me forever. I saw it as a cruel twist of fate, a bitter lesson carved deep into my soul. I saw it as punishment from God; a judgment commanding me to live with guilt for the rest of my life. I spent a long time in desolation. For what felt like an eternity, I was plagued by auditory hallucinations and sleep paralysis. The weight of my decision pressed down on me like an unbearable burden. Even in sleep, I could not escape. I would wake in the middle of the night, drenched in sweat, my ears ringing with cries I could not silence. The guilt gnawed at me, carving itself into the deepest parts of my soul. I questioned everything. Had I been too hasty? Had fear clouded my judgment? Had I abandoned my child out of selfishness? No answers came—only silence, only regret. The pain settled into me, becoming a part of who I was.

Years later, I became a nurse working in the recovery room of a surgery department. I believe it was meant to be. Perhaps it was a calling—an atonement, a way to confront my past, to care for others in their most vulnerable moments, just as I had once been vulnerable. Each day, I witness patients awakening from anesthesia, their eyes fluttering open in confusion, fear, or relief. I hold their hands, stroke their foreheads, and reassure them with soft words. Some wake up weeping without understanding why. Others emerge in pain, their bodies remembering the trauma even before their minds do. I watch over them, ensuring they are safe, easing their distress, offering comfort.

In those quiet moments, I wonder, am I also tending to the wounds I cannot see? Am I, in some way, caring for the life I once lost? I do not know. But what I do know is that my hands, once burdened with regret, now find purpose in healing.

Although I do not take to the streets holding anti-abortion signs, I dedicate myself daily to work that feels like atonement. To teenage girls who treat abortion as their primary method of contraception, I earnestly appeal to the sanctity of life. To women grieving the loss of their unborn child, I share my own story filled with regret and pain, walking alongside them in their sorrow.

I do not preach, nor do I judge. I simply listen, hold their hands, and let them know they are not alone. I see the weight of their choices in their eyes, the silent grief they carry, and I offer what I can; a touch, a word, a presence that understands.

Every day, I spend a set time in silent prayer for all aborted and stillborn babies. I fervently hope that no more unborn lives will be sacrificed due to the selfishness, fears, or unpreparedness of adults. With each quiet moment, I ask for peace for the souls who never had the chance to take their first breath. I pray for the grieving mothers, for those who made difficult choices, and for those who never had a choice at all. May love, responsibility, and compassion replace neglect and regret. May every life, no matter how fragile or brief, be cherished.

Chapter 5

Prayer

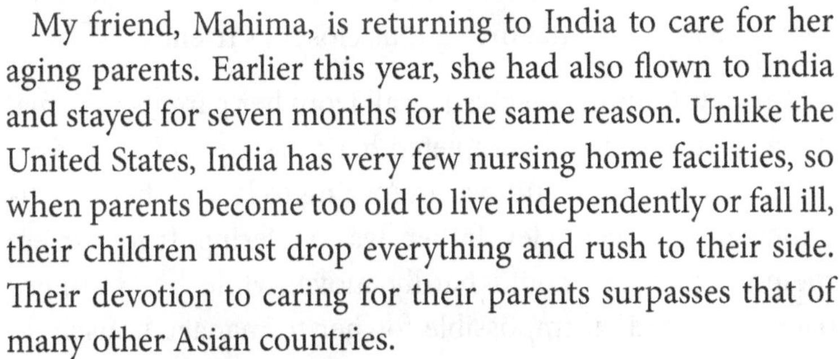

My friend, Mahima, is returning to India to care for her aging parents. Earlier this year, she had also flown to India and stayed for seven months for the same reason. Unlike the United States, India has very few nursing home facilities, so when parents become too old to live independently or fall ill, their children must drop everything and rush to their side. Their devotion to caring for their parents surpasses that of many other Asian countries.

The concept of filial piety is deeply embedded in Indian culture, where children are expected to provide physical, emotional, and financial support to their parents. There is no question of whether they should—they simply must. It is a responsibility that is ingrained, an unspoken duty that is honored with great reverence. Mahima, like many others, does not see this as a burden but rather as a privilege. It is a chance to give back, to care for those who once cared for her, and to express love in its purest form: through presence, sacrifice, and unwavering commitment.

Mahima is 56 years old. We became friends while studying nursing together. I fell in love with the Indian food she made. Whenever she had the chance, she would make chapati for me. When coming to school, she always brought a container of chapati along with a vegetable dish to pair it with just for me. Her stir-fried okra and lentil curry are also exquisite. During the week, she was busy studying, but every weekend she prepared a week's worth of meals and stored them in the refrigerator or freezer. When she called to say, "I'm cooking something you've never tried before, why don't you stop by? Let's eat it while it's warm," I would drop everything and rush to her house. Her kitchen, filled with the warm aroma of spices, felt like a place of comfort, and her hospitality made each meal an experience rather than just food. Even now, whenever I smell cumin, coriander, or turmeric, I think of her, the love she poured into every dish, and the laughter we shared over meals that brought us closer as friends.

One day, Mahima received a call from her parents in India. It was just as she had completed her nursing studies, passed the licensing exam, and was preparing to launch her much-anticipated career. Her father was suffering from severe memory loss and could hardly move, while her mother's back pain made it impossible for her to manage household chores. Without a second thought, Mahima flew straight to India.

She left behind the career she had worked so hard to build, her dreams put on hold indefinitely. She never complained, never hesitated. Her parents needed her, and that was all that mattered.

I couldn't help but admire her. How many people would make such a sacrifice so willingly, with no resentment or regret? While some spend their lives chasing success and personal fulfillment, Mahima simply answered the call of duty, driven by love and an unshakable sense of responsibility.

Mahima comes from a Brahmin noble family, is of the highest caste or varna in the Hindu religion. Most of her relatives, living in both India and the United States, are doctors or lawyers. Her husband is an architect working for a construction company in Santa Monica. She has a son who is a computer engineer and a daughter with a doctorate in psychology. Despite her prestigious background, she has never once flaunted it. Her humility and simplicity are so admirable that they bring tears to my eyes.

The day before Mahima left for India, she called me. She asked if I wanted to have some chapati. I ran over to her place without hesitation. Her hands are small, yet with those small hands, she cooks so quickly and skillfully, as if roasting beans over a flash of lightning. I enjoy watching her cook even more than eating the food itself. Above all, her technique for making chapati is almost magical. She swiftly prepares the paratha dough, pinching off small portions and rolling them out into flat, round shapes about the size of a pancake. She then cooks them over a gas flame, flipping them like roasted seaweed, and they puff up like round balls—a clear sign there were no holes left in the dough.

I marveled at how effortlessly she moved, as if every motion had been rehearsed a thousand times over. But behind those practiced hands was a heart full of love—a love that stretched across continents, calling her back home, pulling her away from the life she had built here. As I bit into the warm, fragrant chapati, I realized that this might be the last meal she cooked for me in a long time. I wanted to memorize every detail—her delicate hands working the dough, the soft hum of the gas stove, the rich aroma of spices filling the air. With each bite, I silently wished for her safe journey, for her parents' health, and for the day we would sit together again, sharing another meal, just like this.

There is something inexplicably special about Mahima's cooking—something beyond just ingredients and technique. As she places the cooked chapati onto a plate and seamlessly moves on to rolling and cooking the next, the stack grows taller and taller in no time. Her hands move with effortless grace, each motion filled with an instinctive rhythm that years of practice have honed.

Her okra dishes and lentil soup are unmatched in flavor; no one can replicate them. No matter how much I try to mimic her methods, my okra always turns out watery, mushy, and limp. My lentil soup carries the raw, uninviting scent of uncooked beans. Even when I use the same Indian vegetables she carefully cultivates in her backyard, the taste never comes close to hers.

Perhaps the missing ingredient is something intangible; the warmth of her hands, the love she pours into every dish, the quiet devotion with which she prepares meals for those she cares about. It's a lesson I've learned many times before: food is more than just sustenance; it carries memory, love, and connection. And now, as I watch her cook for the last time before she leaves, I wonder when I will taste her chapati again.

Mahima showed me her freezer, which was neatly packed with small plastic containers of food. "These are for my husband and daughter while I'm in India," she explained. Though she planned to stay for four months and knew this amount of food would be far from enough, she said she had done her best. "Every day, I prepared a little extra and froze it," she shared with a quiet smile. I felt guilty toward my own family. Despite countless trips and business travels, I had never once prepared meals in advance for them. What truly humbled me, though, were her next words: "Every time I made a dish and packed it into a container, I prayed for my husband." Her words struck me. I stood there, looking at the simple, practical act of love neatly stacked in her freezer, feeling utterly small in the face of her unwavering devotion. It wasn't just about the food. Each container held her care, her prayers, and her silent sacrifices. And in that moment,

I realized how much love can be woven into the smallest, most ordinary actions.

A cousin-in-law, Eunhee, from Canada once stayed with my in-laws for a few weeks. The food she made had an exceptional warmth to it. Every time I ate her cooking, I felt comforted. It was as if her warm dishes extended to my heart, leaving me at ease. At first, I did not understand why. I simply bowed my head in admiration of her dedication.

One day, I discovered her secret. As soon as she opened the rice cooker, she would draw a large cross over the steaming rice. Then, each time she scooped rice onto a plate, she would carefully draw another cross. She explained that it was her silent prayer, wishing health and blessings for everyone who ate the rice she served.

No wonder the food she made tasted so special. It wasn't just the ingredients or her cooking skills—it was the sincerity, the love, and the silent prayers infused into every dish. Perhaps that's what makes certain meals unforgettable. It's not only about the recipe but about the hands that prepare it and the heart behind it.

Eunhee's quiet prayer over rice reminded me that even the most ordinary moments can be transformed into something sacred. The love we embed in our actions, whether seen or unseen, has the power to comfort, heal, and uplift.

Watching her, I was struck by how sacred and admirable her actions were, and my heart was instantly warmed. I realized that cooking wasn't merely an act of preparing food. That simple yet profound gesture transformed an ordinary meal into a sacred act of love. It wasn't just about feeding the body; it was about nourishing the soul.

Eunhee's devotion, embedded in the rhythm of daily life, made me reflect on the way I approached my own responsibilities. How often had I rushed through my tasks without pausing to imbue them with meaning? How many meals had I served without considering the hearts of those who would eat them? Watching her, I realized that love could be expressed not only through words but through the smallest, most habitual actions done with intention and sincerity.

Mrs. Francis is a 93-year-old Mexican grandmother with terminal liver cancer. Her abdomen was so swollen with ascites that even taking a single breath was a struggle. When the doctor approved her discharge, respecting her family's wish to care for her there without surgery, she sat upright in bed and began to dance. Her face lit up with a radiant smile as she showered the doctor's hands with countless kisses. Raising both hands high, she repeatedly declared, "May God bless this man!" She offered words of blessing to everyone who entered and left her hospital room.

There are so many good people in this world. Who said this earth is full of only deceitful and bad individuals? In countless places, there are people offering prayers, petitions, and earnest pleas, selflessly pouring out their hearts for others. Whenever I encounter such people, I am deeply humbled, realizing how sterile and self-absorbed my own life often feels in comparison.

I want to live a radiant life, one that shines with warmth, kindness, and purpose. I want to live a life of prayer, where each thought, action, and moment is infused with gratitude, love, and quiet devotion.

For a Beautiful Today

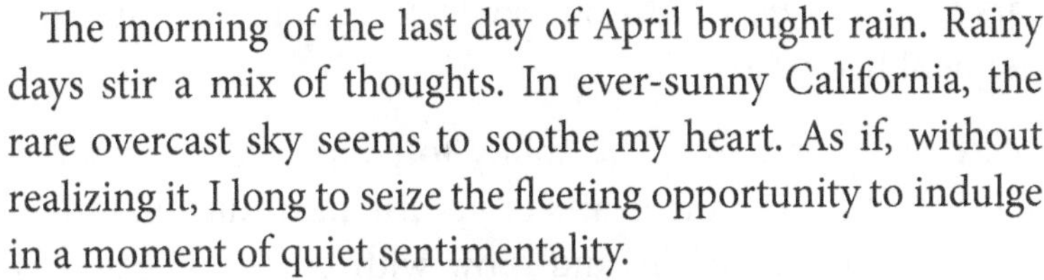

The morning of the last day of April brought rain. Rainy days stir a mix of thoughts. In ever-sunny California, the rare overcast sky seems to soothe my heart. As if, without realizing it, I long to seize the fleeting opportunity to indulge in a moment of quiet sentimentality.

As I grow older, I find undeniable truth in the saying that, with age, one naturally turns toward spiritual and aesthetic pursuits rather than material wealth. I wholeheartedly agree that the human soul has the capacity to ascend to infinite nobility through practice and refinement, or to descend into utter depravity through neglect. Perhaps it is the overcast sky this late April morning, or the gentle whisper of misty rain, but I feel a deep longing and thirst for life—as if it were something distant and just beyond my reach. Though I often despair at the sorrow woven into the fabric of existence, I cannot help but love life still.

How should I live? The life I am currently enjoying is merely a borrowed moment, a fragment of time ultimately surrendered to death. How can I find happiness within it? Perhaps the answer lies not in seeking grand, everlasting joys but in embracing the fleeting beauty of each passing moment. In cherishing the warmth of a morning sunbeam, the quiet comfort of shared laughter, the tenderness of a loving touch. If death is inevitable, then let life be radiant, even in its impermanence. Let me live with intention, with gratitude, with love that leaves a mark even as time carries it away.

I think of Miss Olga, one of my nursing professors. She was the one who eased our anxious minds, filling the exam room with the calming melodies of Mozart. She was the one who sacrificed precious class time to show us beautiful films, silently watching as we cried, her own eyes brimming with tears. Every word she spoke did not merely pass through our ears but sank deep into our souls, lingering long after the moment had passed.

She had a rare gift. The ability to plant seeds of wisdom and inspiration in the hearts of her listeners, allowing them to take root beautifully and grow with grace. Whenever I think of her, phrases like "May God's blessings be with you" and "Because of love" naturally come to mind. She was more than a teacher; she was a mentor who poured every ounce of her knowledge into her students, leaving behind a legacy of generosity, wisdom, and unwavering kindness.

She suffered a brain injury over a decade ago. After surgery, she grappled with impaired memory, her once-sharp mind clouded by confusion. Yet, through a long and arduous journey of rehabilitation, she emerged transformed, reborn as someone new. Gone was the cunning and quick wit that once defined her; in their place, she radiated peace and joy.

She became a quiet blessing to those around her. In her presence, people felt love, comfort, and gratitude flowing effortlessly. Strangely, they found themselves drawn to her even more than before. No longer did anyone feel the need to compete with her or outshine her. In her simplicity, she had gained something far greater, an unshakable serenity that softened hearts and brought people together.

Watching her lecture with sweeping gestures as she moved between the desks often reminded me of the fluid movements of a Mazurka steps, a three-beat dance that originated in Poland. Her presence, far from petite, seemed to glide effortlessly and confidently, weaving through the small classroom space as if it were a grand stage. She commanded the room with grace and energy, each motion carrying the rhythm of an unspoken melody. As I observed her, I couldn't help but wonder, was human nature itself originally composed from musical notes? The way she moved, the cadence of her voice, the pauses between her words, it all felt orchestrated, as if she was conducting an invisible symphony of thought and emotion. When she slowed her movements and said, "This is what life is," my heart would swell, inexplicably moved by the weight and beauty of her words.

Miss Olga's words still resonate vividly with me:

"A wise person is someone who always strives to learn.

A humble person is a frog who never forgets their time as a tadpole.

A content person is someone who does not complain about the portion they have been given.

A strong person is someone who can restrain their burning desires.

A gentle person is someone who is thankful for the reality they are in."

Her wisdom was never forceful, never spoken as a lesson to be memorized, but rather as gentle truths offered with kindness. Even now, I find myself reflecting on these words, measuring my own life against them. Have I truly embraced learning? Do I remember my own humble beginnings? Am

I content with what I have, strong in the face of temptation, and grateful for my reality?

Miss Olga's voice, calm yet resolute, continues to echo within me.

"Do not hurt your parents' hearts. When you play, forget everything else in the world and play. When you work, devote yourself entirely to your task."

Her stream of proverbs seemed endless. Even abstract or ordinary words sparkled when they flowed from her lips. There was a rare magic in the way she spoke—simple truths became profound, and everyday wisdom carried a weight that lingered in our hearts.

The time spent with her was truly precious and beautiful. Each moment felt like a gift, a lesson wrapped in warmth and sincerity. She did not just teach; she inspired. Her presence alone was enough to make us feel like we had stepped into a world richer in meaning, fuller in grace. Even now, the echoes of her wisdom accompany me, like a guiding light through the complexities of life.

These days, I find myself missing her more than ever. Whenever my hectic daily life feels like it is being criticized as a product of greed, I think of her. Simply remembering her brings me comfort. Her voice, her wisdom, and the way she moved with effortless grace through the classroom; these memories settle my restless heart. She was a reminder that life is not just about ambition and endless striving but about presence, gratitude, and depth. Even now, in the whirlwind of responsibilities and expectations, her words whisper to me like a gentle breeze, urging me to slow down, to live with intention, and to embrace the beauty in each moment.

I now fully understand and resonate with her advice to become a healthy egoist. I realize that forgiving is for my own peace, loving is for my own happiness, and understanding is for my own freedom. I know now that in order to give love that is healthy and genuine, I must first love and respect myself. Self-worth is not selfishness; it is the foundation upon which love can be shared without depletion. The more I embrace myself with kindness, the more freely I can extend grace to others. True generosity of spirit does not come from self-sacrifice alone but from a place of inner wholeness. She taught me that, and now, I live by it.

Even so, I still falter, stumble, and break, bleeding in the process. Where is the flaw? I need to reassess the guiding principles of my life. How far have I strayed from the path I originally pursued? How much of my determination remains to rise above material attachments and elevate the value of my life? Where has the resolve gone? The one that once declared, “Loneliness is worth it if it means uplifting my spirit”? Have I lost myself in the noise of the world, in the ceaseless tug-of-war between expectations and desires? The ideals I once held so firmly seem to have loosened their grip. I must find my way back. Not to some rigid doctrine, but to the quiet, unwavering compass that once guided me to be the person who embraced solitude as a means of growth, not defeat.

April is passing. Spring is leaving. On this final morning of April, I find myself missing Miss Olga more than ever. Her voice, once filled with wisdom and warmth, echoes in my mind. Her gentle yet unwavering gaze, the way she carried herself with effortless grace, all comes rushing back. She was more than a teacher; she was a guide, a presence that illuminated the path ahead. Perhaps it’s the fleeting beauty of spring, the way blossoms fall before they’ve been fully admired, that reminds me of her. Like the season, she never lingered too long in one place, always moving, always giving, leaving behind lessons that settled quietly in the hearts of those who truly listened.

Chapter 5

Ice Cream Social Day

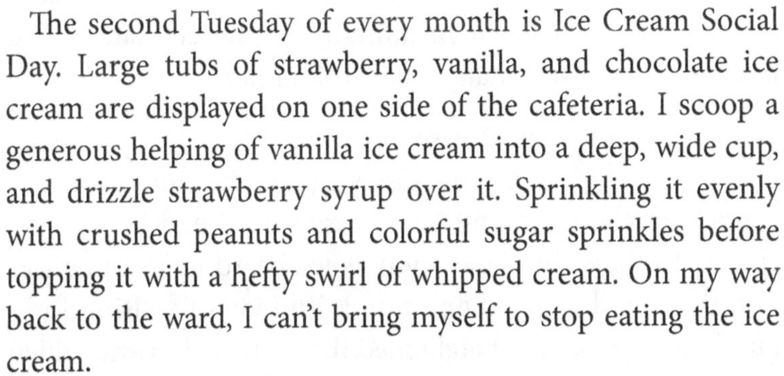

The second Tuesday of every month is Ice Cream Social Day. Large tubs of strawberry, vanilla, and chocolate ice cream are displayed on one side of the cafeteria. I scoop a generous helping of vanilla ice cream into a deep, wide cup, and drizzle strawberry syrup over it. Sprinkling it evenly with crushed peanuts and colorful sugar sprinkles before topping it with a hefty swirl of whipped cream. On my way back to the ward, I can't bring myself to stop eating the ice cream.

By the time I reach the ward, half of the ice cream is already gone. The sweetness melts on my tongue, a small indulgence in the middle of a demanding shift. I tell myself I'll eat just one more bite, but my spoon keeps diving back into the cup.

The Ice Cream Social is a brief moment of joy in the hospital. A fleeting escape from the beeping monitors, hurried footsteps, and the weight of life-and-death decisions. It's a reminder that even in a place of suffering and healing, there is still room for simple pleasures.

Hospital staff are strictly limited in where they can eat. This policy is designed to maintain professionalism and uphold a trustworthy image while minimizing exposure to potential hospital pathogens. There is even a rule prohibiting the transport of uncovered food to prevent accidents, such as someone slipping on spilled food. Yet, on Ice Cream Social Day, all these restrictions seem to fade.

On Ice Cream Social Day, the usual rigid policies seem to loosen, if only for a little while. Nurses, doctors, and staff members walk through the halls, balancing their cups of ice cream with childlike delight. Conversations that are usually hurried and clinical take on a lighter tone, punctuated by laughter and the occasional joke about who got the biggest scoop. Even the most exhausted faces brighten momentarily. In break rooms, at nursing stations, people sneak in spoonfuls between tasks. It's a rare moment of shared indulgence, a small but meaningful reminder that, amidst the chaos of the hospital, we are still human.

Since the morning, Nurse Ariel and I had been excitedly looking forward to it. At precisely 2 p.m., the announcement came over the intercom: Ice Cream Social had begun. We rushed to the cafeteria as soon as we heard it. The line was already long, but we didn't mind. The joy of waiting for a guaranteed treat only heightened the anticipation and added to our delight.

As we stood in line, the scent of freshly scooped ice cream mixed with the faint aroma of coffee from the nearby station. The sound of cheerful chatter filled the air, staff members greeting each other, joking about how many toppings they could pile on before their cups overflowed. When it was finally our turn, Nurse Ariel carefully assembled her masterpiece: a towering scoop of chocolate ice cream drizzled with caramel sauce, sprinkled with crushed cookies, and crowned with a swirl of whipped cream. I, on the other hand, stuck to my vanilla base, drenched in strawberry syrup, with a generous handful of nuts for crunch.

Balancing our treats like prized possessions, we exchanged excited glances before taking our first bites. The cold, sweet cream melted instantly on my tongue, sending a wave of pure happiness through me. At that moment, all the stress of the morning, the fatigue of long shifts, and the constant beeping of monitors seemed to dissolve.

"This," Ariel declared between bites, "is the best part of the month."

I couldn't argue with that.

We strolled along, gleefully licking our overflowing ice cream and laughing loudly. One of our supervisors, Lou, passed by and playfully cautioned us not to get too excited. With a wink, she joked that an excess of sugar might leave us so energized we'd end up handling weak and groggy post-op patients a bit too roughly. I quipped back that the sugar rush would only make me kinder, but he upped the ante with a mock warning: "Keep eating like that, and you'll gain weight. Jane, didn't you just complain about feeling heavier from the cafeteria food? You're probably putting on three pounds just today." I chuckled, brushing it off, boldly declaring that even if I gained ten pounds, I wouldn't trade this joy for anything.

Ariel burst out laughing, nearly dropping her spoon. "That's the spirit!" she cheered, raising her cup in a mock toast. Lou shook her head with a smirk. "Well, don't come crying to me when your scrubs start feeling tight." I shrugged dramatically. "Then I'll just get bigger scrubs. Happiness is worth a size up." The three of us shared a good laugh before Lou waved us off and disappeared down the hallway. Ariel and I continued our stroll, savoring every last bite of our indulgence.

Back in the ward, the usual hum of hospital life resumed, the steady beeping of monitors, the soft murmur of nurses exchanging updates, and the occasional chime of a call bell. But for those few sweet moments, standing in line for ice cream like carefree kids, we had escaped into a world of simple pleasures.

I glanced down at my now-empty cup and sighed contentedly. "Totally worth it," I whispered to myself before tossing it into the trash and heading back to work.

I grabbed Ariel's arm. "Ariel, what if the hospital caves to the complaints about health or obesity and cancels Ice Cream Social Day? I'd cry my eyes out. Mmm, this is so good." Ariel's blue eyes sparkled for a moment, then shifted to gray. She spoke seriously, "Jane, too much pleasure is sinful."

I nearly choked on my last bite of ice cream. "Sinful? Ariel, it's just ice cream!" She shook her head, her expression unreadable. "Jane, haven't you ever noticed? The things that bring the most pleasure always come with a cost."

I frowned, licking the last traces of whipped cream from my spoon. "I think you're overanalyzing this. It's just a little joy in the middle of a tough shift. Nothing wrong with that." Ariel sighed, swirling the melting ice cream in her cup absentmindedly. "I know. But sometimes, I wonder, are we indulging too much? Not just in sweets, but in distractions, entertainment, comfort? Do we ever stop to think about what we're avoiding by chasing constant pleasure?"

Her words lingered in the air between us, heavy and unexpected. I glanced around at the busy ward, where nurses bustled from room to room, tending to patients who carried burdens far greater than a simple debate about indulgence. I nudged her lightly with my elbow. "Okay, philosopher Ariel, you win. Next time, I'll reflect deeply before scooping my ice cream."

A small smile broke across her face. "I'm just saying, balance is everything." I grinned. "Fine, balance it is. But I'll still cry if they ever cancel Ice Cream Social Day." She let out a soft laugh. "Me too, Jane. Me too." We finished the last of our treats in thoughtful silence before tossing our cups away and stepping back into the rhythm of our demanding but meaningful work.

With a serious disposition no less than hers, I paused for a moment to think. "Ariel, would you scold your son or daughter for being so happy they could hardly contain themselves? Wouldn't you be delighted, too? I believe our Heavenly Father feels the same way. Is it really a sin for us, who live in constant tension, to take just one day to feel joy? Oh, forget it—I'm going to finish this ice cream and, at least for this moment, I want to be happy. I'm going to fully enjoy the sense of taste He's given me. If it feels uncomfortable, I'll just drop the adjective 'too much.' That way, 'pleasure is a blessing,' right?" She readily agreed, and our spirits lifted once more.

Ariel's serious expression softened, and a slow smile spread across her face. "You know what, Jane? You're right. Maybe we spend too much time worrying about whether we deserve happiness instead of just accepting it as a gift." I nodded, feeling lighter. "Exactly. We see so much suffering here. If we can't embrace the moments of joy that come our way, how can we ever hope to share joy with our patients?"

Ariel laughed. "Now you sound like a philosopher." I grinned, raising my empty cup like a toast. "To balance, to blessing, and to next month's Ice Cream Social." She clinked her spoon against my cup. "Amen to that." With that, we tossed our cups away and walked back to the ward, a little more at peace than before.

Ice Cream Social. Just the sight of large bowls brimming with various ice creams and an array of toppings is enough to feel full. I am grateful for the hospital's warm consideration in comforting and caring for the hearts of staff who juggle the roles of caregiver, doctor, and colleague, often caught in conflict and enduring challenges with patience. I appreciate the system that allows us, who are often confined to a somber environment, to pause briefly and catch our breath.

The cheerful chaos of Ice Cream Social provides a rare, sweet pause in our demanding routines. For a brief moment, we set aside the weight of the hospital's relentless pace, the tension of life-or-death decisions, and the emotional exhaustion of comforting others. Instead, we indulge in something simple, something joyful. I am grateful for this small tradition, a hospital's way of saying, "We see you. We appreciate you. Take a moment for yourself." It's a reminder that even in a place of suffering, there is room for delight. A simple scoop of ice cream, shared laughter, and a fleeting moment of carefree pleasure can be surprisingly healing.

Dear friend, I invite you to the Ice Cream Social. If there is tension among colleagues, share this ice cream and let it melt away. If your heart is weary, soothe it with this smooth and creamy delight. Life should not be lived like a rigid, joyless plank of wood. Savor this ice cream as it gently dissolves in your mouth. Rejoice when you are happy. Grieve when you are sad. Let the sweetness remind you that even in the hardest moments, there is still something light, something simple, something worth enjoying. Even amidst responsibilities and struggles, give yourself permission to pause, to breathe, and to taste the goodness life has to offer.

Dear friend, come to me as I eat this ice cream. I will hold you close, embrace your pain, and kiss your forehead with care. Let the cold sweetness soothe not just the tongue but the heart. Let the moment stretch beyond words, melting away sorrow, if only for a little while. In this brief respite, know that you are seen, you are heard, and you are loved.

Eyes

When I converse with people, I often focus on their eyes. It feels less like I am speaking to a person and more like I am engaging in a conversation with their gaze. When introduced to someone for the first time, I frequently find myself unable to recall their name, clothing style, or the color of their outfit once we part ways. Yet, the expression in their eyes stays with me for a long time. My habit of staring directly into someone's eyes often elicits mixed reactions. From Americans, it earns trust, as they perceive it as attentiveness and genuine engagement. However, among Koreans, it sometimes leads to misunderstandings; they may find it bold, arrogant, or even confrontational. Perhaps, eyes are the truest form of language, revealing what words often conceal.

I remember an elder I interviewed while working at a publishing company as a reporter. He was the chairman of a major Korean corporation and found it intriguing that he had never met a woman my age who was not intimidated by him. It was likely because I looked him straight in the eyes as we spoke. He realized, perhaps for the first time, that he had unconsciously grown accustomed to women lowering their gaze in his presence. At first, he found my bold eye contact deeply unsettling, but upon reflection, he admitted that it actually put him at ease. He said he could share his past so openly because, through my gaze, he felt truly understood.

When I was still unfamiliar with American culture, one of the memorable mistakes I made involved eye contact. I was scolding my eldest child, who was in elementary school, sitting him down for a stern lecture. My seven-year-old kept his head upright and stared directly into my eyes. Outraged, I demanded to know how he could dare look his mother straight in the eye so brazenly. Bursting into tears, he explained that he was showing he was carefully listening to me. He said he'd learned at school that looking away while someone speaks is disrespectful. The words I intended to use for scolding vanished somewhere, leaving me with nothing but a deep sense of guilt and embarrassment.

Somewhere along the way, I developed the habit of looking closely into a person's eyes while they speak. Perhaps it is a behavior I unconsciously adopted while living in Western culture, where maintaining eye contact is seen as a sign of attentiveness and respect when listening to someone.

Raising three teenage children, I make a conscious effort to maintain eye contact with them. Late at night, when their bodies are weary and their defenses are low, I take the opportunity to speak with them one-on-one, looking directly into their eyes. In those moments, the seemingly impenetrable walls of their secret world crumble with surprising ease. They open up about boyfriends, girlfriends, the feeling of a first hug, and their future plans, they become ready to share anything. I also use this time to bring up the things I have wanted to say throughout the day, whether it is advice, discipline, or words of encouragement. With their hearts already open, understanding comes effortlessly. Holding back certain words during the day and addressing them in the evening has proven beneficial in many ways. It allows emotions to settle, preventing hasty reactions, and provides the space to communicate calmly and thoughtfully. The saying "time heals all things" is undeniable truth.

I reflect on my childhood. I don't have many memories of meeting my parents' eyes. They always felt distant and reserved, leaving me cautious around them. I grew up in a culture where looking at my parents or elders during scolding was unthinkable. It was considered proper etiquette. Making direct eye contact with an adult was seen as a defiance, a challenge, or even rebellion.

I sometimes wonder if my prolonged struggles with independence and direction in life stemmed from never having learned to read my parents' eyes. Had I grown up looking into their eyes, perhaps I would have understood their sincerity and love more quickly and intimately. Maybe I could have reassured them, easing their worries, even just a little. After all, looking into my parents' eyes would have meant that they, too, were seeing mine.

I often witness Americans getting nose-to-nose with their opponents during sports matches, glaring fiercely at each other in intense standoffs. It's a battle of willpower, expressed through their gazes. Having grown up in a culture where even glancing at someone you dislike is considered excessive, I initially found it comical to watch them, drenched in sweat and reeking, inching in to get even closer to their opponent's face. Now, I see it differently. I understand it as an effort to close the distance and convey their truth as directly as possible. I interpret their intense gaze as if they are saying, "Look at your reflection in my eyes and recognize your own faults." Their widened eyes seem to demand that their opponent see and acknowledge the truth for themselves.

When someone's words or actions upset us, our first instinct is usually to look away. We turn our face to the side or shift our gaze elsewhere. An unspoken warning that says, "No matter how much you try to persuade me, I will not listen." It is a refusal to acknowledge the truth, a silent protest against exposing or revealing one's own. This is why looking into someone's eyes is such a powerful act. Making eye contact signals a willingness to accept the other person's truth and a readiness to reveal your own. How beautiful is the expression "our eyes met"? It expresses harmony of the heart, a deep understanding of another's truth, and a connection with their soul. It is an unspoken permission to let another see into one's own truth and spirit.

There is a hearing-impaired person in my family. When he is sad, angry, or unwilling to listen, he tightly shuts his eyes, sealing off the only window through which he can connect with others. But is this only true for those who are deaf? Even those of us with the ability to hear often close our eyes before we cover our ears. Closing our eyes is more than just a physical action, it is an act of shutting out the world, a refusal to engage with the truth that lies before us. It is a way of retreating inward, of blocking out not only sound but also the unspoken emotions and realities reflected in another's gaze. Perhaps, more than we realize, true listening begins with keeping our eyes open.

I once assisted a surgeon performing a procedure to realign the muscles of the eyes. It was astounding to see just how many muscles make up the eye and how intricate and delicate they are. Even now, I can vividly picture the surgeon's intense focus and unwavering dedication throughout the long hours of careful work.

Each tiny adjustment had to be precise, fractions of a millimeter determined whether the patient's vision would align correctly or remain skewed. The surgeon worked in absolute concentration, hands steady, eyes unblinking, adjusting and fine-tuning the delicate muscles that controlled the direction and movement of the eye. Watching the procedure, I was struck by the realization that our eyes, which we use so effortlessly every day, depend on such complex and precise mechanisms to function properly.

I couldn't help but think, if realigning the physical muscles of the eyes requires such meticulous effort, how much more effort is needed to realign the gaze of the heart? Just as a skilled surgeon carefully corrects the pathways of vision, perhaps we, too, must practice refining our perspective; to adjust our way of seeing the world, others, and even ourselves.

There are people whose eyes remain pure and innocent, regardless of age. Meeting them feels like receiving an unexpected gift, filling the day with joy and warmth. When I gaze into the eyes of those shaped by deep wisdom and inner strength, eyes that radiate peace and kindness, I feel comforted, as if I am understood without a single word. What once seemed like a curious phenomenon begins to make sense during conversation. Their words, gentle yet filled with conviction, mirror the warmth in their gaze. I find myself nodding in agreement, realizing that their eyes perfectly reflect the beauty of their dreams, their passion, and their sincerity. It is as if their eyes have absorbed every moment of love, every lesson learned through hardship, and every quiet act of kindness they have given and received. I am reminded that the eyes are not just windows to the soul but also mirrors of the heart. They reveal the depths of one's experiences, the clarity of one's conscience, and the richness of one's spirit. No matter how much time passes, the eyes never lie.

I recognize the meaning of eyes that convey rejection—eyes that silently declare, "I am of a different class than you." They hint at the mistaken notion that equality among humans is merely an illusion. Such a gaze can feel almost like a threat. It stings more than being rejected with words, leaving behind a deep sense of loneliness and humiliation. In front of such people, I find myself making more mistakes, as if stripped bare, exposed, and ashamed. A cold, dismissive gaze has the power to freeze the world around me.

It builds an invisible wall, erecting a barrier stronger than any spoken insult. No matter how confident or resilient I may feel, the sharpness of that look cuts deep, leaving an ache that lingers long after the moment has passed. And yet, just as eyes can wound, they can also heal. A single glance of warmth, understanding, or encouragement has the power to erase doubt, to mend what is broken, to remind us that we are seen—not as lesser, but as whole.

As a nurse, I encounter eyes that express a multitude of emotions, the eyes of patients. Some shine with a pure determination to heal, filled with the hope of returning to the life they knew. Others reflect a quiet surrender, an acceptance that worldly desires no longer hold sway over them. Their eyes speak volumes, telling stories of pain, courage, fear, and resilience in a way that words never could.

Whenever I feel weary of life's struggles or overcome with resentment, I think of their eyes. In them, I find a reflection of life's deepest truths, stripped of illusions. I learn the secret to clarity of vision; to see what truly matters. The eyes of my patients remind me how fleeting and fragile our existence is, how foolish it is to stake everything on things that will one day fade. I come to realize how futile many of the things we stake our lives on truly are, as if we could live forever in these fragile bodies. And yet, within that fragility lies something profound, a beauty in the way we hold on, in the love we share, in the small yet significant ways we comfort and care for one another. Looking into their eyes, I understand that to truly see is not merely to look, but to recognize, to accept, and to cherish the moment we are given.

I have also seen eyes filled with rage and despair, the eyes of those who unleash their inner turmoil onto others, wounding both themselves and those around them. These are the eyes that burn with resentment, that seek someone to bear the weight of their suffering. They glare at the world with silent accusations, believing that someone healthier, luckier, or better off should suffer in their place. In the presence of such a gaze, I instinctively hold back my words and restrain my actions. Any provocation is strictly to be avoided. I tread carefully, not out of fear, but out of a quiet understanding that their pain runs deeper than words can reach. Their fury is not truly directed at me, it is a desperate cry, an unspoken plea for relief from a burden too heavy to bear alone.

I have learned that the only response to such eyes is patience. Not every battle needs to be fought, and not every wound can be healed with words. Sometimes, simply standing firm without retaliation, without feeding the fire, is the only way to offer solace. Over time, even the most tormented eyes may soften; not because they have been defeated, but because they have been understood.

I enjoy observing the many expressions in people's eyes on the ward—it feels like uncovering the secrets of life. There is a thrill in it, an unspoken intimacy that transcends words. Is there any expression more honest than that of the eyes? No matter how much one tries to conceal their inner world through composure or willpower, the eyes never lie. They betray fear, sorrow, relief, or even the flickering hope that lingers in the depths of a weary soul. I believe that by looking into someone's eyes, I can sense their inner order, catching even the slightest tremors of emotion; the silent struggles, the unshed tears, the quiet determination. In that sense, I suppose I carry a certain bias, I tend to judge people based on the messages their eyes convey. A gaze that holds warmth and sincerity draws me in, while a cold, indifferent stare makes me instinctively step back.

Perhaps this is an unfair way to perceive others. After all, not everyone is comfortable revealing their emotions through their eyes. Some guard their gaze as a shield, while others, worn down by life's burdens, have simply forgotten how to let their true selves shine through. But even in the most guarded eyes, I find clues. Small, fleeting glimpses of who they truly are beneath the masks they wear.

While I love the innocence in a child's eyes, I am even more drawn to eyes that have deepened and become clearer through years of hardship and steadfast love. Eyes that have witnessed sorrow yet still choose to see beauty. Eyes filled with understanding and tolerance, shaped not by fleeting joys but by endurance, forgiveness, and quiet strength. Such eyes do not burn with intensity or demand attention; rather, they hold a quiet radiance, like the last light of dusk settling over the horizon. They do not judge hastily but instead reflect patience, as if they have seen enough of the world to know that nothing is ever as simple as it seems.

When I meet such a gaze, I feel a sense of peace. It is as if those eyes are telling me, "I understand. I have been where you are, and I see you as you are." There is no need for pretense, no need to hide behind walls. In those eyes, I glimpse the kind of wisdom I hope to carry one day, the kind that comes not from knowledge alone, but from a heart that has been tested, broken, and made whole again. They are not weak or ignorant, relying on others for support, but rather eyes that lift up and strengthen those who are fragile. They belong to those who have suffered, yet refuse to be defined by their suffering, who, instead of being weighed down by pain, have transformed it into quiet resilience. These are the eyes of those who understand that true love is neither mere theory nor fleeting emotion, but a continuous act of giving, a choice made again and again. They do not love with words alone, but with presence, with sacrifice, with a heart that has learned to endure.

To be in the company of such souls is a rare privilege, a blessing that humbles and inspires. Oh, may their peace extend to me. May I, too, be touched by their love. And may my own eyes, someday, reflect the same depth of understanding, the same unwavering kindness, so that I might offer others the quiet strength that has been so graciously given to me.

What kind of gaze do I carry? What impression do I leave on others? Have my eyes reflected kindness and understanding, or have they been clouded by impatience, indifference, or weariness? I cannot help but wonder how many silent cries for comfort I have overlooked, how many opportunities for connection I have let slip away.

Looking back, I feel a deep sense of regret for the years that have passed. Days spent aimlessly, without the awareness or wisdom to cultivate the truths reflected in my eyes, the unspoken expressions of life, love, and longing mirrored within them. What stories have my eyes told without my realizing? Have they whispered warmth and sincerity, or have they unknowingly conveyed distance and restraint? I long to possess eyes that can convey heartfelt love to even just one person, even for a single moment. But no, more than that, I wish to live a life filled with such moments. I want to be someone whose eyes radiate light, whose gaze soothes the wounded, whose silent presence brings comfort. I want to multiply those moments, to nurture them, to share them freely.

If love can be felt in a single glance, then may my eyes never be void of it. If understanding can be granted in the meeting of two gazes, then may I look upon others with all the tenderness and depth I wish to receive in return.

Chapter 5

An Afternoon in the Operating Room

Today is a heavy day. Among the various surgical cases, there are three leg amputations. By some coincidence, all three patients require above-the-knee amputations on their right leg. They are long-term diabetes sufferers who, over the past several years, have repeatedly entered the operating room; each time losing a part of themselves; blackened toes, decaying ankles, and necrotic flesh along their shins, cut away piece by piece.

For them, this is not just another surgery, it is the culmination of years of silent suffering. The final, irreversible severance of what remains. Each time they have left the OR before, they carried with them the fragile hope that it was the last time. That perhaps, with careful management, they could prevent further loss. But today, the unspoken understanding settles over them. This time, there is no turning back.

I think of the weight that must press on their hearts. The sorrow of witnessing one's own body diminish, the fear of what life will look like from now on, the struggle of accepting a new reality. Have they made peace with this moment? Or do they still cling to the disbelief, the desperate wish that it wasn't happening?

In the recovery room, I know I will see their faces. I will be the first to witness their initial reactions; the shock, the numbness, the silent tears. I will hold their hand, offer words of comfort, adjust their blankets with extra care. But what words can truly console a person who has just lost a part of themselves? One of them has already lost the left leg. Today, he will wake up to the reality of life without either. The sterile air in the operating room, despite the constant ventilation, will still be laced with the distinct, heavy scent of cauterized flesh and bone. The sharp whir of the electric saw and the rhythmic suctioning of blood will form an unrelenting backdrop to the day's work.

These are the sounds and smells that no longer startle me, yet they never truly fade into the background. They settle somewhere deep in my consciousness, emerging at unexpected moments. Like when I peel an apple, the scent of the blade against fruit momentarily taking me back to an OR filled with the acrid smoke of burning flesh.

There will be no outward display of mourning in the operating room today. The surgeons will work methodically, their hands steady and their minds focused. The scrub tech will anticipate each instrument before it is asked for. The circulating nurse will monitor the patient, making sure every detail of the procedure flows seamlessly. And yet, beneath the surface of this clinical efficiency, there is an unspoken weight in the room. Does the patient know that his lost limb will be sent off for disposal like medical waste? That something that has carried him for decades will no longer be part of him, reduced to just another object to be discarded?

I brace myself for the moment in the recovery room. The moment when his consciousness fights through the layers of anesthesia, and reality crashes down. The moment when his hands instinctively reach for a leg that is no longer there. And then, the stillness—perhaps a tear, perhaps a quiet nod of acceptance, or perhaps just the emptiness of someone too exhausted to react. How do I comfort a man who has lost his last piece of independence? What words could possibly make it better?

The first patient, who had just been taken into the operating room, is now being wheeled back out. All because of a tiny pill, a blood thinner taken the night before, a single misstep in preoperative preparation. It should have been stopped at least five days before surgery. For a patient facing a major operation, it is a dangerous drug, increasing the risk of excessive bleeding and making it nearly impossible to control hemorrhaging during the procedure. It was caught at the very last moment, just as the team was about to make the first incision. A final pre-surgical review saved both the patient and the surgical team from a potentially catastrophic situation.

The anesthesiologist, in a calm but firm tone, made the call to abort the procedure immediately. The circulating nurse swiftly notified the OR coordinator, and within moments, the patient was on their way back to the ward, surgery postponed, and the operating schedule rearranged.

For the patient, the delay is both a blessing and a disappointment. The emotional toll of preparing for an amputation, psychologically bracing oneself for the permanent loss of a limb is tremendous. Now, they must endure this weight for another week or more, knowing they will have to go through the entire process of pre-surgical clearance once again.

For the surgical team, the mix of relief and frustration is palpable. Time has been lost, the case schedule has been disrupted, and yet, the alternative, proceeding with the operation under dangerous conditions, could have led to tragic consequences.

One oversight, one forgotten pill, and everything comes to a halt. It is a sobering reminder of how fragile the balance is in surgery—how a simple detail can mean the difference between life and death.

Things have become complicated. The ward nurse, the operating room nurse, the surgeon, and the anesthesiologist are all involved, and the matter has escalated into an emergency. The surgical instruments had already been opened and arranged, the sterile field meticulously prepared; a costly mistake in both resources and time. At this point, there's no room for shifting blame, making excuses, or pointing fingers. Every second spent on accusations is a second wasted in problem-solving. The focus now is on damage control: rescheduling the surgery, ensuring the patient's safety, and recalibrating the surgical team's workflow for the day.

The OR coordinator scrambles to adjust the case schedule, calling in another patient who had been prepped for surgery later in the afternoon. The circulator works quickly to document the aborted procedure, while sterile processing is notified to reprocess and re-sterilize the instruments.

The anesthesiologist is already at the patient's bedside, explaining the reason for the delay, addressing concerns, and reinforcing the importance of following preoperative instructions. Meanwhile, the ward nurse, caught between following physician orders and the reality of patient compliance, feels the weight of the oversight.

It is a stark reminder of how interwoven every role is in patient care. A single missed detail can send ripples across multiple departments, turning a carefully orchestrated surgical plan into a chaotic reshuffling of resources and responsibilities. Mistakes in medicine are rarely individual failures; they are systemic, a shared responsibility in a delicate web of communication.

The OR, once bustling with preparation for the amputation, now stands in a momentary lull; surgical drapes untouched, the empty table a silent witness to what almost happened. But soon, the next case will be brought in, and the rhythm of surgery will continue, as it always does.

Canceling a surgery at the last moment is never an easy decision, but I am grateful to Dr. Perez, the anesthesiologist, for making the call with conviction. "The patient's safety comes first," he says, giving a subtle wink. "Stopping now is the smartest choice—it is the only choice that truly benefits everyone." His firm declaration—that a patient's life cannot be weighed against the financial loss of a canceled surgery—commands my deepest respect. In a field where efficiency and cost-effectiveness often battle against ethical decisions, his words serve as a reminder of our core duty as medical professionals.

I watch as he calmly explains the situation to the surgical team, his voice steady and reassuring. There is no frustration, no sense of blame, only a clear commitment to doing what is right. The OR team begins to dismantle the sterile field, and the patient is carefully wheeled back to the pre-op area. The disappointment on the patient's face is evident, yet it is met with Dr. Perez's unwavering reassurance: "This delay is not a setback, it's a precaution for your safety. We'll get you back in here when the time is right."

His words are not just for the patient; they are for all of us in the room. A reminder that in medicine, the hardest decisions are often the ones that uphold our highest duty: to protect, to heal, and, above all, to do no harm.

A woman in her fifties, who had just woken up from an endoscopic gallbladder surgery immediately asked for her necklace. She explained that it was the only keepsake from her mother, who had passed away 20 years ago, and she had never once taken it off. The necklace, a fine gold chain as thin as thread, was brought to her in a Ziploc bag. When I took it out, the links tangled tightly into a knot. With unfocused eyes and trembling hands, still groggy from the anesthesia, the patient desperately tried to untangle the knots. Seeing her struggle, I gently took the necklace from her shaking hands. "Let me help you," I said softly. Her teary eyes met mine, filled with gratitude and urgency.

I carefully examined the delicate gold chain, its fine links wound into an intricate tangle. Years of never removing it had caused the knots to tighten, and now, in her post-operative haze, her desperate attempts only made them worse. I reached for a pair of sterile tweezers and, with steady hands, began to work through the knots. The room was quiet except for the rhythmic beeping of the monitors. The patient watched me closely, her breathing still labored from the anesthesia. With each small movement, I could feel the weight of her emotions. Her attachment, the memories, the unspoken longing for her mother, all woven into this fragile piece of jewelry.

Dr. Johnson, who had been listening to our conversation, approached quietly. He perched on the edge of the patient's bed and laid the necklace out carefully on the mattress. With his head bent low in concentration, he began working on the knots. The sight of him in that moment was strikingly beautiful. He was utterly focused, as if performing a delicate surgery; his focus was unwavering. I watched his hands. Hands that had meticulously sutured wounds, steadied trembling hearts, and guided life back from the brink. Hands of extraordinary precision. Hands that spoke of quiet determination. Hands that seemed destined to heal and restore. A gift of nature.

Finally, he stood up and exclaimed, "Done! Here you go." The fully untangled necklace shimmered as it dangled from his hand. The patient's eyes welled with tears as she took it from him, her fingers trembling with emotion. She thanked him repeatedly, her gratitude overflowing not just for the successful surgery, but for this simple, heartfelt act of kindness. In that moment, I realized something profound: healing in a hospital isn't always about medicine, procedures, or clinical expertise. Sometimes, it's about restoring the small, deeply personal things that tether a patient to their identity, their past, and their love.

The ICU (Intensive Care Unit) called. A young female patient who had undergone a hysterectomy yesterday due to prolonged bleeding had taken a turn for the worse overnight. She had been transferred from the general ward to intensive care, and there were questions regarding her surgical records. A heavy feeling settled over the Unit.

Just yesterday, she had been so full of anticipation, eagerly planning a pilgrimage to Turkey once she recovered. Now, everything had changed. The bright hope in her voice, the excitement in her eyes as she spoke of her travels. All of it felt like a distant memory, replaced by the cold, clinical reality of beeping monitors and urgent consultations.

After completing our rounds, we gathered in the break room, huddled together, easing into conversation starting with the weather. As we spoke and laughed, a quiet realization settled among us. We were fortunate to have this moment, to be able to talk and smile after such a long and exhausting day.

In that small space, amid the scent of coffee and the lingering echoes of the OR, we warmed our hearts with a simple truth: happiness is not something that arrives on its own; it is something we must create for ourselves, even in the midst of life's chaos.

The afternoon sunlight pours through the recovery room window in a brilliant display. That is enough for today. I've lived fully. The countless steps taken, the hands that soothed, the words exchanged, all of it was enough.

The salad I didn't finish earlier in the day will remain uneaten after all. Some things, like a half-eaten meal, can be left behind without regret. But today? Today was lived completely.

Chapter 5

The Principles of Relationships

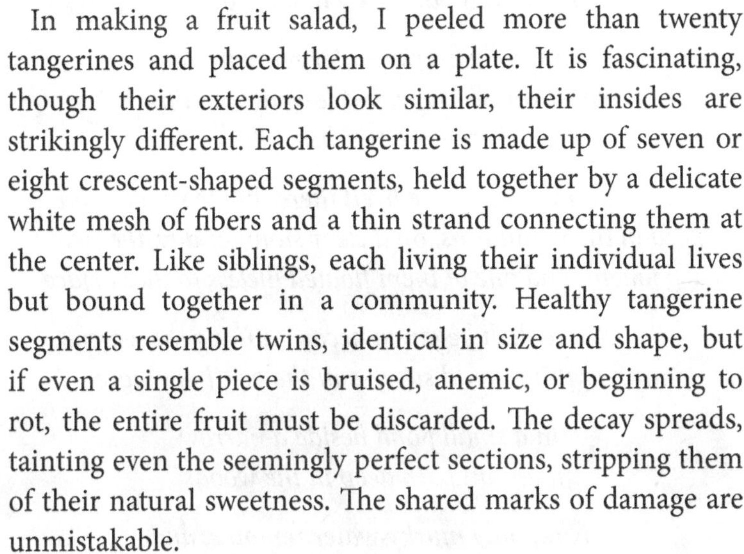

In making a fruit salad, I peeled more than twenty tangerines and placed them on a plate. It is fascinating, though their exteriors look similar, their insides are strikingly different. Each tangerine is made up of seven or eight crescent-shaped segments, held together by a delicate white mesh of fibers and a thin strand connecting them at the center. Like siblings, each living their individual lives but bound together in a community. Healthy tangerine segments resemble twins, identical in size and shape, but if even a single piece is bruised, anemic, or beginning to rot, the entire fruit must be discarded. The decay spreads, tainting even the seemingly perfect sections, stripping them of their natural sweetness. The shared marks of damage are unmistakable.

Isn't it remarkable how a single bruised segment can affect the entire fruit? In many ways, relationships function the same way. A family, a team, a friendship. Each is a delicate balance of individuals bound together by invisible threads. If one person suffers, the weight of their pain inevitably seeps into the whole. Just like the tangerine, no relationship exists in isolation. The well-being of one influences the harmony of all.

Just like a tangerine cannot preserve its freshness if even one segment begins to decay, a person who isolates themselves in the name of self-preservation ultimately withers. Hatred, jealousy, exclusion, and division eat away at the spirit, much like rot spreading through the fruit. True protection doesn't come from standing alone. It comes from fostering harmony, healing wounds, and nurturing the connections that sustain us.

The lyrics of the song "A Small Pond" came to mind.

In a small pond beside a narrow
mountain path deep in the woods

Now, only murky water remains, and
nothing lives there, but long ago, in this
pond, there were two beautiful carp

It is said that they once lived there. In the small pond
deep in the mountains, on a clear summer day, the two
carp fought, and one of them floated lifeless to the surface

Its delicate flesh began to decay, tainting the water,
until nothing could survive in the pond anymore

In a small pond beside a narrow
mountain path deep in the woods

Now, only murky water remains, and
nothing lives there anymore

The tragedy of the small pond is not just the loss of its beauty but the consequence of a single moment of conflict. The two carp, once thriving together, allowed a moment of discord to destroy not only themselves but the entire ecosystem that sustained them. The water, once clear and full of life, became stagnant, unable to support anything anymore.

How often do we see this in relationships? A single act of hatred, a single unforgiving moment, can poison what was once pure and thriving. Just as the pond could not cleanse

itself after the loss of one carp, relationships, too, can crumble when conflict festers without resolution. In the end, the pond, once vibrant, is now lifeless. Serving as a quiet reminder that destruction often begins from within.

We, who share the same time and space, are inevitably intertwined, bound by an invisible yet unbreakable thread. Is there anything, whether material or spiritual, that sustains me, which I have attained entirely on my own? The answer is clear: nothing exists in isolation. Every breath we take, every thought we form, every bit of nourishment we consume is in some way a product of others.

Coexistence is not a matter of preference; it is a necessity, an undeniable truth woven into the fabric of life itself. To reject it is to deny reality. Whether we acknowledge it or not, our lives are deeply interconnected, and only by embracing this truth can we begin to cultivate harmony and understanding.

My 17-year-old son was hit by a drunk driver, who struck his bumper. He was on his way to a restaurant to meet his friends for dinner. When my son suggested exchanging information, the large-built driver instead threatened him with a raised voice. As soon as his friends got the call, they all rushed to the scene. While my son was struggling to handle the situation, seven strong, multinational friends surrounded the driver, and only then did his aggression subside. The driver was handed over to the police, who arrived shortly after. The group then went to the restaurant together and celebrated their friendship. My son was deeply moved. Each friend was just a teenager, awkward and fragile in their own way, but together they were like an impenetrable fortress. He said his friends felt like true brothers.

Thinking about the encouragement and comfort my son received from his friends warmed my heart. It must have been a precious experience for him, realizing the value of neighbors who care for him, even if they are not bound by blood. As I listened to his story, a line from Yoo Anjin's poem Jiranjigyo, 'Dreaming of the Sweet and Noble Friendship' came to mind: "If a person shares love only with their wife, husband, their siblings, or children, how could they ever find true happiness?"

The poem beautifully captures the essence of human connection beyond familial ties. True happiness often comes from the bonds we form with those outside our immediate family—friends, mentors, colleagues, and even strangers who show us kindness in unexpected moments.

It must have been incredibly reassuring for my son to realize that love and support can come from friends just as strongly as from family. These friendships, built on shared experiences, loyalty, and mutual care, create a kind of chosen family. A network of people who stand by each other through life's uncertainties.

We are not meant to navigate life alone. The warmth of friendship, the kindness of neighbors, and the presence of people who genuinely care make life richer and more meaningful.

When a patient's life is in danger, a Code Blue is activated. In that moment, the assigned medical staff drop everything and rush to the patient, engaging in a desperate battle between life and death. I watch as they form a tight circle around the patient—a barrier meant to physically hold onto life.

Seeing them rejoice after saving a life fills me with profound emotion. Even in failure, no one grieves alone; solace is found in shared comfort. Rarely is the joy of living together felt as deeply as in these moments, when a quiet assurance emerges: if I were ever in danger, the hands of strangers would reach out to protect me, just as I witnessed today.

Yes. I am my neighbor, and my neighbor is me. At this very moment, someone shivers in the cold, searching for food in my place. Someone faces the threat of an armed robber instead of me. Someone works over 16 hours a day in my stead, while another weeps because they have no job.

The burdens I am spared today are carried by another. The suffering I have avoided has found someone else. This world is not made up of isolated lives—we are woven together in an intricate web, each of us bearing the weight of another's hardship, whether we realize it or not. How, then, can I claim that their struggles have nothing to do with me?

How valuable have I truly been to my neighbor? I have failed to extend a warm hand to those who are lonely. I have not shared enough of my time or heart. With a deep sigh, I reflect on myself, hoping to do better. Hoping to become someone who notices the quiet struggles of others. Hoping to be a presence that offers comfort, even in silence.

Life is fleeting, and no one can predict when they will need the kindness of a stranger. Perhaps the simplest acts of warmth, a smile, a listening ear, a moment of shared humanity, are the most impactful. I want to live with open hands, ready to give and receive, because in the end, we are not meant to walk this journey alone.

A moment of silence for my neighbor, for someone out there. Extending that silence to include myself as well, because we must live together, because our happiness must be shared. We are like tangerine segments, invisibly but firmly bound to one another, back-to-back, heart to heart.

Jane Ha

In Search of My Identity

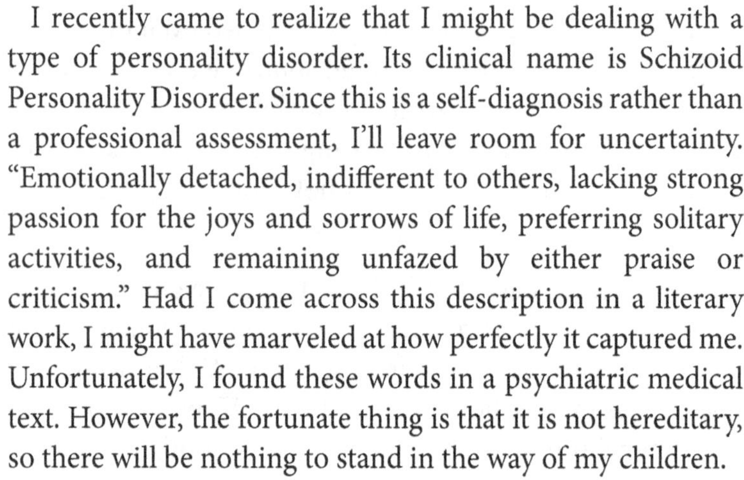

I recently came to realize that I might be dealing with a type of personality disorder. Its clinical name is Schizoid Personality Disorder. Since this is a self-diagnosis rather than a professional assessment, I'll leave room for uncertainty. "Emotionally detached, indifferent to others, lacking strong passion for the joys and sorrows of life, preferring solitary activities, and remaining unfazed by either praise or criticism." Had I come across this description in a literary work, I might have marveled at how perfectly it captured me. Unfortunately, I found these words in a psychiatric medical text. However, the fortunate thing is that it is not hereditary, so there will be nothing to stand in the way of my children.

To be indifferent to life is considered a personality disorder. I can accept the idea of emotional deficiency, but to go beyond that is unsettling. It is disheartening to realize that what I once believed to be my own unique emotional disposition has instead contributed to the definition of a clinical condition. What baffles me even more is the claim that such individuals are often described as "imaginative and creative." I may not have much energy for life, but one way or another, whether by choice or circumstance, I am managing to get by. And as someone who is a writer, possessing a rich sense of abstraction should not be something to be ridiculed, should it?

This disorder lacks the qualifying symptoms of schizophrenia; the emotional ups and downs are not severe, and a sense of reality is maintained. Phew, thank goodness. Didn't I almost end up wandering alone without any family? The prognosis for people like this is described as "mediocre," neither good nor bad. Such individuals are said to be unsuited for business but well-suited for solitary tasks, like working night shifts at a post office, sorting mail alone. An unnervingly precise diagnosis.

The suggested treatment for people with this disposition is, essentially, to leave them alone. Let them do what they wish on their own terms. Whether they eat porridge or rice, do not interfere. Since they naturally seek the shadows, allow them to live as they are. I must say, I find this approach quite appealing. More active methods involve developing emotional expression through psychodrama or recreational activities, as well as enhancing interpersonal relationships through group therapy.

There is no person or object I am so deeply attached to, whether out of love or hate, that I feel I couldn't live without them. I do not have a strong desire to distance myself from others, nor do I refrain from doing what I want for fear of others' opinions.

What fascinates me is that I have already overcome or am in the process of undergoing the very treatment outlined by experts. In a way, I have been practicing self-directed cognitive therapy through reading, writing, traveling, and meditation. Without ever consulting a psychiatrist, I have instinctively chosen the means to sustain myself. Isn't it remarkable to have unknowingly navigated my own path to healing? Humans are, after all, innately wired to survive.

One day, I made up my mind to be happy. If life must be endured, I decided, I might as well make it enjoyable. Now,

I channel my energy into seeking out joy and embracing moments of fun. As I spend more time with others, I even hear the unexpected remark that my expression looks brighter.

I prefer blending into a crowd rather than standing out—this way, I can keep my solitude hidden. Immersing myself in psychological films and books has likely made the contours of my mind more flexible over time.

I once believed that my neurosis stemmed from a childhood shaped by blindness and deprivation. But that is not the case; this is simply my nature. And that is a relief. Knowing that I am not some enigmatic anomaly, but rather someone who fits within a classified framework of psychopathology, is strangely comforting. If the cause is understood, the outcome can be anticipated. If a condition can be diagnosed, then a treatment must also exist.

One day, I asked my family and close friends if they had ever noticed any signs of psychopathology in me. Taken aback, they unanimously replied, "No, you are more normal than normal."

Uncovering the true nature of my mind is fascinating. Life is an endless journey of discovery and wonder.

Mother and Daughter

I drove toward the ocean. It was a Saturday afternoon. With my left hand on the steering wheel, I held my mother's hand tightly with my right. It had been nearly two weeks since she arrived from Korea. Yet, we still had not found a quiet moment to sit down and talk. She spent her days at home, reading, doing laundry, or cooking. Some days, she didn't even step outside the front door.

I was too busy. With a five-day workweek, countless on-call, standbys, and callbacks, I couldn't manage a single leisurely outing with my mom. Even after work, I was either glued to my computer writing or driving over an hour to literary gatherings in downtown LA, often returning late at night. There were many moments when I didn't even have the energy to exchange a word with her.

It was a scorching day in July, with the intense sun blazing down. The numerous beaches along Pacific Highway were packed with people. Searching for a quieter spot, I ended up driving all the way to Malibu Beach. Parking the car near a restaurant adjacent to a private beach, I suddenly found myself in an awkward situation.

Since we hadn't planned for a beach trip, we were completely unprepared. I grabbed a large towel from the car seat and spread it over the sand. Holding up a wide-brimmed golf umbrella for shade, it suddenly felt as though the entire world had shrunk to just my mother and me. In front of us, waves rolled gently onto the shore, while to our side, a weathered ridge, sculpted by the tides, stretched out in quiet serenity.

My mother, as if she had decided to open the door to her heart, began to speak. Stories spanning over twenty years surfaced from the depths of her memory, shaking off the dust and announcing their presence: "Here I am." It was like watching a sweeping panorama unfold before me. In every scene, my mother was the protagonist. Her tears, her suffering, and her endurance were woven into each moment.

In the past, I often found my mother's perspective on the world frustrating. I would cut her off with sharp rebuttals, questioning how she could think that way and effectively silencing her. No matter how many times I resolved to simply listen without interrupting, my impatience always won. But this time, something was different. I found myself accepting her thoughts and the angle of her perspective just as they were. I listened, not to refute, but to understand. It made me wonder, was I finally maturing?

My mother said, "I had planned to take this story with me to the grave, but here I am sharing it with you now," and she kept talking without pause. "Mom, let it all out. Tell me everything in your heart. I am here for you," I said. At that, she nodded gently, like a meek child. By the time we headed up to the restaurant, it was dark, and the night air had turned chilly. Walking arm in arm with her, I felt the warmth of her presence, the undeniable reality that I still had a mother by my side. My eyes grew warm with emotion.

Even as I looked at my mother, it didn't feel real. Hers was the face I had always longed to see, the voice and presence I had missed so deeply. Yet, even with her right in front of me, I already missed her. Even as I held her hand, it didn't fully register. I knew that once she returned to Korea, I would be left feeling dazed and empty. The moment felt fleeting, like a dream I would wake from too soon.

This evening, my mother retreated to her room early, saying she didn't want to disrupt her daughter, who was racing to meet a writing deadline. She had likely spent the entire day alone in a stuffy house with no air conditioner turned on in hot weather, and now, even as night fell, she remained by herself. Yet, before she had even left my sight, I already missed the comforting warmth of her touch.

I took my hands off the keyboard and knocked on my mother's door. For this moment, while she is by my side, I want to cherish her fully as mine. I wish there would always be someone to answer, "Yes, my dear," whenever I call out, "Mom."

Jane Ha

I Will Love in the Name of Love

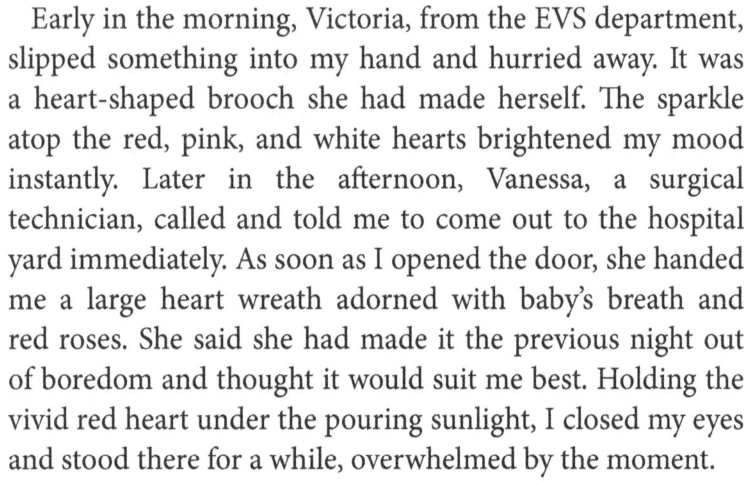

Early in the morning, Victoria, from the EVS department, slipped something into my hand and hurried away. It was a heart-shaped brooch she had made herself. The sparkle atop the red, pink, and white hearts brightened my mood instantly. Later in the afternoon, Vanessa, a surgical technician, called and told me to come out to the hospital yard immediately. As soon as I opened the door, she handed me a large heart wreath adorned with baby's breath and red roses. She said she had made it the previous night out of boredom and thought it would suit me best. Holding the vivid red heart under the pouring sunlight, I closed my eyes and stood there for a while, overwhelmed by the moment.

Today is Valentine's Day. Has the season of love arrived already? The roses in the garden haven't even bloomed yet, and winter's breath still lingers in the air. Perhaps love isn't about reaching full bloom, it might be the essence of something still ripening, the beauty found in its unripe, unfolding state.

I meditate on a love that transcends human limitations, escaping the weariness of fleeting affection. Ah, Genghis Khan's falcon comes to mind. A story I often recall for comfort whenever I feel wronged by my one-sided love. When I struggle to understand the intentions or heart of someone I love, I remind myself not to fixate solely on what is visible. There is always a deeper meaning beyond

my limited perception. This tale serves as a lesson, not to act recklessly in the face of emotion, but to trust that some truths lie beyond the reach of short-sighted judgment.

It was a scorching summer day. Genghis Khan, weary and parched during a hunt, was desperate for water. Reaching a ravine, he saw drops of water trickling down from above. He quickly held out his precious silver cup and managed to collect a few sips. Just as he was about to drink, his beloved falcon swooped down and overturned the cup, spilling the precious water. This happened a second time. By the third attempt, Genghis Khan had already drawn his sword. When the falcon struck the cup, sending it tumbling down the mountainside, his fury consumed him, and he struck the falcon dead with a single blow.

Overcome with thirst and anger, Genghis Khan decided to climb higher in search of the water's source. Finally reaching the top, he saw a massive snake coiled in the center of the spring, releasing deadly venom into the water. The water he had so desperately longed to drink was flowing down from that poisoned spring that was contaminated with the venom of a viper.

In that moment, he realized the truth: his faithful falcon had been trying to save his life. Grief and regret overwhelmed him as he cradled the lifeless bird in his hands. His impatience and impulsive judgment had cost him a loyal companion.

Genghis Khan's falcon. Did it hesitate, even for a moment? Staring at the flashing blade in its master's grip, it must have been heartbroken, yet it had no choice but to knock over the cup. From its vantage point in the sky, the falcon had seen everything, fully understanding the situation. There was no other way, it had to save the master it loved. The falcon likely remembered the love and care its master had shown over the years and forgave him in advance. Even as it faced misunderstanding and death, it remained steadfast. The falcon's love was not expressed through words but through sacrifice, proving its devotion in the purest way possible.

This story lingers in my mind whenever I find myself feeling wronged, misunderstood, or hurt by those I love. It reminds me that not everything is as it seems, that love sometimes appears in the form of denial, resistance, or even pain. There are moments when, in our narrow perception, we mistake protection for betrayal, wisdom for obstruction, and care for cruelty. But love, true love, often operates beyond the limits of our understanding. Perhaps, in those moments, the greatest act of trust is to pause, step back, and look deeper.

We often hear stories of people who, when faced with accidents or life-threatening situations, receive invaluable help from strangers. A common thread in these tales is that these "angels" were, at some point in the past, recipients of similar acts of kindness from strangers. Pay it forward: a chain of love that continues to grow and extend. A kindness once received does not wither away; it transforms into another act of goodwill, passing from hand to hand, heart to heart. This silent, unbroken thread of compassion weaves through time, binding us together in unseen yet profound ways.

Those who have been saved from death understand that their life is now a gift, a second chance. That is why they do not hesitate to risk their own lives to save others. Is there anyone among the living who has not, at least once, brushed against the edge of death? There were strangers who revived our fading breath, who lifted us from agony and embraced us in our weakest moments. My being alive today, then, is the result of someone's love and sacrifice. If so, how can I let this life pass by meaninglessly? If I am breathing, it is because love has sustained me. Now, it is my turn to extend that love—to carry forward the kindness that once saved me.

It is the season of love. So, I must love. Even animals know how to repay a debt of love—how can humans dare to turn away from it? Even when it feels exhausting, I must still love. As an investment of the heart. In the name of love. Not out of duty, but as an investment of the heart. Not for reward, but in the name of love itself.

The purple magnolias in the hospital yard are in full bloom, dazzlingly gorgeous. I long to love and be met with love in return. I want to be loved and to give that love back, wholeheartedly and without hesitation.

Chapter 6

What You Can Buy With $1,000

The Equation of Love

Living and Loving

For the Sake of Life

The Weight of the Day

The Priorities of Life

My Sentimentality for Pasadena City College

Heart of the Mountain, Heart of the Water

My First Experience

A Student Nurse's Letter to a Teenage Mother

Lecture on Communication Skills for Nurses

While Putting on Make-up

My Name is Jane

Jane Ha

What You Can Buy With $1,000

Last week, our speech class kicked off with a debate on the topic, “Finding the Perfect Spouse: What You Can Buy With $1,000.” The exercise presented a list of roughly ten traits, each assigned a specific monetary value. For instance, sharing the same ethnicity was valued at $500, and having similar hobbies at $250. Good character, appropriate height and weight, a positive attitude, and shared future goals were each assigned $250. Abstaining from smoking and drugs was valued at $150, wealth at $600, physical attractiveness at $500, intelligence at $250, and being fashionable at $500.

The rule was simple: you could choose the qualities of your ideal spouse, but you had to do so within a strict $1,000 budget. If you spent $500 on physical attractiveness, there wasn't much left to invest in any other trait. Nevertheless, many students boldly opted for that option. Interestingly, the desired qualities in a spouse varied significantly depending on gender, region of origin, and age.

I allocated $500 for ethnic background and $250 each for good character and a positive mindset, leaving no funds for shared hobbies or future goals. It wasn't that I dismissed qualities like intelligence; rather, they were pushed down my priority list and ultimately sacrificed. When I reviewed the list of attributes I had chosen—irrespective of their assigned costs—it became clear that I wasn't a practical person. Watching teenagers, half my age, confidently make

pragmatic, materialistic choices, I briefly wondered whether I was driven by intellectual vanity or if I had simply wasted my life being out of touch with reality.

Mr. Mike asked whether it was truly necessary to invest so heavily in ethnic background and if I regretted doing so. Even though there were many Asian students in the class, only two of us chose to invest in that ethnicity—and I was one of them. This naturally piqued his curiosity about my reasoning.

I was at a loss for words. I wasn't driven by nationalism, nor did I harbor any particular preference or conscious awareness on the matter. Yet, remaining silent felt disrespectful, especially as the teacher patiently waited for a logical explanation. At the same time, simply replying "just because" would have bruised my pride. Had he criticized me for spending such an absurd amount without clear reasoning, I would have had no defense.

Mr. Mike was a man of wisdom, someone with an exceptionally open heart—an exceedingly rare find. His question, delivered with a piercing gaze that seemed to see straight into the depths of my soul, made me pause and reflect on whether my decision had truly been the right one. After a tumultuous 20-year career in law enforcement, he had returned to university, pursued further studies, and earned a doctorate. A question from someone with such a wealth of life experience deserved nothing less than a thoughtful answer.

He was kind to me. In keeping with his preference, I called him by his nickname, Mike, instead of the formal "Mr. So-and-So," and that simple gesture transformed the entire semester into a delight. It felt less like a conventional speech class and more like sharing genuine friendship with him. Every time I presented in class, he filled my evaluation sheets with encouraging words and praise, lifting my spirits immeasurably. He truly knew how to protect and uplift those who were vulnerable. Perhaps he sensed that without his support, I might have struggled to thrive in this foreign land.

I felt compelled to offer an explanation. "I believe anyone can be generous and pleasant in a good environment, but a person's true character is revealed during tough times. In those moments, sharing a common background or culture might make emotional connection and understanding easier. After all, isn't emotional compatibility the foundation of love?" My response was so textbook-like and uninspired that I felt frustrated with myself for saying it.

Why am I so insistent on choosing the same ethnicity? Perhaps it's because, while humans are inherently solitary, I place a certain trust in shared ethnic traits. To share those deeply buried, indescribable subconscious emotions, isn't it essential to have the bond of a common heritage?

If a relationship with a spouse of the same ethnicity becomes strained by differing perspectives, personalities, or hobbies, the resulting resentment might even be more intense than in a relationship with someone of a different background. When cultural differences exist, one might approach the relationship with an inherent understanding of those distinctions. However, sharing the same blood and language can sometimes lead to unrealistic expectations, as one may inadvertently treat the other as an extension of oneself. Even so, the ability to love—and even argue—in the same language remains a beautiful thing. These conflicting thoughts alone were enough to give me a headache.

Mike gave me a faint smile, as if to say, "You still have a lot of growing up to do." I felt disheartened. I tried to counter by saying, "Look, that trait is the most expensive on the list.

Isn't that proof of its importance? If it lacked significance, they wouldn't have set the price so high." Even as I presented my case, my heart remained far from satisfied.

Before I knew it, it was time for the presentations. Eighteen-year-old Annie, who had allocated $600 for "wealth," $250 for "good character," and $150 for "not using drugs," delivered her playful and charming speech, offering a glimpse into the mindset of the younger generation. She explained that although wealth might seem expensive, investing in it addresses multiple issues at once, making it a cost-effective choice. There was no need to separately prioritize traits like refined taste or a preference for luxury brands, since wealth inherently provides access to such things. She argued that having money not only allows one to diversify and develop hobbies but also cultivates a more relaxed and generous character. As long as her ideal partner avoided drugs and exhibited good character, she felt she could easily overlook differences in ethnicity, height, or weight.

As Annie spoke, sighs of admiration filled the room. Her charming, logical, and persuasive arguments truly shone. Amid murmurs of "That's not a bad idea," it was clear that some students wished they'd thought along similar lines. Watching my classmates become deeply engrossed in this hypothetical debate brought a quiet smile to my face. How often does reality align with our desires? Reflecting on the trial and error they'd face before realizing that evoked a different kind of sigh.

Wealth is undeniably beneficial. Living as a wealthy person undoubtedly makes life more pleasant, sparing one from the hardships of scarcity. It is wonderful to have the means to give generously and maintain a positive outlook on the world. As Annie pointed out, modern wealthy individuals often exhibit better character than those less fortunate. They are less likely to harbor a distorted or embittered view of life; instead, they tend to be straightforward and open-minded. When shown love, they trust it sincerely, embrace it wholeheartedly, and reciprocate with equal warmth.

Despite all the clear advantages, something still makes me hesitate to choose wealth. It isn't because I belong to an older generation clinging stubbornly to Puritanical self-denial, nor did I grow up believing that modest living is inherently virtuous. I harbor no prejudice or aversion toward wealth; I simply need to uncover the reason behind this reluctance.

When one evaluates the world's worth or judges character solely through the lens of money, attempting to solve life's deeper values with riches, or dismissing anything beyond material wealth, it strikes me as an incurable malady. The notion of reducing everything to material terms or, worse, trying to purchase love with money feels like an intolerable affront. There are countless precious spiritual values in this world that simply cannot be bought.

The thought of materialism trampling those values was almost unbearable. A person enslaved by wealth is likely to lead a lonely life, and the idea of sharing life's journey with such an individual seemed like a dreadful nightmare. Instead of risking the desolation that immense riches can bring, I found myself preferring a life of poverty enriched by a healthy mind and spirit.

While I was lost in thought, the class debate showed no sign of ending. Finally, Mr. Mike stepped in to mediate. He emphasized that everyone has the freedom to make their own choices and that it is crucial not to harbor prejudice against the values others choose. He noted that all the world's misfortunes stem from prejudice; a point with which I wholeheartedly agreed. Believing that only the values I hold or the choices I make are best is a selfish perspective. Respecting others' choices is fundamental to living a harmonious life. Life gains its true meaning when my values blend beautifully with those of others, creating a radiant harmony.

Now it was Mr. Mike's turn to deliver the conclusion. With a casual air, he stated, "No matter how lofty your philosophies or ideals may be, human relationships ultimately boil down to money and sex." We could hardly believe our ears. In an instant, the class fell silent; most had undoubtedly expected a metaphysical or profound conclusion.

I was deeply shocked. Realizing that a teacher I had admired held views so utterly different from my own, and that he would present such a simplistic, shallow conclusion in front of the class left me dumbfounded. Either he was remarkably worldly, or I was overly idealistic. Perhaps he was an honest realist, while I was merely a dreamer lost in idealism and wishful thinking.

How many years will it take for each of us to discover the values we hold as the greatest? The truth is, there is no universal timeline—each of us must embark on our own unique journey. For some, clarity may dawn in just a few pivotal moments, while for others, the path to understanding our core values could be a lifelong endeavor.

Jane Ha

The Equation of Love

"If there are a hundred people in this world who love you, I am one of them.

If there are ten people in this world who love you, I am one of them.

If there is only one person in this world who loves you, that person is me.

If there is no one in this world who loves you, then I no longer exist."

It is a truly heartfelt verse. The confession, "If there is only one person in this world who loves you, my dear, that person is me," sounds incredibly sweet at first. It makes one wonder; if only there were someone truly worthy of such love, or if only I could experience receiving such pure devotion, or even if I could offer such profound love just once in my life.

When you reflect on it deeply, the story becomes intensely profound. When someone you love, no matter the reason, becomes unable to reciprocate that love, or when circumstances render them seemingly unlovable by anyone else, it's incredibly challenging to continue loving them unwaveringly.

At the hospital where I'm currently doing my clinical training, I care for a patient named Aradia, who suffers from multiple complications. She depends on a feeding tube inserted through her stomach for nutrition. The nursing assistant who cares for her is Jay, a robust man in his early thirties. With his tall stature, large eyes, and strong features, he handles even the most demanding tasks with remarkable ease and efficiency.

Yesterday, while I was administering finely ground medication through the feeding tube connected to Aradia's stomach, she sneezed unexpectedly. The sudden jolt caused the medication to backflow, soiling her gown and bed linens. Since she is completely immobile, the thought of changing her linens on my own was overwhelming, leaving me no choice but to ask Jay for help. In response, his eyes widened in mock shock as he exclaimed, "Oh my God! I'm going to kill you!" while spinning around in exaggerated circles. He remarked that he had just finished replacing her linens. When I pleaded, "Please forgive me," he asked if I was really scared, if he appeared genuinely angry, and joked that if so, he might have a future in acting school. He chuckled to himself, clearly amused.

Today was the day to bathe Aradia. Feeling awkward about sharing the small bathroom with Jay while assisting in washing her, I insisted on handling it alone. Jay merely smiled and asked why I was being so formal. "Fine, but if you call for me, you're dead," he joked, adding that he would wait right outside the door and that I should call him anytime I needed help.

He already knew; I would have no choice but to call him. Bathing a 160-pound, immobile patient was no easy task. When I finally asked for his help, he stepped in with practiced ease. He washed her chest, underarms, and groin without hesitation, moving confidently and efficiently, as though it were second nature to him.

After finishing the bath and drying Aradia with a towel, she unexpectedly had a bowel movement. We waited patiently until she was done and then cleaned her again. Together, we struggled to lift her and transfer her back to the bed. Just as we were about to put on a fresh diaper, she had another accident. Looking at the newly soiled bed linens, I sighed in dismay, saying, "What do we do now?" Jay reassured me, saying it was fine. With remarkable speed, he replaced the sheets and neatly tucked the corners, his calm efficiency making the situation feel less overwhelming.

After Jay left the room, I looked at Aradia. Her freshly cleaned face remained devoid of expression. In her youth, or before illness took its toll, she must have been beautiful. Perhaps she once lived a remarkable life, cherished deeply by someone who loved her intensely. But now, in her vulnerable, exposed state, she no longer stirs desire in anyone's heart. No one questions a young man like Jay bathing her alone—her current condition has seemingly erased the essence of who she once was in the eyes of the world.

As I gazed at her, the lines from The Equation of Love suddenly surfaced in my mind. I couldn't help but wonder; were they merely poetic words, detached from the harsh realities of life? But then, shaking my head, I dismissed the thought.

To look upon a soul trapped in a broken body, suffering, and to love that soul to the very end is no easy task. Yet, it is made possible by one thing: love. Love is an equation. For the equation to balance, there must be an equal amount, or at least a corresponding measure, of substance on both sides. In other words, if I love someone, that love will inevitably be returned. Love is without deceit, after all.

To love someone until the very end, or to be loved until the end myself, requires that I know love today. Even if, one day, my body is cared for and tended by the hands of strangers, love will make me eternally beautiful. Even if it seems unrealistic, like something out of a poem, now is the time to love. Love is not just a fleeting emotion but a choice, a commitment, and an investment in the essence of our humanity. When we give love freely, without hesitation, we create a world where dignity and compassion endure, even in the most vulnerable moments.

If you have been holding back the words "I love you," then today, my dear, say them. Say, "I love you." Let love be spoken, felt, and lived—before time takes away the chance to express it.

Jane Ha

Living and Loving

Today was my day in the neonatal ward. I accompanied a new couple to the hospital entrance as they prepared to leave with their newborn. They carefully strapped their 27-hour-old baby into the car seat, fumbling nervously, uncertain of what to do next. Watching the father hover protectively, I considered the weight now resting on his shoulders. The responsibility of providing everything this tiny life would need would surely drive him to work even harder in the days to come.

Under the scorching sun, he sweated, tilting his head in confusion as he struggled to secure the baby's car seat. Watching him, I felt a pang of compassion. "Yes, that's how life goes. You fumble through it, sweating, and you feel frustrated along the way." I glanced at the woman beside him, silently watching her husband, waiting patiently. "Dear lady, I hope you continue to look at your husband with the same patience and warm gaze until the very end."

I gazed at the baby. Even the faintest breeze seemed to make it squirm, as if the sunlight were already too bright. Its tiny body was so delicate and beautiful. Little one, how many beads of sweat and tears must you and your parents shed before your innocence and fragility give way, allowing you to grow resilient against life's trials? One day, that sweet and peaceful expression might be etched with worries, concerns, and discontent; how I wish I could spare you from that.

They were finally ready to leave. As I folded the wheelchair that had carried the mother, I offered a word of advice. "Be patient. There will be many things that require patience. It is through patience that you become true parents." Then, as if I were their own parent, I added, "When raising your child becomes difficult, remember the emotions you felt the very first time you held your baby. Recall the way your hands treated them like a precious treasure."

The young couple nodded eagerly, promising they would remember my words. The faces of the new mother and father shone with joy and hope. "I hope your baby becomes a great blessing to you. May you build a happy and beautiful home together with your little one," I said. As they smiled brightly and waved, I waved back, wholeheartedly wishing them a future filled with happiness.

That's right, you don't need to know. You don't need to know that the human heart beats more than 30 million times a year. Or that countless blood cells travel through over 80,000 kilometers of blood vessels to sustain life. Or that 10 billion nerve cells, each performing its role brilliantly, allow us to fully experience this world and love it deeply.

You only need to marvel at the eyes glistening with moisture, the radiant skin, and the muscles that respond with such sensitivity and harmony. Simply admire the masterpiece of life, where everything works together in perfect cooperation. As long as there is wonder and gratitude, life will never feel too burdensome.

Today, I bid farewell to six couples. Watching them care for each other so tenderly and interact with such warmth and caution brought me joy. Surely, in their own ways, they will help make the world a more beautiful place. They will stumble, fall, and break along the way, but one day, they'll experience an epiphany and think, Ah, so this is what it was.

With eyes full of wonder, they'll occasionally admit, I didn't know this before.

As their babies grow and life's experiences accumulate, their perspectives will deepen. Even when they feel sadness from the futility of life or sorrow from the inevitable tragedies of the human condition, they will carry on, continuing the journey of living without pause.

Everyone's life eventually ends. How wonderful it would be if we all carried compassion and tolerance toward one another. If only we could maintain the same careful attitude and gentle heart throughout our lives that we show when caring for a newborn baby. If we trusted and respected each other, strove not to inflict harm, and refrained from casting harsh, judgmental looks—imagine what a beautiful world this would be.

Chapter 6

For the Sake of Life

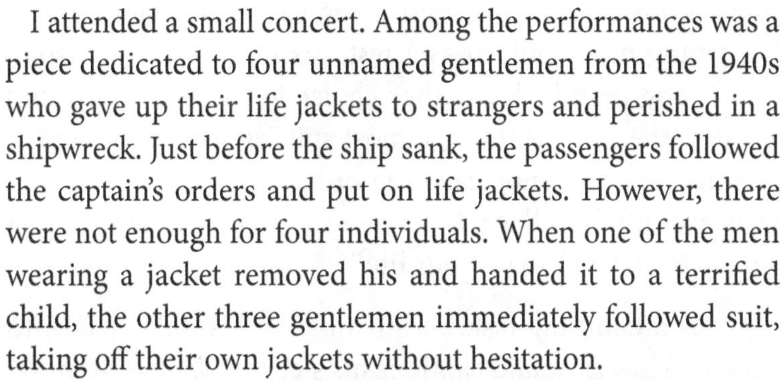

I attended a small concert. Among the performances was a piece dedicated to four unnamed gentlemen from the 1940s who gave up their life jackets to strangers and perished in a shipwreck. Just before the ship sank, the passengers followed the captain's orders and put on life jackets. However, there were not enough for four individuals. When one of the men wearing a jacket removed his and handed it to a terrified child, the other three gentlemen immediately followed suit, taking off their own jackets without hesitation.

On the deck of the sinking ship, as water rose to their necks, those wearing life jackets held the hands of the four who had given theirs away. Together, they sang a tearful song until the ship disappeared beneath the waves. Listening to the deep, resonant tuba and the solemn beat of the drums, I felt as though the spirits of these noble individuals, who selflessly gave up their chance at life to save strangers, were present in the music, stirring my heart and soul. The performance drew me into thoughts about the depth of awareness that selfless souls might possess. As I absorbed the subdued, somber melody, a story illustrating the preciousness of life surfaced in my mind.

India, where Hinduism is the predominant religion, shares a border with Pakistan, where Islam is the majority faith. In a border region, a young Pakistani man, a Muslim, happened to see a cow that had wandered over from India. Unaware of the consequences, he slaughtered it for food, only to be caught by Indians and brought before the governor. The death penalty was a given under the circumstances. However, the young man pleaded for mercy, explaining that his elderly mother was waiting for him back home, and without him, there would be no one to care for her. The governor investigated his claim and found it to be true.

The governor, moved by the thought of the young man's mother, decided to give him a chance. He declared that if the young man could pass a test, his life would be spared. The young man had no other choice but to comply. A cup filled to the brim with oil, almost spilling over, was handed to him. The governor gave the order: "Carry this cup and walk around the village. If you return without spilling even a single drop, I will spare your life."

It was a daunting task, but it was also his only chance to survive. How slow and cautious his steps must have been! By sunset, he returned to the governor after completing a full circle around the village. Not a single drop of oil had spilled from the cup.

The governor asked, "As you walked around the village, what did you think of its sights and the warmth of its people?"

The young man bowed his head deeply and replied, "I am sorry. I was so focused on not spilling the oil in the cup that I couldn't spare a thought for anything else or dare to look around."

In the end, he was allowed to return home.

Life is so precious that it demands our complete focus, leaving no room for distraction. Such unwavering concentration is never excessive when it comes to the value of life. Just as one's own life is precious, so too is the life

of others—a simple truth embodied by those who live it through their actions. Those who recognize the equal worth of all lives and are willing to sacrifice selflessly for others are the ones we call saints. In that sense, even ordinary people have a path to sainthood.

Is giving up one's life for strangers, like the four gentlemen on the shipwreck, the only act of true value? Love, understanding, tolerance, and forgiveness are the driving forces that nurture life. While it is not easy to give one's only life for others, offering your heart and extending forgiveness are not so difficult. After all, these acts ultimately benefit yourself. Monk Beopjeong, a famous Korean writer, also says that forgiveness is not so much an act of compassion toward others as it is a way to gather and restore one's own scattered self? With a compassionate heart toward all living beings, one can abundantly preserve and save life.

Today is a day to clothe yourself with an awareness of the value of life and the humility it demands. It is the bare minimum weapon we need to stand against the dark, bleak, and dehumanizing logic of the world.

Jane Ha

The Weight of the Day

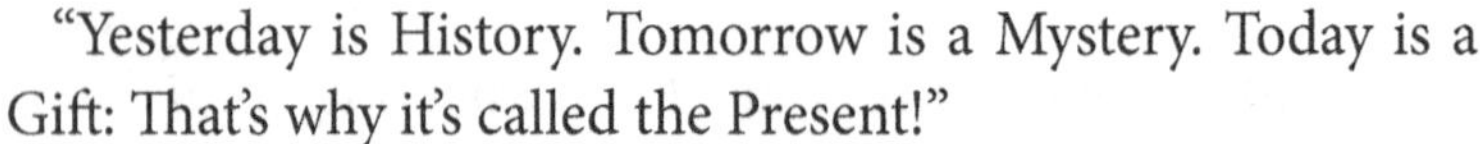

"Yesterday is History. Tomorrow is a Mystery. Today is a Gift: That's why it's called the Present!"

It is a phrase written on the chalkboard in the dining hall of the psychiatric ward where I have been training for four weeks. As I read it, all the chaos of the world seems to fade away, and a sense of peace washes over me. The words feel like a gentle reminder—not to be overwhelmed by the weight of yesterday, today, and tomorrow all at once. Instead, they seem to encourage me to take life slowly, embracing each moment as it comes.

Over the past month, I have spent time conversing and engaging in activities with individuals battling mental illness. In their presence, I have felt emotions and drawn inspiration that no theory or textbook could ever fully explain. There were people who did not fit neatly into the errors and absurdities of this world, souls who wandered because they could not make sense of society. Some fell into deep depression or lost their grip on their sanity because enduring reality in a rational state was unbearable. Others grew up in broken homes, carrying the deep roots of despair, anger, and victimization. They were pure and delicate souls, vulnerable enough to expose the very depths of their inner selves and speak of their emotions with honesty and calmness. Their struggles with mental illness were, in truth, desperate cries for survival. For without "madness," they would have had no choice but to succumb to death.

D, who paces nervously, asking what to do with a life he feels he has ruined.

R, who shakes her head, saying the world is too frightening.

L, who sobs uncontrollably, saying she feels unbearably lonely and wishes someone would love her.

J, a fragile transgender individual who chose to become a man because of the father who shielded him with warmth amid his mother's severe abuse—the only source of comfort in his life.

K, who says his soul has always been female, acknowledging that living as a woman is not easy but has no regrets about becoming one.

S and N, tormented by voices commanding them to kill their father, mother, spouse, or children, trapped in the grip of horrifying hallucinations, battling suicidal impulses moment by moment.

These are people who, despite wanting to give up, walked in on their own, determined to change their lives because they could no longer continue living as they were. They endure today while crying out in the throes of withdrawal from drugs, alcohol, and cigarettes. Many are tormented by physical illnesses intertwined with their mental disorders, their bodies and minds trapped in relentless agony. A significant number are HIV-positive, struggling moment by moment to manage their fear and anger. Some, rejected by both society and family for being gay or lesbian, still yearn desperately for the love and acceptance of those who cast them aside. Others have no place to go after discharge, their futures uncertain. Some break down in tears when speaking of their goals for life beyond the hospital walls, knowing how fragile their hopes are. Many of them will likely end up back on the streets, wandering until the weight of the world becomes unbearable, until one day, they return here, their diagnoses compounded by even more ailments.

They struggle desperately to belong to the very society we often grow weary of and wish to escape. They long for recognition and understanding from a world that coldly dismisses those it deems different; without hesitation, without guilt. It is a society where fathers, brothers, and mothers commit acts of sexual violence, where the very people meant to protect can become the source of unimaginable pain. And yet, despite it all, they dream of returning to that same society, soothing their wounded bodies and hearts while learning how to love themselves. For them, today is not merely an extension of yesterday. Each moment is an urgent future—a fragile dream they cling to with all their might.

"Yesterday is History. Tomorrow is a Mystery. Today is a Gift: That's why it's called the Present!"

No matter how much effort we put in, we cannot change the past. The only thing we have control over is the perspective we choose to take on it. As for tomorrow, no one knows what it will bring. We cannot predict even the next moment, let alone what might happen an hour from now.

Compared to yesterday and tomorrow, today truly is a gift. No matter how small or imperfect it may seem, a gift is something to be accepted, never rejected. It is only right to receive it with gratitude. We must embrace the gift of today with thankfulness and enjoy its blessings to the fullest. Dwelling on the past and wasting today in regret or worrying about tomorrow and squandering the precious moments of the present, only leads to loss. By fully

recognizing, cherishing, and making the most of today, we create a beautiful past and pave the way for a hopeful future. Remember, the present moment we are living now is the future someone longed for yesterday. Yet, unable to see it, they closed their eyes forever.

"What is your goal for today?" The question, posed by the group therapist to the patients, struck a chord. What is my goal for today? How should I live this gift of a day, one that can become a beautiful history and a foundation for a hopeful tomorrow? Neither the pain of yesterday nor the uncertainty of a tomorrow filled with twists and mysteries has the right to disrupt today. This moment, the one I am breathing in right now, belongs entirely to me.

The gift of today, newly arrived, is truly beautiful.

Jane Ha

The Priorities of Life

When faced with life's challenges, I am always caught off guard. What's curious is that, despite having encountered and overcome countless difficulties, each new challenge feels entirely fresh, leaving me just as unprepared as before, as if I had built no immunity to hardship at all.

In such moments, I reflect on the priorities of life. What choice will allow me to lose the least, or better yet, is there a way to overcome this challenge without losing anything at all? The truth is: nothing can be gained without letting go of something else. So, what should I relinquish, and what should I hold on to in order to emerge from this hardship with valuable wisdom?

Everyone has their own priorities in life, and they vary widely. However, the formula for determining those priorities is the same: focus first on what you consider most important, and then take care of everything else.

Not long ago, I had the opportunity to witness a performance about the priorities of life. Though simple, it left me deeply inspired and profoundly moved.

Professor Ms. Cervenka entered the classroom, but unlike other days, she was silent. There was no bright smile, no cheerful greeting. Instead, she placed a large, transparent glass jar on the lectern. Without a word, she began filling it with golf balls until it appeared full. She gave the jar a gentle shake, allowing a few more golf balls to settle in. Then, for the first time, she spoke. "Does the jar look full to you?" she asked. We all agreed that it did.

Next, she poured small pebbles into the jar. They trickled down into the seemingly full space, filling the gaps between the golf balls. She shook the jar lightly again, allowing more pebbles to settle in. Then she repeated the question: "Do you agree that the jar is now full?" We nodded.

Using the same method, she added sand, which seeped into the even smaller spaces between the pebbles. Finally, she poured four bottles of beer into the jar, the liquid absorbing into the sand until the jar could take no more. At last, the jar was truly full.

Finally, Ms. Cervenka looked around the room and smiled.

"This jar represents life," she began. "The golf balls symbolize the most important things in your life—your family, spouse, health, children, friends, and those you pour your passion into that drive you. Even if you lost everything else or lacked some of the less critical things, as long as these remain, your life will still be as full as this jar."

"The pebbles represent material things like your job, house, or car. The sand represents all the small, insignificant things beyond what I've already mentioned."

She then posed a question: "What would happen if you filled the jar with sand first?" We thought for a moment before she answered us. "There would be no room left for the golf balls or even the pebbles. Life works the same way. If you spend all your precious time and energy on trivial things, you'll never have space for the things that truly matter."

"Focus on what truly brings you happiness. Spend time playing with your children, and don't neglect your health.

Make time for the people you love. There will always be time for work, cleaning the house, throwing parties, or fixing a leaky faucet."

I realized that while what and how much we fill our life's jar with is important, the order in which we fill it matters even more. The principle that prioritizing the most precious things first naturally creates space for everything else was a newfound revelation. The idea that as long as life is filled with what truly matters, the rest may be lacking but will not leave us feeling empty was deeply reassuring. Moreover, knowing that no matter what we choose to fill our lives with, and regardless of the order, there is always room for the small joys of life, symbolized by the space for beer, was an unexpectedly comforting thought.

A person with clear and definite priorities in life is truly a happy person. How often can problems be solved, and the world transformed, simply by adjusting one's mindset or reordering priorities? When life feels chaotic, Ms. Cervenka's voice echoes in my mind reminding me that life is, at its core, nothing more than an empty jar—so do not be afraid, but first, take care of your priorities.

My Sentiment for Pasadena City College

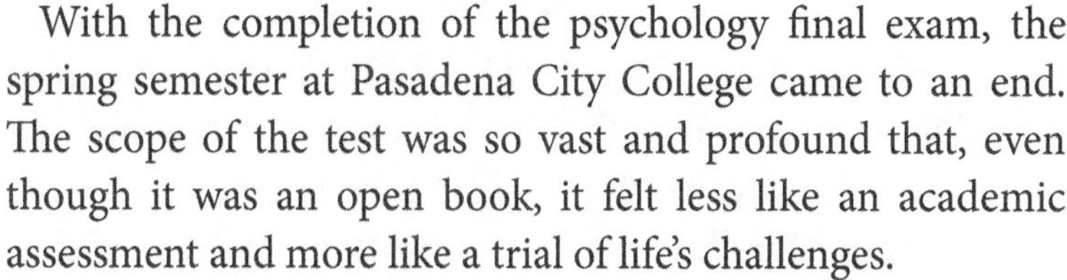

With the completion of the psychology final exam, the spring semester at Pasadena City College came to an end. The scope of the test was so vast and profound that, even though it was an open book, it felt less like an academic assessment and more like a trial of life's challenges.

As I handed in my paper, I told the professor how much I had truly enjoyed his class and how his lectures had sparked moments of fiery inspiration about life. The white-haired professor, who had poured out countless propositions and truths about life like blessings in every session, simply nodded repeatedly. It seemed as though all his usual words were tucked away, leaving only a brief but meaningful reply: "May you have a good life."

As I walked out of the classroom, a wave of emotion washed over me, marking the end of a challenging semester. There were countless moments when I wanted to give up, when doubts crept in and tested my resolve. The relentless cycle of weekly exams, countless assignments, and demanding writing projects often felt overwhelming, making me want to collapse under the weight of it all.

I was even tempted to settle—to study just enough, to accept a mediocre grade, to simply get through it. But is it true that as we age, we become more fixated on doing things thoroughly? That we refuse to cut corners, not because we have to, but because we want to?

The sensitivity and abundant passion I once had have grown dull, layered with the dust of time, leaving me feeling fragile. Yet, through the cracks of this fragility, an uncompromising stubbornness has emerged. Though clumsy and full of flaws, I've earned the nickname "Miss Naïve." I have somehow developed an inability to settle for less in certain areas. Especially when it comes to studying; the idea of "good enough" is something I simply cannot tolerate. If, after giving my best effort, there are still concepts I cannot grasp, I can blame my IQ, my lack of study strategies, or even the language barrier. But knowing the core of the lecture, understanding what and how to study, yet walking into an exam unprepared due to circumstances beyond my control—it feels unbearable. Though my stubbornness has made things harder for me, it has also pushed me to make the most of every spare moment and to practice the art of deep, unwavering focus.

It was a challenging yet deeply fulfilling time. I had the opportunity to meet many people who approached life with sincerity and depth, as well as exceptional professors who embodied the true essence of a scholarly attitude. It was also rewarding to become adept at navigating the school system and making the most of its resources. What made the experience even more meaningful was that many of the professors were around my age. This allowed me to deeply resonate with the direction and purpose they were pursuing in their own lives, making my journey feel all the more connected and inspiring.

One of the professors once said that as knowledge increases, so too does anguish—that greater understanding often leads to deeper loneliness and suffering. A nineteen-year-old student challenged this idea, asking, "How could gaining more knowledge possibly make someone sad and troubled? Shouldn't it bring pride and happiness?"

The professor, caught off guard and momentarily at a loss for words, seemed unsure of where to begin or how to explain. Watching this exchange, I subtly nodded, silently conveying my agreement and understanding. There were many moments like this; moments when, without speaking, we could acknowledge a shared truth: the weight of time is never light.

It was a great school. It was clear that the institution was committed to providing resources and faculty for those eager to learn, making genuine efforts to be accessible to its students. For just $11 per unit, students could attend lectures taught by UCLA professors with doctoral degrees. Every laboratory was equipped with high-tech electron microscopes, each worth thousands of dollars—more than enough for the number of students. And in a place where human cadavers were provided for basic physiology experiments, the school fostered an environment where meeting with professors and engaging in meaningful discussions was always encouraged and accessible.

As I hurried toward the parking lot, I suddenly stopped in my tracks. California's May had unfolded across the campus flowerbeds, filled with roses of every kind, blooming in abundance. I thought to myself, "Why are there so many roses on campus? When did they bloom so beautifully?" It was only today, for the first time, that I noticed just how many roses there were, and how stunningly they flourished on the very campus where I had spent so much time studying.

I crouched by the flowerbed and gazed at the blossoms. They seemed to be a hybrid of climbing roses, their delicate petals layered upon one another in tightly packed blooms. The soft pink and white hues blended so harmoniously, radiating a brilliance that was almost blinding. Each petal was so gracefully shaped, and the fragrance was impossibly sweet. Looking at the fresh, vibrant blossoms, I couldn't help but let out a sigh of admiration. Amid the hurried moments of life, these flowers had quietly bloomed, faded, and bloomed once more; their beauty unfolding whether or not anyone noticed. Traces of the wind's fleeting presence lingered among them.

I bid farewell to the trees standing by the parking lot, the roses in the flowerbeds, and all the familiar sights around me. "Have a great summer. Live well, and I'll see you again in three months."

On the way home, I thought about a world as lovely and fragrant as a rose—a life lived slowly enough to never miss its beauty.

Heart of the Mountain, Heart of the Water

Right after finishing my final exams, I set out for a trek on Mt. Baldy. There, a grand celebration of nature was in full swing. Bright yellow blossoms from the forsythia family blanketed the mountain, adorning it with vibrant color. Everywhere, Yucca cacti had sent up thick, towering flower stalks, crowned with delicate white blossoms that gleamed like festival lanterns, dazzling in their brilliance. Until they bloomed, I had not even noticed their presence. A carpet of tiny purple wildflowers stretched before me, their delicate petals swaying in the breeze alongside an array of blossoms in every color. There was harmony in their movement, a radiant joy, and a pure, untainted life. The sight was so breathtaking that for a moment, I felt as though I could scarcely breathe.

Amid the charred remains of trees blackened by last year's wildfire, clusters of green vines had emerged, weaving a strange and striking beauty. A world made beautiful through sacrifice, where giving and receiving became one, evoking a quiet awe. It was, in every sense, breathtaking.

I saw the wide-open heart of the mountain; expansive, welcoming, alive. Who would have thought the mountain's heart could be so vibrant and radiant with all its dazzling colors? Who would have imagined it to be so intricate and delicate? With a genuine sense of being warmly welcomed, I found myself drawn deeply into the world the mountain had invited me to explore.

The mountain was simultaneously full and empty, overflowing with trees, flowers, water, wind, and clouds, yet vast and open in its stillness. In its empty spaces, there was acceptance, forgiveness, and healing, wisdom and love born from overcoming pain. As I gazed upon the fields and slopes, brimming with harmony and peace, a deep sense of happiness settled within me. Watching the world sparkle in its purity brought an effortless smile to my face. The world is so beautifully balanced. Faced with such fullness and quiet maturity, I could not help but bow my head in reverence. In that moment, I began to understand why being embraced by the mountains awakens a sense of sacredness in the heart.

The mountain does not lie. Each peak stands at a height that reflects the depth and maturity it has cultivated within. It does not fill itself with empty air to boast or deceive. It simply exists in quiet strength, humble and true. In the presence of something so majestic and genuine, I find myself naturally humbled, my own sense of self gently lowering, as if bowing before wisdom far greater than my own.

The stream was full and alive, its flowing waters carrying a refreshing, rhythmic sound. Along its banks, several aspen trees had fallen, their trunks now stretching across both sides of the rushing current, carried by its force and speed. Watching this quiet cycle of creation and decay, I felt a solemn reverence for the beauty inherent in nature's endless transformation.

I dipped my feet into the stream, and the icy water sent a sharp, invigorating jolt through me. This purity, so untouched now, will one day bear the scars of the world, carrying its burdens and traces before ultimately reaching the sea. It will be a long journey.

I spoke to the water. "I'm graduating the day after tomorrow. The past five years feel like a dream. Finishing my studies at this late stage in life has left me with emotions too complex to contain. I'm afraid to step into society. At an age when the knowledge and experience accumulated over years should bloom into a peak of maturity and completion, I am only just beginning. Can you understand the feeling of trembling with the uncertain steps of a beginner? I'm also anxious about picking up the many responsibilities and obligations I postponed under the guise of studying. How should I live? How will my life unfold?"

The water flowed ceaselessly. It rushed forward with urgency, yet when it met an obstacle, it did not resist. It paused momentarily, swirling in quiet reflection, before being carried onward by the force of new waves pressing from behind. In that movement, the heart of the water spoke to me.

"Do not be afraid. Do not rush, and do not cling to regrets. Look at me. I have a much longer journey ahead than you, yet I am not impatient. I simply flow continuously at a pace that suits me. There's no need to reach a specific destination. Not all water has to reach the ocean. The journey itself matters. Flowing gently, rather than rushing, allows me to appreciate the beauty around me. It is meaningful to move slowly, to quench the thirst of those nearby and take in the world along the way. Even if I stop midstream, it is not a failure. Where I pause, I can nurture a single wildflower, and that too would be worthwhile."

The heart of the mountain reached out to me. "Look at me. A mountain cannot exist without embracing many things. It cannot be filled with only what is beautiful and good. Sadness, pain, and loneliness must blend together in harmony to create a world as breathtaking as this. You must learn to embrace it all."

I descended the mountain with a sense of lightness. My mind was filled with fresh energy, a gift from the mountains and water, and my body felt as if it could fly. That night, I dreamed. "If you look at the mountains, the water—at us—and observe nature, wisdom will come to you." All night long, I drifted in and out of sleep, hearing the soft, whispering voices of the mountains and water.

My First Experience

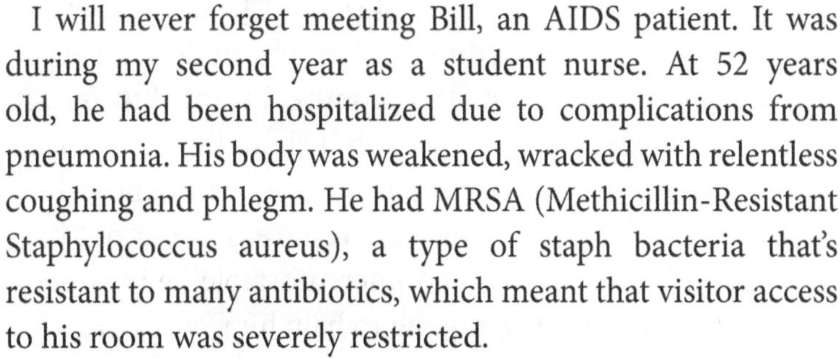

I will never forget meeting Bill, an AIDS patient. It was during my second year as a student nurse. At 52 years old, he had been hospitalized due to complications from pneumonia. His body was weakened, wracked with relentless coughing and phlegm. He had MRSA (Methicillin-Resistant Staphylococcus aureus), a type of staph bacteria that's resistant to many antibiotics, which meant that visitor access to his room was severely restricted.

Entering his room required wearing a special mask, gloves, gown, and even shoe covers. Naturally, the staff avoided going in unless absolutely necessary, and even then, they would leave as quickly as possible. The lighting was dim, at Bill's request, to ease his discomfort. A humidifier continuously released steam to aid his breathing, making the air thick with moisture, leaving everything damp to the touch. The moment you stepped inside, a wave of sorrow seemed to wash over you.

I felt a profound sense of pity for him. As I checked his blood pressure, I noticed his arm was drenched in sweat. He mentioned that he hadn't been able to wash at all during the three full days since his admission. When I offered to help him clean up, he expressed gratitude but insisted it wasn't necessary. I suggested bringing in another colleague if he felt uncomfortable, but he replied that as long as I didn't mind, he had no objections.

The nursing assistants flatly refused my request. Even Lupe, with whom I was usually close, shook her head decisively. They reasoned that, since he could move on his own, he could bathe himself if he truly wanted to. They also pointed out that he would likely be discharged in a day or two and could bathe properly then. Besides, they added, a simple sponge bath wouldn't make much difference anyway.

I resented my colleagues. How could they dismiss a sponge bath as insignificant? If they didn't want to do it, it would have been better to just admit it. A stubborn determination rose within me. Once I made a promise, I wanted to keep it. If I wasn't willing to follow through, I shouldn't have offered in the first place. Thinking about the hurt he might feel if I backed out only strengthened my resolve. I could not bear the thought of how sticky and uncomfortable he must have felt. No matter what, I was going to help him.

It was likely sheer determination that pushed me forward. For a brief moment, I hesitated at the thought of handling this task alone. But the conclusion was clear—I had to help him, no matter the reason. He had the right to be cared for with dignity. The only reason he endured in silence was because he carried the weight of how the world viewed people like him.

In the end, I entered his room alone. Due to the nature of his illness and to protect his privacy, I closed the door and drew the curtains. His body was so emaciated that his protruding bones had chafed his skin, leaving behind raw sores. Under the dim light, as I carefully cleaned his frail body, my mind swirled with countless thoughts.

It was my first time encountering the naked body of a man who wasn't family. Not only did I have to look at it, but I also had to clean it with my own hands. I repeated a mantra to myself: "I am not a person. I am not human. I am a robot tasked with cleaning a patient's body. Robots do not think. My only goal is to complete this task. Nothing more." There was no need to think. I must not think.

I realized then the power and allure of a uniform. Wearing it gave me courage I never knew I possessed. Outside the hospital, I wonder if I could ever summon such bravery. For Bill, it worked the same way—he placed his complete trust in me simply because I was wearing a uniform. That single garment gave him the assurance to surrender himself to my care. I did what a person in uniform is supposed to do. I mixed soap into warm water and meticulously washed every part of his body, leaving no area unattended.

I gently dried his body with a clean towel. After helping him into a fresh gown, he finally spoke. "Thank you." Come to think of it, he hadn't spoken a single word during the entire process, and neither had I. Though our words remained unspoken, the mutual awkwardness and tension were unmistakably present.

As I was leaving the room, he added, "In my entire life, no one has ever treated my body with such care. Especially in the 13 years I've been in and out of hospitals with AIDS, I've never once felt love through anyone's touch. I don't know when my life will end, but I will never forget your touch, Jane, for as long as I live."

I felt both fear and awe. It was as if I had been handed the keys to heaven—I was overwhelmed with happiness. How profound it is for my presence to be etched into someone's memory. What could be more precious than knowing that my touch has brought gratitude and love into another's life?

I often wonder about him. Where is he now? What is he doing? Is he even still alive? He said he would never forget me, yet I find that I cannot forget him. Every time I care for an AIDS patient, I think of him. His quiet voice saying "Thank you" still echoes vividly in my mind.

A Student Nurse's Letter to a Teenage Mother

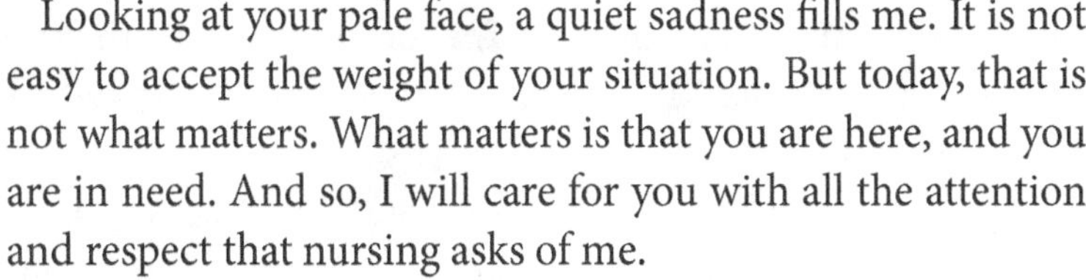

Looking at your pale face, a quiet sadness fills me. It is not easy to accept the weight of your situation. But today, that is not what matters. What matters is that you are here, and you are in need. And so, I will care for you with all the attention and respect that nursing asks of me.

Sixteen. Such a tender, blossoming age. You carry a name as beautiful as music, and a face even lovelier than that melody. With long, jet-black hair flowing down your back, you should be laughing with friends, perhaps stressing over SAT prep or Advanced Placement exams, a high school junior caught up in ordinary things. But instead, you lie in a hospital bed, your thoughts already with the 18-month-old child waiting at home, while your arms cradle the second baby you gave birth to just yesterday.

That's right. You had no way of knowing. Spinal anesthesia kept you free from pain, and with a curtain drawn across your chest, you never even saw it happen. While the anesthetist and nurse stayed close, the gynecologist made a careful incision in your lower abdomen and brought your baby into the world. All you felt was a brief pressure. A gentle tug in your belly. You were breathing in quiet, soothing oxygen as a new life took its first breath.

So much blood was pouring out. The surgeon's blade moved swiftly across the soft curve of your lower abdomen.

With a wide iron retractor, he and his assistant folded back the pale layers of tissue, revealing the womb beneath.

I stood quietly at the edge of the operating field, my breath caught somewhere between awe and disbelief. There it was—your uterus, open and exposed, its shape both familiar and strange. Then, through the incision, a new life slowly emerged. The baby's head appeared first, glistening and fragile, guided gently by skilled hands.

The surgeon worked with calm precision. Blood vessels were sealed with flashes of light. The torn uterus was stitched with practiced ease. The scent of burned flesh lingered in the air, sharp and metallic. Blood rushed into the suction tubes with a sound that seemed too loud. Droplets splashed onto the surgical drapes. I blinked hard, again and again, as dizziness crept into my chest. For a moment, I thought I might collapse.

And yet, just beyond the drape, you were speaking with the anesthesiologist. A light voice, casual and unshaken, floated above the noise of the room. It was a conversation about the weather.

Sydney,

I recently learned that your school provides a daycare center for the babies born to students like you, allowing young mothers to continue their studies. I was stunned to hear that, as long as space is available somewhere on campus, you and your boyfriend are permitted to be physically intimate without restriction.

When I read about your five pregnancies, three abortions, and now a partial hysterectomy, I was overcome with sorrow and disbelief. I can hardly imagine the weight of all you have endured—especially beginning with your first pregnancy at the age of eleven. It feels almost beyond comprehension.

Yes, I know. Statistically, you are not alone. In America, nearly one million teenage girls become pregnant each year. That means about four out of every ten teenage girls will face pregnancy before adulthood. Each year, around half a million babies are born to teenage mothers—many of them unprepared emotionally, psychologically, or financially for the weight of parenthood. As difficult as it is to believe, the numbers remain consistent. A significant number of girls who experience pregnancy in their teens become pregnant again within a year. Of those second pregnancies, nearly forty percent end in abortion.

Some say that teenage mothers need stricter moral or character education. Others go so far as to suggest that the availability of pain-free childbirth encourages pregnancy, arguing that young mothers should be made to endure labor pain as a deterrent.

But the truth is, the fault lies with us—the adults. I accept that responsibility without hesitation. It is the failures of grown-ups, the flaws in the world we created, that have left young people like you to carry such heavy burdens.

I do not say this out of pity, nor simply as an apology. Somewhere along the way, my sense of responsibility turned into something else. Something quieter. Something deeper. A feeling I did not expect.

Sydney,

Tomorrow you will be discharged, and next week I will be working at another hospital. Most likely, we will never meet again. Still, I find it hard to leave your room. I keep lingering near you, and I ask myself why. It is because I feel love for you. You smile when I say that. But there are people in this world, people like me, who believe that when an unknown life is lost, something within them is lost too. You are a part of me. And so, loving you feels as natural as breathing.

Sydney,

This world is wide and filled with beauty. Your youth is a precious gift that will never return. I hope you will finish high school, gain skills that empower you, and grow strong enough to stand on your own. When you reach my age, may you look back without regret. May your path ahead be blessed and full of light. Take good care of your two little ones. Raise them with love.

Goodbye, Sydney.

Chapter 6

Lecture on Communication Skills for Nurses

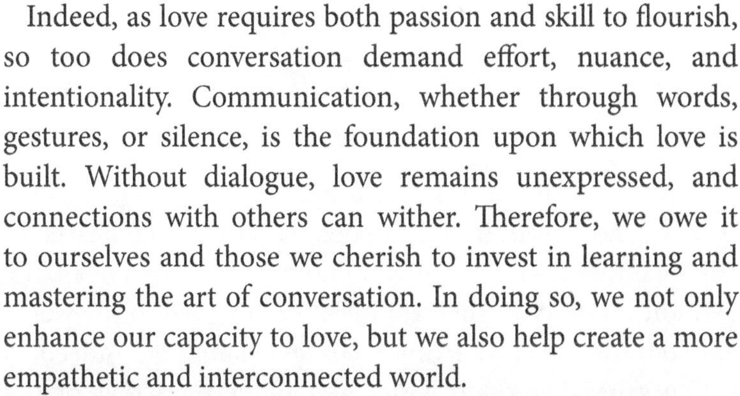

Indeed, as love requires both passion and skill to flourish, so too does conversation demand effort, nuance, and intentionality. Communication, whether through words, gestures, or silence, is the foundation upon which love is built. Without dialogue, love remains unexpressed, and connections with others can wither. Therefore, we owe it to ourselves and those we cherish to invest in learning and mastering the art of conversation. In doing so, we not only enhance our capacity to love, but we also help create a more empathetic and interconnected world.

Conversation is essential to understanding and feeling the heart of another. While some argue that connection can occur without words, truly deep understanding requires a foundation built on countless dialogues over many days. Even Yeomhwa Sijung, the Buddha's silent transmission through a flower, and Yeomhwa Miso, a knowing smile, are subtle forms of communication that connect hearts.

Words are indispensable; they have the power to wound or to heal. Through words, people forge camaraderie, become adversaries, or build lifelong alliances. Words can lead to marriage, and they can also cause separation.

The "Nurse's Communication Techniques" course I studied last semester was incredibly valuable. It taught me that effective and active communication is not just a professional skill, it is essential for building trust and fostering genuine connections with patients. While non-verbal cues and attitudes can often be conveyed naturally, without verbal dialogue to support or follow them, misunderstandings can arise. Without words, even actions lose their strength.

Patients open their hearts only when they feel a genuine sense of trust. It is only when they do so that we can truly connect with them and foster hope for a swift recovery. A patient's full cooperation is crucial in medical care; if they lie or withhold the truth, gathering accurate information becomes challenging, often leading to inadequate care. Trusting a stranger with their body and mind is no small task for anyone.

Nurses' communication techniques are a profound skills that reaches deep into the soul. Opening the hearts of patients, those who are already hurt or vulnerable, is truly extraordinary. With such abilities, reaching out to the world and our neighbors becomes far less daunting. Indeed, a patient's heart is often softer and purer than that of the average person, which can make genuine connections easier to forge. Nevertheless, I believe that by developing and practicing effective dialogue skills in nursing, we naturally enhance our capacity to communicate with the world at large.

Skilled nurses are effective communicators. This does not mean they talk excessively but rather that they know how to say the right words at the right time and place. They can read the patient's emotions and deliver information with appropriate depth and sensitivity. A good nurse possesses the ability to truly listen, offering patients a sense of comfort and emotional stability with warmth and compassion. Ultimately, nursing is a profession that cannot be sustained without a genuine love for people.

Silence can be the most powerful form of communication. It means not reacting to every word; rather, allowing the other person the freedom to express themselves completely. This approach is especially effective for those who tend to be overly talkative or prone to complaints. By maintaining silence, you create a space where you can observe their emotions and attitudes, gently encouraging them to lead the conversation.

At the same time, effective nonverbal communication is crucial—body language and facial expressions serve as essential complements to our silence. If these cues aren't aligned with your true intent, silence can easily be misinterpreted as indifference or disregard. Truly mastering this technique requires more than mere practice; it calls for a deep reservoir of life experience and wisdom, allowing you to know when silence can indeed speak louder than words.

There is also a communication technique known as "offering self," where a nurse willingly shares time and space with a patient. Phrases like, "Let's walk to the dining hall together," "I'll stay by your side for a little while," or "Would you like some help chopping the carrots?" demonstrate a nurse's readiness to offer both time and presence. This simple act of sharing creates a space for connection and comfort, allowing patients to feel seen, heard, and supported in their journey toward healing.

Showing empathy is not easy. Truly understanding and sharing someone else's feelings goes far beyond mere sympathy; it demands a deep sensitivity to the emotions and concerns of others. For instance, a nurse might gently say to a patient, "Being hospitalized must be very difficult for you," or "That problem seems to be causing you a lot of distress," or "You seem quite down this morning." These statements exemplify empathetic communication.

Recognizing and validating the emotions of a patient who is struggling with separation from family, disrupted routines, financial burdens, and the uncertainty of the future requires significant emotional energy and commitment.

Focusing is also a vital communication skill. When a nurse senses that a patient is struggling to understand or address a particular issue, focusing comes into play. It involves gently guiding the conversation so that the patient can confront and clarify the situation at hand. This process helps the patient pinpoint the root of their distress and articulate their concerns, paving the way for a more targeted and effective intervention. In doing so, the nurse not only assists in resolving the immediate issue but also empowers the patient to take an active role in their own care.

Restatement is another highly effective communication technique. It involves rephrasing what the other person has said, using similar words to reflect understanding and encourage further conversation. By restating the patient's words, you provide valuable feedback that shows you are truly listening, and you invite the patient to elaborate on their feelings. This technique often takes the form of a question. For instance, if a patient says, "I suddenly feel anxious this morning," you might respond with, "Are you feeling tense?" Similarly, if they say, "I want to be alone. I'm in pain," you could reply, "You're not feeling well, are you?" These responses not only confirm that you understand the patient's experience but also gently prompt them to provide more details, deepening the conversation and enhancing mutual understanding.

The sixth technique is validation. This approach is used to confirm information or seek further clarification from the speaker. Examples of guiding validation include phrases like, "So, if I understand correctly…", "What I'm hearing is...", "Would it be accurate to say that...?", "Your intention seems to be...", and "Based on what you just said, am I right in thinking...?" These techniques are essential for accurately reflecting the speaker's emotions without exaggeration or understatement, so that they feel truly heard and understood.

The final technique is dealing with the here and now. This approach helps focus the patient's attention on the present moment and the immediate issue at hand. For example, a nurse might say, "The issue you're currently facing is..." By directing the patient's thoughts to the present, this technique minimizes distractions from past regrets or future worries, enabling them to address their immediate needs more effectively.

There are also significant barriers to effective communication—such as offering unsolicited advice or showing overt approval or disapproval. Ultimately, the decision must rest with the patient, and it is the nurse's role to empower them to make choices for themselves. Unhelpful statements like, "In that situation, you probably had no other choice," "You did the right thing," or "You shouldn't be so angry about this" fail to center on the patient's emotions or experiences. Instead, they reflect the nurse's own judgments and opinions, which can limit the patient's autonomy and inhibit self-reflection. To truly support and empower patients, nurses should focus on active listening, validation, and encouraging patients to explore and articulate their own feelings and perspectives.

Clichés and false reassurances are not effective communication techniques. Statements like, "You will feel better tomorrow," "Everything will be fine," or "Don't worry," often do little more than leave the patient feeling isolated and misunderstood. Rather than offering genuine comfort, these phrases may inadvertently make patients feel that their unique experiences and emotions are being dismissed. Instead, what patients need is to feel truly heard and understood, not merely reassured by empty platitudes.

"Why" questions can often make patients feel interrogated or judged. For example, asking, "Why did you do that?" "Why do you feel this way?" or "Why didn't you call the doctor at the time?" can come off as accusatory or judgmental. In contrast, using questions that begin with "who," "what," "when," "where," or "how" tends to foster a much gentler and more supportive conversation.

Minimizing a patient's emotions is a sure way to shut down meaningful communication. Statements such as "Don't worry," "That's not a problem," "Don't think that way," "You shouldn't feel so down," or "That scar will fade with time" can leave patients feeling dismissed rather than understood. These remarks fail to validate their emotional experiences, instead imposing a viewpoint that undermines their feelings. Instead, we must strive to acknowledge and validate what patients are experiencing, ensuring they feel truly seen and heard.

Defensive language may offer the nurse a sense of protection, but it is not an effective communication strategy. Statements such as, "What do you mean this hospital is unfriendly? This ward provides the best service." "I'm doing my best right now." "Everyone has to wait their turn." "Don't talk to me about that awful food." "That's not my responsibility."

These types of responses tend to frustrate and alienate patients, making them feel unheard and invalidated. Instead of shielding themselves with defensive remarks, nurses should strive to engage in open, empathetic dialogue that validates the patient's experiences and fosters trust.

Focusing on irrelevant issues, avoiding a patient's concerns, or deflecting responsibility are all forms of ineffective communication. For example, statements like: "If you're so worried, ask the doctor about it," "Why don't you talk to…?" "If it's about that, ask the dietitian," all dismiss the patient's immediate concerns and make them feel that their worries are being brushed aside. Such responses fail to validate their experiences, leaving them feeling isolated and unsupported. Effective communication involves acknowledging the patient's feelings and addressing their concerns directly, rather than deflecting responsibility onto someone else.

Learning these communication techniques left me perplexed. I questioned the necessity of all these methods. Even if I understood them in theory, how challenging would it be to apply them in real-life situations? I worried that attempting to use these techniques might come across as manipulative or insincere. If they resulted in forced or fake emotions, what good could they possibly do? Simply mimicking these approaches like a parrot might not inspire professional trust; instead, it could give off a sense of clumsiness or superficiality. Perhaps the effective use of good communication is reserved for those who have first mastered their own emotions, where genuine care naturally precedes technique.

I have always struggled with communication. I'm slow to grasp situations and hesitant to make judgments. It's almost unbelievable that I stepped into the medical field; a realm where sharp awareness, quick decision-making, and integrative thinking are indispensable. The fact that I haven't been pushed out of this demanding world and have managed to persevere until now feels nothing short of a miracle.

I have my own approach to communication: "Live as you are. Speak as you think. The best life is the simplest life. The best thoughts are those expressed without overanalyzing. Just say what comes to mind, simply and honestly."

But wait; expressing thoughts as they are, without embellishment or omission, requires profound self-discipline. I also understand how bold and reckless such an approach can be. That is why I have established my own set of rules:

Do not wound the other person's heart. Speak the truth, but first, pass every word through a filter—removing the harsh thorns and sharp stones so that only gentle, rounded words remain. Stay silent when silence is needed. Endure when patience is required. No matter how good the words may be, reduce them by half before speaking.

These guidelines help me balance authenticity with compassion, ensuring that my communication remains both honest and kind.

Ah, how wonderful it would be if I could truly live by those rules. I know you're smiling, and I can almost hear your voice saying it's an impossible dream. Having failed to adhere to even one of those guidelines, I resolved to adopt another: remain silent instead. Yet even that comes with its challenges. Whenever I do speak, my untrained tongue and clumsy lips betray me, and unintended words spill out like discordant notes. How many times have I regretted what left my mouth the moment it was spoken?

It is often said that speaking well begins from within. The proverb, "People speak as their hearts are full of," reminds us that the quality of our words reflects the condition of our inner world. To speak with grace, we must first cultivate a kind and sincere heart—one filled with thoughtful intentions and genuine feelings.

I try to live by the lessons I've learned from teachers and books, but to be honest, I often fall short. Still, the following are the things I hope to learn and put into practice.

Nurture Your Inner Life: Spend time reflecting on your values, experiences, and the things that truly matter to you. A heart rich with understanding and empathy naturally gives rise to authentic expression.

Practice Active Listening: By truly listening to others, you learn to understand different perspectives and nuances in conversation, which in turn helps you express yourself more thoughtfully.

Engage in Thoughtful Reflection: After conversations, take a moment to consider what went well and what might be improved. Over time, this reflection will refine your ability to articulate your thoughts.

Express Yourself Honestly: Even if you feel your technique is still developing, speaking from a place of sincerity and authenticity will resonate more than perfectly polished words.

Embrace Silence When Needed: Sometimes, pausing before you speak allows your genuine thoughts to settle and come through more clearly.

Ultimately, while technique is important, sincerity and kindness are what truly make communication effective. As we continue to fill our heart with good thoughts and genuine care, our words will naturally become a true reflection of who we are.

I think it was meant to be that I became a nurse. Through conversations with my patients, I feel I'm being guided to look inside myself and to practice the art of communication.

I wish that every word I speak could bring positivity and comfort, that I might always say the right thing at the right time and place. The art of communication as a nurse is an endless challenge, one I may never fully master, yet each conversation is a step toward growing more compassionate and effective in my care.

While Putting on Makeup

I stood in front of the mirror to do my makeup for an evening outing. As I applied my foundation and reached to shape my eyebrows, my hand hesitated. My eyebrows—untouched by a professional since the beautician styled them on my wedding day—had grown wild and unkempt. I thought of an acquaintance who frequented a skincare center for facial massages, wrinkle treatments, eyelash extensions, eyelash perms, and even maintained a tattoo for perfectly natural eyebrows. She always insisted that there was more to be done. For a moment, I felt a pang of sadness, realizing that, unlike many who invest time and effort into their beauty regardless of age, I seemed to be the exception. Yet that feeling was fleeting. As I applied my lipstick, I was struck by how futile all of this seemed. When life ceases, none of it matters; over time, nothing remains beautiful forever.

Later, I was reminded of my physiology class that afternoon. We had observed a human dissection, studying the body of a woman who had donated herself to science. Preserved in formalin, she lay there in a yellowish, clay-like state, impervious to decay, as her muscles, organs, and every anatomical detail were examined meticulously. Looking at her, the saying that life ultimately returns to dust felt profoundly real. A mix of emotions: compassion, respect, and an indescribable heaviness washed over me, leaving me in a complex, reflective state of mind.

The records showed that she was 62 years old and had passed away from coronary artery failure, a consequence of lung cancer that had metastasized from uterine cancer and compressed her heart. I couldn't help but wonder how excruciating it must have been for her to breathe. Her right lung was utterly destroyed by cancer, its structure unrecognizable, while her left lung was severely marred by black spots. Among the students, there was much speculation; some suggested she must have been a heavy smoker, while others blamed the polluted air of Los Angeles. There was no shortage of theories about the cause of her tragic condition.

During her lifetime, how much joy and sorrow must this woman have experienced? Was she a cherished daughter, a loving mother to many, or perhaps someone who navigated life's complexities entirely on her own? Her elegant figure and striking beauty hinted at a life once defined by grace. The delicate sweep of her eyelashes, the softly contoured lines of her face, the straightness of her teeth, and her meticulously groomed eyebrows all spoke of a time when beauty and refinement were celebrated. Her narrow shoulders and well-proportioned body, along with unscarred leg muscles, exuded strength and vitality, a testament to a life lived with purpose and resilience. Yet, the fine, delicate hairs on her legs seemed to whisper secrets of a life now gone, evoking an inexplicable sadness within me, as if they murmured stories of both cherished moments and profound loss.

Even with her body now broken and ravaged, she selflessly donated it to benefit future generations. Instead of resting peacefully and returning to the earth, she remains here, subjected to the hands of countless students. Regardless of the life she once lived, she has now been reduced to a serial number, a mere scientific specimen for research. In time, her body will deteriorate beyond even the potent preservation of formalin, and it will no longer hold value as a medical teaching tool.

We thoroughly examined her lungs, internal organs, and even her most private parts. My colleagues pressed on her spongy lungs, grasped her perineal muscles, and gave them a slight shake. One of them whispered that her pancreas was larger than he had imagined and that her diaphragm was thicker than expected. I couldn't help but wonder, what would she think if she could hear our irreverent conversation?

I looked upward, mascara wand in hand, but I stopped. What is the point of applying foundation to conceal acne scars and fine wrinkles, or brushing a pink hue over pale, faded lips with lipstick? One day, all of this will return to dust. With life and death standing so close together, why does life have to feel so burdensome? Once we lie in the earth, everything will find peace. What use is pride, when all of it is fleeting? Instead of dwelling on what will inevitably fade, I should embrace those I love one more time and never hold back the words, "I love you." Tears well up in my eyes.

Jane Ha

My Name is Jane

This spring semester, my clinical nursing instructor is Mrs. Davis. Her short, tightly curled hair is dyed a bright yellow, giving her a somewhat masculine appearance at first glance. However, her smooth, radiant skin and slender, graceful figure make her an increasingly captivating African American woman the more I observe her.

Before she took attendance, she had each of us pronounce our own names so she could learn them correctly. When it was my turn, I spoke my Korean name, then mentioned that I preferred to be called Jane. She asked if she could try saying my Korean name herself, and to my surprise, she pronounced it remarkably well, unlike most Americans I'd met. I expressed my gratitude and amazement, and she followed up by asking if there was a particular reason I preferred the name Jane.

I saw this as a good opportunity to explain the background. I shared that my Korean name is based on logograms, so its meaning can change entirely depending on how it is pronounced. When my name is pronounced correctly, it evokes a warm, familiar image. However, most Americans mispronounce it as Jongka, Jungka, or Jonga. Hearing my name mispronounced in this way, especially with harsh sounds, makes me feel as though my very identity is being distorted and my dignity diminished. That's why I don't feel comfortable when people attempt to use my Korean name.

After I finished my long explanation, she nodded in understanding. She shared that her name, Lois, is meant to be pronounced Loyce, yet people constantly call her Louis without even asking. She said she struggles to correct them each time, as it is her own name, something she cannot simply ignore. She empathized with my frustration.

Twenty years ago, when my husband came to Korea to marry me, he had no suitable place to stay and lived at my parents' house until the day before our wedding. One morning, while my mother and I were cooking in the kitchen, there was a sudden commotion. Listening closely, I realized it was my soon-to-be husband calling from the next room, "Ha-Jeong-a!" I was stunned. Why Ha-Jung? My name is Lee Jung-Ah. It was shocking to think that the name I had grown so accustomed to for 24 years could suddenly change so easily. The realization that my name could be combined with someone else's surname and called differently was a jarring experience.

Unbelievable! That timid-looking man must have some serious nerve. How dare he lie in bed and call out so loudly? And of all places, in my parents' home!

We are not even married yet! In front of my strict and formidable parents, who still find the American custom of a wife taking her husband's surname unfamiliar, how could he so casually change my name and call me by a different last name?"

I felt so embarrassed in front of my parents that I couldn't lift my head. Later, I heard my husband explain that he had done it on purpose, as if to tell them, "Your daughter now belongs to someone else, so it's better to accept it sooner rather than later." When I heard the full story, I could not help but laugh.

During his stay in Korea, my husband repeatedly called my name everywhere, always prefixed with his surname. Had the shock and humiliation of that moment in front of my parents been too overwhelming? Somehow, after that, I found myself accepting Ha-Jeong-a without resistance. It was as if I had resigned myself, what could possibly be more surprising or embarrassing than what had already happened? And before I knew it, Ha-Jeong-a had become my name.

When my surname changed, my life shifted entirely. I had to leave my homeland, share a bed, and meals with one man. Having been raised with my mother and three sisters in a close-knit household, I wasn't accustomed to the thoughts and behaviors of men. My youngest brother was far too young to offer any guidance, and my father was such an imposing figure, someone I hardly dared to approach.

After marriage, walking together with my husband often made me smile. I couldn't help but chuckle, wondering how my father would react if he knew his unmarried daughter was strolling arm-in-arm with a man in broad daylight down a busy street. Despite spending evenings out drinking with his friends, my father would always call home at sundown to ensure all his daughters were safely back.

If my sisters or I weren't home before sunset, my father's wrath was swift and stern. Staying late for evening study sessions was simply unthinkable. I recall when I was in my third year of middle school, both my homeroom teacher and the academic advisor came to our house. They explained that I consistently excelled in advanced classes but never participated in the school's special study programs. They pleaded with my father to allow me to attend, emphasizing the importance of supporting my future. My father flatly refused. "A daughter? I don't want to turn her into a machine that only studies. I love my daughter more than you do." The teachers left empty-handed. I was overwhelmed with embarrassment toward my teachers and resentment toward my father. All I could do was sigh deeply, caught between gratitude for his care and frustration over lost opportunities.

When I was accepted into college, my mother gave me a stern warning: "Don't get involved in any romantic relationships. The moment you start dating instead of focusing on your studies, your college education is as good as over. Not only that, but you'll block the path for your younger sisters. As the eldest, you must conduct yourself properly so your sisters can also attend college. Be mindful of your responsibilities."

Her words carried the weight of expectation and sacrifice. It wasn't just about my own future, it was about setting the precedent for my sisters, ensuring they, too, would have the chance to pursue higher education.

When I sat across from a male classmate in a café, sipping tea, I often felt uneasy. Am I setting a bad example for my younger sisters? We would get along well as friends, addressing each other as "hyung" (brother) or "unnie" (sister), but things became awkward whenever the guy began expressing deeper feelings. I knew it wouldn't be long before I'd have to ring the metaphorical bell of farewell. It always puzzled me: why did men insist on narrowing the scope of their relationships with women they found agreeable? Why were they so quick to abandon a pleasant friendship in favor of something more exclusive? Some seemed eager to bring an abrupt end to what could have been a beautiful connection.

One male classmate laughed out loud when I told him I was not allowed to date. He claimed it was his life's mission to teach me what romance truly was and pestered me about it for quite some time. Looking back, it remains a fond memory.

No matter how others perceived me, I was genuinely serious about it. After all, this was about my sisters' futures. When I think about it, it feels unfair. I had to constantly turn away, unable to experience a deep and meaningful romance with any of the wonderful men I met. I sacrificed emotions I might never reclaim, setting aside fleeting moments of connection for a duty I believed was greater than my own desires. In the end, all three of my younger sisters went to college. They'll likely never know the immense sacrifices their eldest sister made; the significant, often painful choices I endured—for their sake.

When I first arrived in the United States, my husband gave me the name Jane. He explained that it was easy to pronounce since it didn't contain challenging letters like R or F, and it matched the initial of my Korean name, making it a natural choice. I accepted the name Jane for my own reasons. I thought, "After all, my last name has already changed; what difference does changing my first name make? Having an English name won't make me an American anyway."

Looking back, I wonder if my destiny began to slowly shift course from that moment. Didn't our ancestors regard names as profoundly significant? In the study of "Seong-myeong-hak" (the traditional Korean belief that a person's character and destiny are foretold in their name), changing or adopting a new name is no trivial matter. According to this perspective, a change in name can lead to a change in the person themselves. At the time, I didn't realize how true that could be.

There was another reason I came to love the name Jane: Charlotte Brontë's "Jane Eyre." Jane was a woman who loved with profound, anguished devotion. Even when her beloved's circumstances turned bleak, her love did not fade; instead, it burned even purer and stronger.

She was lonely and unfortunate; yet possessed an inner beauty and maturity. She longed endlessly for independence and freedom. I especially loved that she was not portrayed as conventionally beautiful. That made her even more compelling.

There's yet another reason. The pronunciation of Jane sometimes resembles 죄인 "jaein" criminal or sinner, in Korean. Saying, "My name is 죄인 "jaein" (sinner)," may sound pitiful, but to me, it holds deep meaning. Every time someone calls my name, I am reminded of my flaws and prompted to practice humility. The awareness of being a sinner serves as a catalyst, helping me to honestly confront my shortcomings and strive for self-improvement.

The stereotypes associated with the name Jane aren't bad either. It is often interpreted as "one who accepts" or "one who is hidden." It aligns perfectly with my own desire—to embrace the world while remaining quietly unseen, living freely without interference.

When I started attending a Korean church in America, I noticed that most of the women kept their maiden names. Some would teasingly ask, "How much must you love your husband to give up your pride and even change your surname?" Explaining it felt too complicated, so I would just laugh and reply, "I love my husband so, so much!"

Why didn't I keep my maiden name? As a descendant of a proud noble lineage, why did I act as though I lacked a sense of identity? Though I wasn't proactive in the decision, I didn't resist or reject it either. Why did I accept it so easily? It feels a bit unfair to blame my husband entirely, he wouldn't have insisted if I'd truly wanted to keep my maiden name. At one point, with someone's help, I even considered reclaiming my original surname. But by then, it felt too late. People found the idea awkward, saying my married surname suited my name better and looked more beautiful. They said it felt expansive and vibrant, even joking that I'd married well. I didn't feel like explaining that is because of the harmony of consonants and vowels or arguing that they were just used to hearing my name with my husband's surname. So, I let it go.

Truly, no one forced me, so why did I not only change my surname but also my first name? It wasn't simply because I live in America. Not all women who immigrate here change both their first and surname as I did. There must have been deeper, more fundamental reasons, rooted in my subconscious, that influenced my decision.

Perhaps I saw this as a chance to finally cast off the shadows of my youth. Maybe I longed to begin again; to live as if I had been reborn. It's possible I simply wanted to embrace hope and start a new life on unfamiliar soil. Or perhaps, after all these years, I just wanted to be free of the burden of a name that was too beautiful to bear.

My name was excessively pretty, and people who met me with expectations shaped by it often seemed disappointed. They would say, "Your name is so beautiful," and I could almost hear the unspoken thought that followed: "But you don't quite match it." Their awkward chuckles stung, and each time, I felt a quiet ache.

These days, I joke, "Since I'm not beautiful, at least my name should be, it makes things feel a little less unfair." But back then, it hurt. I felt guilty, even ashamed, as if I had personally let people down by not living up to the name I carried.

My husband once said, "Your face is just like your name: graceful and intelligent, something that grows on you." I was so moved, I let everything go. Looking back, I wonder, did I marry him for that one moment of healing? At the time, it felt as though his words had quietly erased all the wounds my name had ever left behind.

Since childhood, I never once thought of myself as pretty. If someone ever called me beautiful, I assumed they were teasing me. I must have been wounded more deeply than I realized. I often resented my mother, asking, "Why did you give me such a pretty name when you did not make me pretty to match?" Living alongside my three unusually beautiful younger sisters, I always felt alone.

When I was in middle school, there was a charcoal briquette factory along the way to school. A man from the factory would suddenly appear whenever I passed by and strike up a conversation. "My pretty one, you're three minutes early today." "Pretty one, why didn't you come to school yesterday? I thought my eyes would fall out waiting for you."

It wasn't that I found it uncomfortable that the briquette factory man, dressed in his soot-covered work clothes, took an interest in me. What upset me was being called "pretty one" when I didn't feel I was. He continued to call me "pretty one" until I graduated from middle school, but not once did I truly accept the word for its intended meaning. Perhaps I didn't even bother to connect it to myself, as if it had nothing to do with me. Yet, I never considered taking a different route to avoid him. Seeing him did not bother me enough to change my path.

I lived in Korea for 22 years, and now I've spent 20 years in a foreign land. Here, my American friends call me Jane. They say my name as they pat my shoulder, embrace me, and sometimes even weep beside me. On my voicemail, the word Jane plays softly, naturally, as if it had always been mine.

Between the names Ha Jeonga and Jane, a vast river flows. Ha Jeonga wears neat formal attire, her makeup precise, her hair carefully styled. She carries herself with quiet poise, meeting the world with composed, deliberate grace.

Jane, by contrast, goes barefaced, her acne scars plainly visible. Her straight hair is pulled back with a simple clip. She wears jeans and slippers, a backpack slung over one shoulder, moving through life with the ease of someone who no longer worries about how she is seen.

Those who know me as Jane are often surprised, even wide-eyed, when I show up dressed in formal attire. They say I look like a completely different person. It's amusing. Though it's not intentional, I have, in effect, become someone who lives between two extremes, a sort of double personality. I navigate back and forth between these two identities, adapting my actions and speech to fit the circumstances and the role I am expected to play in each moment.

While living in this land, my consciousness has changed as much as my name and surname. I have, in many ways, become a different person. Even if I hadn't changed my name while living in Korea, I could never return to the youth and passion I had 20 years ago. Time alone would have reshaped me. However, the changes I've undergone here are distinctly different from those I would have experienced had I remained in Korea. My consciousness can never fully return to the way it was when I lived there.

When my mother visited from Korea some time ago, she remarked that I seemed much stronger and sharper now. I laughed as I replied, half-joking and half-serious, "No, Mom, I've always been strong. You just didn't notice." She couldn't seem to let go of the image of me as her child who was gentle, naïve, and prone to tears. I had often heard her say, "Your tears flow like water from a leaky straw shoe; they never dry up. You'd give your liver away if it didn't hurt." It seemed my mother was grappling with a shift in her long-held perception of me, a contrast to the values and memories she had firmly associated with my younger version of me.

The last time someone complimented my mother, saying, "You have a very smart daughter," she was taken aback, saying she found it hard to believe. After spending three months with me, she admitted, "I never realized my daughter carried such a fiery passion in her." What could this fiery passion be that my mother claims to have discovered? How does she see this flame in me, something even I am unaware of? She said it felt as though she was meeting an entirely new version of me. I told her, "Well, my name has changed, so of course, I am not the same person you once knew." And it is true. If culture is embedded in language, then adopting an English name is not a simple or insignificant change. It carries a far deeper transformation than it may seem.

Why must changing my name come with such an elaborate explanation? Suddenly, it all feels cumbersome and unnecessary. Perhaps trying to justify it only makes it stand out more. Mrs. Davis is a prime example. From the very first meeting, she may have seen me as someone overly particular about something as simple as a name. She doesn't let anything I do pass without notice. During a recent class, she asked all nine of my fellow students to discuss the psychological state of surgical patients. Then, saving me for last, she called my name, "Jayne," with deliberate emphasis on the "Jay." She asked me to share something that hadn't already been mentioned by the others.

Whenever she widens her large eyes even further and deliberately enunciates "Jaaayne," my heart sinks. When she fires off her piercing questions, it feels as if my chest freezes. This is the same instructor who, during an early morning clinical, sent Chloe home in tears because she hadn't sufficiently studied her patient's condition and medications. Now it's 10 a.m., time to administer medication to the patients, but instead of attending to the other nine students, she has singled me out and won't let go. What is her intention? Has she made it her mission to shape Jane into an exceptional nurse?

I still cannot tell whether her focus on me is positive or negative. I have an ominous feeling that this semester will be anything but easy. Looking back, perhaps my mistake was not choosing to stick with my Korean name when she pronounced it so well during our first meeting. Or perhaps the real misstep was changing my name in the first place. What am I to do now?

Epilogue

Sharing the Heart Behind *Code Blue*

Jane Ha

Sharing the Heart Behind *Code Blue*

We live in an era overflowing with information, where it's possible to acquire vast knowledge even without firsthand experience. Yet this abundance presents a modern dilemma: knowledge alone cannot transform our character or the way we live. To truly improve, both our body and mind must recognize and embrace the need for change. It isn't enough to understand intellectually; we must also feel it in our hearts. True transformation doesn't come solely from the intellect; it must resonate in the heart. Only when the heart is moved does the will for change arise, and with sustained determination, the body eventually follows.

I believe that, regardless of the era, we are inherently spiritual beings. I trust that beautiful, moving stories can refresh parched souls and renew our perspective on the world.

I appreciate the hospital environment because it offers a setting where truth is enacted with genuine sincerity. It is a realm free from unnecessary embellishments.

You see things as they are, feel them as they come, and accept or process them accordingly. Here, "yes" means yes and "no" means no. It is a place where these words are taken at face value, without the need for complex interpretation.

Hospitals are not merely spaces where people interact; they are sanctuaries for authentic human connection. In

moments when joy or deep emotion overflows, doctors embrace patients, patients return that embrace, and even nurses share warm hugs with one another, transcending distinctions of gender or age. In these instances, we are reminded that before we are defined by our roles, we are extraordinary beings capable of profound connection.

A hospital is more than just a microcosm of the human world—it is its vivid reflection. Every time I step into the ward, I feel a flutter in my heart. I experience a pure, almost overwhelming joy that makes my heart feel as though it might burst, alongside a despair that plunges me into an abyss of crushing sorrow. When sorrow overtakes me, my energy seems to freeze, tears remain unspilled and even a sniffle is restrained. This surge of emotion resonates in every cell of my body, and though the joy and sorrow I witness are not originally my own, their intensity washes over me like a tidal wave.

Each shift in the ward feels less like merely caring for patients and more like gathering precious gems. The pain, ecstasy, wisdom, and inspiration conveyed through their stories shine brighter than any jewel. In every moment, I awaken to the world with renewed wonder.

After becoming a nurse, I let go of many of my wants. Before this, the desires I clung to had no real substance; they were nothing more than illusions, perhaps mere vanity. My life was filled with so much excess that I never truly understood what I was longing for at my core.

Now, I have become a realist, a true seeker of what is genuine. In a way, I have become a different kind of greedy, desiring only what truly matters. When the body fails, even the noblest mind crumbles. And before the body collapses, the heart often gives way first. To restore the body, the mind must first be strong. But mental well-being does not come from external sources, just as true happiness is not something granted from the outside. Only those who have wrestled with their own suffering can possess an unshakable sense of happiness, no matter the circumstances. A hospital is one of the few places where this truth can be witnessed with absolute clarity.

In the ward, I encounter people of all ages, genders, and nationalities. While subtle differences in culture and lifestyle exist among various ethnic groups, these differences have no bearing on how I approach and care for each person. At some point, I stopped distinguishing between my interactions, whether showing formality with Caucasians, humility with African Americans, or a friendly ease with Latinos and Native Americans. In the face of truth, these distinctions become nothing more than superficial courtesies.

Every day, I witness the transformative power of sincerity. Nothing is more beautiful than honesty. More than merely applying social etiquette or cultural norms, I have come to believe that when dealing with people, all that truly matters is being genuine.

Love and truth transcend cultural differences and social conventions. A beautiful, simple life is a universal aspiration. True beauty flourishes only when accompanied by peace, and genuine simplicity is achieved through authenticity.

Within the ward, I encounter authentic beauty and noble simplicity. How can one not feel their heart stir in the presence of such profound emotion? I witness a delicate harmony, a blend of dignified professionalism and raw vulnerability. It is a beauty that captivates and inspires, over and over again.

I cherish the unique environment of the hospital: a place where character and spirit are refined. Although modern society often nudges us toward indifference, I remain convinced that humans possess warm, compassionate hearts. I believe that a single gesture of placing a warm blanket over someone or wiping away a tear from the corner of their eye can change the course of a person's life.

I often reflect on how we live as if we will live forever yet die as if we never truly lived. I remind myself to expect nothing and to cherish every moment with joy and gratitude. Live well, laugh often, and love much.

My friends, let us love one another. In this very moment when we can see, feel, and touch, let us truly look at one another, share smiles, and extend gentle kindness.

www.ingramcontent.com/pod-product-compliance
Lightning Source LLC
Chambersburg PA
CBHW051815090426
42736CB00011B/1482

* 9 7 9 8 9 9 8 5 6 3 7 0 6 *